Roots in the Air

Value Inquiry Book Series

Founding Editor

Robert Ginsberg

Executive Editor

Leonidas Donskis†

Managing Editor

J.D. Mininger

VOLUME 328

Philosophy, Literature, and Politics

Edited by

J.D. Mininger (LCC *International University*)

The titles published in this series are listed at *brill.com/vibs* and *brill.com/plp*

Michael Krausz
PHOTO COURTESY OF BROOK HEDGE

Roots in the Air

A Philosophical Autobiography of a Philosopher, Artist, and Musician

By

Michael Krausz

With an Introduction by

Andreea Deciu Ritivoi

BRILL
RODOPI

LEIDEN | BOSTON

Cover illustration: "End of Texts," by Michael Krausz, copyright Michael Krausz 2010.

The Library of Congress Cataloging-in-Publication Data is available online at http://catalog.loc.gov

Typeface for the Latin, Greek, and Cyrillic scripts: "Brill". See and download: brill.com/brill-typeface.

ISSN 0929-8436
ISBN 978-90-04-36434-9 (paperback)
ISBN 978-90-04-38801-7 (e-book)

Copyright 2019 by Koninklijke Brill NV, Leiden, The Netherlands.
Koninklijke Brill NV incorporates the imprints Brill, Brill Hes & De Graaf, Brill Nijhoff, Brill Rodopi, Brill Sense, Hotei Publishing, mentis Verlag, Verlag Ferdinand Schöningh and Wilhelm Fink Verlag.
All rights reserved. No part of this publication may be reproduced, translated, stored in a retrieval system, or transmitted in any form or by any means, electronic, mechanical, photocopying, recording or otherwise, without prior written permission from the publisher.
Authorization to photocopy items for internal or personal use is granted by Koninklijke Brill NV provided that the appropriate fees are paid directly to The Copyright Clearance Center, 222 Rosewood Drive, Suite 910, Danvers, MA 01923, USA. Fees are subject to change.

This book is printed on acid-free paper and produced in a sustainable manner.

For Connie, with love ...

Where is the center of events, the common standpoint around which they revolve and which gives them cohesion? In order that something like cohesion, something like causality, that some kind of meaning might ensue and that it can in some way be narrated, the historian must invent units, a hero, a nation, an idea, and he must allow to happen to this invented unit what has in reality happened to the nameless.

HERMANN HESSE

Contents

Acknowledgments   XI

Introduction   1
   Andreea Deciu Ritivoi

PART 1
My Journey

1   My Early Years: Geneva, New York, Cleveland   9

2   Music and My Jewish Question   33

3   Rutgers, London School of Economics, Indiana, Toronto, and Oxford   47

4   Bryn Mawr, Philadelphia, Oxford Again, and Other Places   78

5   My Epiphany and Art   101

6   My Music Again   111

7   My India   135

8   Trajectories and Transitions   148

PART 2
Philosophical Reflections

9   Relativisms   165

10   Interpretation   178

11   Creativity   192

12   Self-Realization   201

Roots in the Air: A Postscript   223

Appendix A: Chronology   225

Appendix B: Select Bibliography of Michael Krausz   240

Appendix C: For Further Reading   245

Bibliography   248
Name Index   257
Subject Index   263

Acknowledgments

To Andreea Ritivoi, who encouraged me to take on the project of my philosophical autobiography, I express my gratitude. Andreea is currently Professor and Head of the Department of English at Carnegie Mellon University. Her research interests include rhetorical theory and Continental philosophy, narrative and identity, exile and transnationalism, Eastern European societies, and controversy. She teaches courses on contemporary rhetorical theory, argument, research methods, international communication, and narrative theory. She has witnessed my activities in my three lives—philosophy, music, and art—as well as heard my reflections about their interactions. We launched the present project in August 2011, when we recorded our initial interview.

In addition to Andreea's invaluable contribution to this volume, I have been most fortunate to have been guided and encouraged by many others throughout my personal and professional development. Foremost, these include my parents, Laszlo and Susan Krausz, my brother Peter, and my darling wife, artist Constance Costigan, who is an unflagging source of support and inspiration to me. Others include:

Mark Adams, Leslie Anderson, David Arben, Shlomo Avineri, Ruth Tiffany Barnhouse, S.R. Batt, Isaiah Berlin, Luis Biava, Guy Blaylock, David Bloor, Phyllis Bober, Zoltan Bretter, Larry Briskman, Richard Burian, David Cast, Kim Cassidy, Stanley Cavell, Jacques Catudal, Vibha Chaturvedi, Armond Cohen, Jerry Cohen, Françoise Cossery, David Crocker, Helena Cronin, Deborah Curtis, Michael Curtis, Rita Czipczer, Ronald de Sousa, Jennifer Dickson, Alan Donagan, Robert Dostal, William Dray, Douglas Duckworth, Arthur and Adrienne Dudden, Craig Eisendratch, Catherine Elgin, Barbara Fiedler, José Ferrater Mora, Roy Fitzgerald, Michael Forster, Harvey and Allyn Fruman, Markus Gabriel, Patrick Gardiner, Herbert Garelick, Jay Garfield, H.I. and Elaine Gates, Carlyle Gill, Josef Gingold, James Grant, Paul Grobstein, Chhanda Gupta, Victor Laks, Lobsang Gyatso, Tenzin Gyatso (The Dalai Lama), Peter Hacker, Gary Hagberg, Audrey Handler, Patricia Hanna, Ron Harré, Judith Harold, Bernard Harrison, Mark and Kathryn Harris, Mary-Jane Hayden, Richard Hicks, Roman Jakobson, Fritz Janschka, Géza Kállay, Michael Johns, Olaive Jones, Jennie Keith, Philip Kilbride, Lorraine Kirschner, Christine Koggel, Thomas Kuhn, Ralph Kuncl, Imre Lakatos, Peter Lamarque, Barbara Lane, Thomas Leddy, Philip Lichtenberg, Tony Litwinko, Walter Lubar, Steven Lukes, Joyce Lussier, Bryan Magee, Michael McKenna, Pat McPherson, Afaf Mahfouz, Ram Mall, Jacques Marchand, Joseph Margolis, Bimal Matilal, Elizabeth McCormack, Jack Meiland, Gary Millier, Josef Mitterer, Jitendra Mohanty, Alan Montefiore, Martin Moskof, Jon

Newsom, Cecilia Nobel, Christopher Norris, David Norton, David Novitz, Hans Oberdiek, Henry Odera Oruka, Giridhari Pandit, Herbert Perr, Karl Raimond Popper, Frederik Prausnitz, Hilary Putnam, Leah Rhodes, M.C. Richards, Arnold Rockman, Ina Roesing, Amélie Rorty, Henry Rosemont, Nathan Rotenstreich, Ngawang Samten, Kenneth Schmitz, Anne and Nick Sclufer, Stephen Sell, Carl Shieren, Murray Sidlin, Harsaran Singh, Anne Shteir, Swami Shyam, Anne Slater, Paul Snowdon, Jill Stauffer, William Stokking, Tracy Taft, Paul Thom, Mark Thornton, Bharath Vallabha, Georg Henrik von Wright, Robert Washington, John Olton Wisdom, Jane Weiss, Harriet Wise, Ulrike Wiesner, James Winn, Mary Wiseman, Harris Wofford, David Wong, and many others.

Michael Krausz front plate photograph is courtesy of Brook Hedge. Constance Costigan photograph is courtesy of Kathleen Buckalew. All other photographs are courtesy of Michael Krausz private collection.

Introduction

Andreea Deciu Ritivoi

The purpose of this philosophical autobiography is more than to present the details of a work and a career. Its dialogic form is designed to dramatize life events as a series of questions and answers and to give readers a vivid understanding that philosophy really is a life project rather than merely an abstract intellectual enterprise. The book offers an account of the making of Michael Krausz's philosophical, musical, and artistic work, with emphasis on *making* as a process and constantly emerging project.

Part 1 is structured around the major developments that define Michael's biography, along with the philosophical, musical, and artistic projects they inspired. Moving between biographical experience and philosophical problems, it defines the contours of a life examined.

The book begins with questions about Krausz's family background, and explores the values and beliefs that underlined his upbringing. Born during World War II in Switzerland, he is the son of two highly accomplished Jewish musicians, Susan and Laszlo Krausz, who came to the United States in the aftermath of the war, having survived the Holocaust in Europe. Krausz's stories about his parents' musical interests and their circle of artist-friends offer a fascinating account of an old world sensibility that he inherited, and these stories set the tone for the entire volume.

Susan Krausz, an extraordinary woman who, as a mother and wife in America while also staying true to her professional and artistic self, was a pianist and composer. Laszlo Krausz was a violist and conductor, who played with l'Orchestre de la Suisse Romande and the Cleveland Orchestra. Painting and drawing was an avocation of his as well. Both parents were not only talented artists, but also complex ones, for whom intellectual development defied narrow specialization and valued broad expertise.

The Jewish identity of the Krausz family, reflecting the cultural ideal of the intellectually assimilated and religiously observant Jewish characteristics of late European modernity, and the tragic death of Michael's grandparents at the hand of the Nazis, underpinned and shaped his emotional and intellectual development.

Growing up with music also shaped Krausz's sensibility in a way that made him intellectually restless, and that might account for the versatility that defines his philosophical and artistic identity. It opened him up to the pursuit of major philosophical questions. His philosophical method is the product of multiple formative influences, starting with those exerted by his family, and beyond that, shaped by his encounters and friendships with several major figures in both in philosophy and in the artistic world. He recounts his discovery of philosophy at Rutgers University, his philosophical awakening at the London School of Economics during his junior year, his graduate work at Indiana University, and the University of Toronto, where he earned his doctorate in philosophy with a dissertation on R.G. Collingwood's theory of absolute presuppositions, under the supervision of William Dray. While preparing that thesis, Krausz spent a year at Oxford, working with Patrick Gardiner, Isaiah Berlin, Rom Harré and others. He later returned to Oxford numerous times as a senior member of Linacre College, and now, as Adjunct Fellow.

Krausz went back to Oxford to teach a joint seminar on relativism with Indian philosopher Bimal Matilal at All Souls College. That resulted in a lasting partnership that inspired and influenced fundamental projects. With Matilal, Krausz began to co-author *Varieties of Relativism*. But before its completion Matilal died. Rom Harré substituted for Matilal to complete that project which became a seminal work. It was also Matilal who encouraged Krausz to turn to Indian philosophies as they bear on relativism. An enduring commitment to India ensued, which would lead to lasting and deeply influential attachments to numerous informants in the fields of Hinduism and Buddhism. These encounters allowed him to broaden his philosophical inquiries with regard to cultural diversity and identity, universalism, cultural relativism, and related themes.

The ambitious scope of the projects to which Krausz has dedicated his life includes, in addition to his unique intellectual profile as a philosopher, being also an accomplished painter, and an accomplished orchestral conductor with national and international experience.

Recounting his childhood in a family of musicians and artist, Krausz stresses that he discovered his own interest in the visual arts later in life, following upon an epiphanic experience at the age of twenty-eight, when visiting the studio of a painter-friend. Surrounded by large canvasses, he experienced what he calls an 'inner necessity' to paint, which he pursued in a life program that has materialized in thirty-seven solo exhibitions to date. His artistic life is intertwined with his personal life. Married to artist Constance Costigan, a noted painter and Emerita Professor of Fine Arts at George Washington University, Krausz inhabits a creative and aesthetic space, which has also influenced his philosophy—especially his interests in interpretation—while being in turn shaped by his other artistic interest in music.

Krausz's musical training—which allowed him to conduct several professional orchestras—made more than a musician out of him: it also exposed him to a philosophy of life, a *Lebensphilosophie*, as he reflects in this book, centered on creativity and on life programs dedicated to trying to live out one's potential. Yet to a reader accustomed to the professionalization of narrowly defined intellectual work, such a broad range of talents and pursuits might leave one incredulous. When pushed to consider whether he might belong more in one field than another, he admitted to the challenges it has posed to him over the years in making him feel as if a choice was in order. He also pointed out that his interests are not mutually exclusive, and expressed his hope that they coalesce somewhere and somehow.

Indeed, they do. Krausz's reflections on his own work reveal the way in which varied interests congeal in a consistent set of endeavors. His intellectual and artistic selves seem inherently multidimensional. He has an uncanny ability to forge and inhabit a conceptual space that transcends the usual disciplinary and intellectual boundaries, and enables him to draw on seemingly irreconcilable approaches. The depth of his work—not only in the domain of analytic philosophy, but also in aesthetics, art theory and criticism, as well as Eastern thought—derives from his reliance on diverse and compelling examples that confer upon his arguments an increased explanatory force. This book will show the working of a mind that can generate and control a diverse and complex discourse.

Krausz's willingness to engage topics that are not commonly discussed in the Anglo-American philosophical discourse—including crucial tenets of the Hindu and Buddhist doctrines—leads to important insights into the limits of interpretation. For example, in his *Limits of Rightness* (2000), he discusses witnessing a dead baby's body floating in the Ganges River. Within one cultural system of interpretation, the body of the baby can suggest malfeasance and prompt a criminal investigation. But in another system, it can invoke a sacred practice and inspire piety. Unafraid to deal with such troubling examples, Krausz also stays away from embracing a blanket cultural relativism, according to which anything goes as long as it accords with a coherent system of beliefs and practices. Krausz has developed a conceptual framework for the study of interpretation, which relies on three constitutive elements: ideals, aim, and objects. He defines an interpretive ideal as the critical stance based on which interpreters decide whether to accept only one interpretation using admissibility criteria to adjudicate among competing possibilities (singularism), or to show a more tolerant attitude and allow that for some objects, and under certain circumstances, multiple interpretations can be admissible (multiplism).

It is tempting to assume that multiplism obtains especially in interpretive efforts we encounter in certain domains, such as the arts. Or, one might assume that singularism and multiplism are each aligned with particular ontological stances. Yet for Krausz, this differentiation is not field-dependent or reducible to the more general distinction between ontological positions.

Indeed, one of the main contributions made by Krausz in his earlier books and reinforced in the present volume is the so-called detachability thesis, according to which interpretative ideals are logically detachable from designated ontologies. Reflecting on the connection between ontology and the ideals of interpretation, Krausz offers the concept of reference frames—schemes of justification that are appropriate for particular interpretations. He discusses them not only as epistemic configurations based on particular criteria of admissibility, but also in terms of their edificatory dimension.

In reconstructing his intellectual trajectory, Krausz revisits the main conceptual tenets of his philosophical inquiry into relativism, interpretation, creativity, and self-realization. He addresses the connection between interpretation and ontology, and offers a compelling discussion of identity-construction. Interpretation and identity are complex domains of inquiry. The lucid and trenchant way in which they are treated in Krausz's books makes his work all the more impressive. Returning to them here, he offers more than a summary of his views. He gives us an account of how his interest in interpretation and ontology emerged and how they fit together in the story of his intellectual and personal life. The result is impressive, because it brings philosophy itself to life in an exemplary fashion.

Krausz also elucidates the way in which his philosophical interests converge in a broader concern with humanism, with a personal program that does justice to one's epiphanic experiences, and a philosophy that provides a conceptual space in which one can live.

I hope readers of this volume will discover and be impressed by the range and versatility of Michael Krausz's conceptual apparatus. He is an ecumenical thinker, willing to contemplate earnestly viewpoints that come from radically different philosophical camps, and to derive useful ideas from opposing directions. He benefits equally from competing philosophical outlooks because they are not the product of a rigid, preconceived schema, but are derived from a broad overview of situations that demand interpretive activity—from practical circumstances to specialized fields from art and aesthetics to culture and interpretation.

Over the years, I have benefitted tremendously from many inspiring conversations I have had with Michael Krausz. This book began as a conversation between us, which we had in Pittsburgh over the course of several days in late summer in 2011. In that conversation—reproduced partly in a revised form in the first part of this book—I asked him questions both as a friend and as an admiring reader who, over the years, has paid close attention to his works. This book grew out of and far beyond that conversation, and as it evolved into a full-fledged philosophical autobiography, my voice appropriately turned into a *rhetorical artifice* (RA) that allows Michael's story to unfold. I do not offer anything substantive in the remaining chapters, and indeed the RA interlocutor is not me but a conversational persona designed to support the flow of the narrative. I am deeply grateful and flattered to know that Michael Krausz continued the conversation he and I began, about his childhood and philosophical education, and continued to reminisce and reflect in an imaginary exchange with me. I encourage readers to imagine themselves asking him questions, as the RA voice does, and to follow his story as if they were talking to him in person. It will be a most gratifying experience.

PART 1

My Journey

∴

CHAPTER 1

My Early Years: Geneva, New York, Cleveland

RA: Let's begin with you saying something about your early years with your family, especially with regard to the historical context within which your early development took place, and how that affected your eventual musical, philosophical, and artistic pursuits.

Michael: My life began on a hopeful note. I mean that literally. I was born on September 13, 1942, in Geneva, Switzerland, which was the second day of Rosh Hashanah—the second day of the Jewish New Year. My father was fond of telling the story about it. While my mother and I were still in the hospital, my father came to visit us. After the visit, he went to Victoria Hall, the home of L'Orchestre de la Suisse Romande, where he was the principal violist at the time. The orchestra was already in rehearsal when he arrived. As he walked down the aisle toward the stage, the venerable conductor, Ernest Ansermet, turned around. After recognizing my father, he stopped the orchestra and asked the musicians to play a D major fanfare in honor of my birth! My father would tell that story as if a great good omen had been bestowed upon me and my family. I've internalized that story so much that I have always been partial to the key of D major! Still, it was a difficult time for my parents. The War was on. It would be three more years before it would come to an end, and another two years after that before our family could immigrate to America. In the meantime, during my very early years in Geneva, I became aware of serious problems.

I can't recall how old I was, but while playing on the floor, I would hear hushed voices talking about death. Later, I became aware that our family was in danger—more particularly, my father's parents, still in Hungary, were in danger. Eventually, I learned that, with many others, they had been killed in a gas chamber.

RA: How did you handle that awareness?

Michael: I now know that very young children go through an egocentric stage, during which they think that the whole world is their creation. Looking back, that appears to have been true with me. I thought that I had created this terrible world. I recall blaming myself for creating a world of death. I recall that already from a very early age, I employed a strategy to withdraw from all the talk about war and death.

I would look up at the ceiling to the furthest point in the room. I would focus my attention at the spot where the two contiguous walls met the ceiling, and imagine that I was there, or, I projected myself as being there. In that way, I tried to remove myself from what was going on in the conversations around me—to remove myself from the horrible things people were talking about. I would do that again and again. In retrospect, you could say I tried to detach myself.

RA: Did your parents notice that you were doing this?

Michael: I can't recall that they did. It was a kind of private habit.

RA: What were your parents like? I understand you also had a brother.

Michael: Yes, Peter. But first, let me start with my mother, although it was with my father with whom I eventually identified more strongly. As I've grown older, I've come to appreciate how exceptional my mother was—as a student, musician, wife, mother, pianist, composer, and confidante to her friends and neighbors.

My mother was born Susan (Suzi) Strauss in 1914, in Stuttgart, Germany. She died quietly in her sleep at the age of ninety-three, in Cleveland. An only child, she was extraordinarily talented and had a single-mindedness about her piano playing. By the time she was ten years old, she knew she was going to be a professional pianist. She entered the Stuttgart Musikhochschule—a college of music—in her early teens, where she worked with some extraordinary people, including pianist, Walter Rehberg. My mother graduated in 1933, at the age of eighteen, being one of the youngest graduates in the school's history. Originally, she had been in touch with Artur Schnabel, in Berlin, and she had intended to go to Berlin to study with him. However, Hitler had come to power in 1933, and Rehberg cautioned her to get out of Germany as soon as possible, because Jews had no future there anymore. Fortunately, she was able to get out of the country right before Hitler's madness began. When Rehberg himself emigrated from Germany to Switzerland to avoid the Nazis, my mother followed him to Lucerne, so that she could continue her piano studies with him. Once there, she also attended master classes under Edwin Fischer, and she studied with Dinu Lipatti in Geneva.

RA: How did your mother meet your father?

Michael: In Luzerne, with Rehberg, she was a guest at a concert in which Rehberg's brother was a cellist. After the concert, she met Rehberg's brother and a colleague of his, a certain Laszlo Krausz.

They married in Basel, in 1935, living in Lausanne from 1935 until 1938, when Peter was born, after which they moved to Geneva. As you know, the war broke out in 1939, but both before and during the war, they would concertize together in Lucerne, Basel, Lausanne, and Geneva; they also played together over Radio Basel, Lausanne, and Geneva. Together, they played a cycle of fifteen viola sonatas representing the history of the development of sonata literature for viola over Station Radio Geneva. They came to be regarded as the leading viola-piano duo of Switzerland. They finally came to the United States in 1947, first living in New York City.[1]

RA: So, how did your parents get the necessary papers to enter the United States? I understand that at that time, you needed an American citizen to sponsor your affidavits. Who sponsored them?

Michael: My maternal grandmother Else Strauss was a second cousin of the movie producer, Walter Wanger, who was married to the actress and movie star, Joan Bennett. They sponsored us. On my father's side, there was Eugene Zádor, the orchestrator for the Hollywood composer, Miklos Rozsa.[2]

RA: How did they fare after arriving in America?

Michael: It seemed like a big struggle at the time. But in hindsight, they did fairly well.

Once in New York City, my mother played piano accompaniment for students at the New York College of Music. She also taught piano students in all five boroughs of the city. Also, she and my father performed professionally at various venues in New York. During the same time, she did postgraduate work in piano pedagogy at Teachers College, Columbia University, where she eventually earned two piano teaching certificates. Despite being a fine pianist, I believe that she was a victim of her own perfectionism. She performed relatively little.

---

[1] The dates noted in this volume have been verified by Susan Krausz's personal papers.
[2] See Joan Bennett, and Lois Kibbee, *The Bennett Playbill*.

RA: How did your mother's professional life unfold from then on, especially by comparison to your father's?

Michael: It wasn't simple. Initially after settling in New York, my father taught at the New York College of Music and played briefly with the Carnegie Hall Pops Orchestra during the summer of 1947. Then, he was offered a position with the Cleveland Orchestra under George Szell. However, my mother insisted that we wouldn't move to Cleveland until a position for her had been secured as well. So, my father left New York in the fall of 1947, to begin his tenure with the Cleveland Orchestra, visiting us in New York when he could. Despite the challenge of being separated for awhile, my mother told me that she found her time in New York to be energizing. She loved the city, regardless of all its challenges.

As it turned out, we moved to Cleveland in 1949, after my father arranged for my mother to teach at the Cleveland Music School Settlement, where she ended up teaching until 1955. She also took over the private students of a teacher who left Cleveland, as well as continuing to pursue her own piano studies with pianist, Leonard Shure, who had been the assistant to Artur Schnabel, in Berlin.

RA: What was working with Shure like for her?

Michael: It was very trying for her. On more than one occasion, she would come home in tears. On her account, he was something of a bully with her. He insisted that she interpret the music only one way—his way.

Many years later, I happened to find a letter that my mother had written about herself, which shows her tenacity. After mentioning Shure's poor treatment of her, here is some of what she said:

> but I stuck it out stubborn as I am, and tenaciously got my Master's degree in music in 1956 at Western Reserve University. After this, I said (to myself), "I will never go back to school." And in 1957, I started work on my doctorate at Case Western Reserve University. My mother called me stubborn, and I think this quality kept me going up to the present ... all of the obstacles that came my way cannot hold me back from my striving to reach my goals, whatever they are, and whatever they were.

My mother was seventy-nine years old when she wrote that. Some years later, she tried to pursue her PhD at Columbia University. She went back to New York for a summer session. Sadly, it did not go well there. But it was her determined striving to achieve her goals, regardless of the outcome, that impresses me about her character.

I must say that my mother's experiences with Shure—at least as I remember her account of them—eventually led me to think of Shure's approach as 'singularist,' as I termed it later. I don't mean that singularists need to be bullies. But the idea that there exists one and only one admissible interpretation in music making remains an anathema for me. I guess we can talk about my views about singularism later on.

RA: Yes. I look forward to that. In the meantime, in what other ways did your mother's professional life unfold in Cleveland?

Michael: In 1956, my mother received her Master's degree in Music from Western Reserve University. In addition to playing with various symphony orchestras on a few occasions, she also performed her own compositions for piano. Her *Piano Picture Book* won her national recognition from *Mu Phi Epsilon*, the National Music Sorority. Edwin Kalmus published those compositions in 1957.[3] Her other compositions include, "Variations for Piano Solo," "Songs," "Piano Sonata," and *Piano Picture Book II*, among many others.

In 1966, my mother joined the music faculty at Western Reserve University, where she remained a lecturer in piano until 1992. Ironically, after her experience with Shure, significant musicians consulted with her about musical interpretations. For example, I remember that when composer, pianist, and conductor Lucas Foss came to Cleveland, he came to our apartment to consult with my mother about Bach's Piano Concerto in D minor. Throughout her life in Cleveland, she also taught piano privately. She did that until the very last day before she died in February 2008, at the age of ninety-three.

RA: You say that besides being a pianist, your mother was a composer. Would you tell me more about the sorts of pieces she composed?

Michael: Yes. She composed in the romantic tradition at a time when atonality was all the rage. Interestingly, she loved and found inspiration in the poetry of the Austrian poet, Rainer Maria Rilke. Sometimes his poetry inspired her compositions. That tells you something about her disposition. In addition,

---

3   Susan Krausz, *Piano Picture Book: Piano Solo*; and *Picture Book*.

my mother was a member of the Cleveland Composer's Guild, which included leading composers of the region, such as Klaus Roy, Herbert Elwell, and Donald Erb. Many of them were men experimenting in the atonal idiom. As a woman and a romantic composer, she felt a bit isolated, although years later, when I got to know Klaus Roy on my trips to Cleveland to visit with my aging mother, I learned that he very much admired my mother as a composer.

RA: This all sounds as if your mother was very busy, indeed. Yet you say that she continued her own studies as well?

Michael: Yes! In Cleveland, on top of everything else that she was doing, she was a composition student of the composer, Marcel Dick. In addition to working with Dick, she traveled to Pittsburgh a few times to consult with composer, Nikolai Lopatnikoff, at Carnegie Mellon University. She did all this working out of our modest living room, which doubled as her studio.

At first, she taught on two very used upright pianos, because that's all my parents could afford. One of the great moments in her life was when they were finally able to afford to buy a Steinway grand. A few years after that first one, she was able to buy a second Steinway, in order to accompany her students. For her, Steinway was the very best. So, that was a huge achievement for her; she had finally achieved her dream.

RA: It sounds as if she was quite an impressive woman!

Michael: I should say so. When she wrote that her mother had called her stubborn, and acknowledged that her mother was right, she was that, indeed—in the best sense of the word. But at the time, I didn't appreciate just how impressive she was. To me, she was just my mom.

RA: Do you recall any especially memorable moments you shared with her?

Michael: Yes. It was special when she would come with me to my violin lessons with Josef Gingold, and accompany me as I played for him. She and I would play together at home quite often. Occasionally, my father would join us. Those moments were always special for me. I especially recall one time when the three of us played the Bach Double Violin Concerto together. Such moments were rare though.

Also special to me were the blessings my mother would give me at the beginning and end of the Sabbath and holidays—and also when we would leave for a trip. Her blessing was an admixture of German, and Hebrew, "*Wir danken dem Lieben Gott für alles Er hat uns gegeben hat und gipt … chaim, sholom, parnose, Amen.*" I roughly translate it as, "We thank God for all he has given us and continues to give … life, peace, sustenance, Amen."

There was such purity in my mother's love. That purity was also present when she made music. I have an extraordinary photograph of her playing at the piano that suggests this to me. Her eyes are closed, as if she were playing to God. I believe that her purity as a musician was connected with her purity in religion.

RA: Was your mother particularly religious?

Michael: My mother's parents were observant Jews, in that they kept a kosher home, but my impression is that they were not extremely religious. Yet my mother's own religiosity grew significantly when, as a teenager, in Stuttgart, she met a young woman, Greta Brom, the wife of a rabbi, who was strictly Orthodox. Under her influence, my mother became very religious indeed.

RA: How did that affect her relationship with your father?

Michael: Before they were married, my mother made it clear to my father that she intended to live an observant Jewish life—to keep the Sabbath and the holidays, to keep kosher, to observe the laws of *mikveh*—the ritual bath after menstruation—and so on. My father was more secular in his early days, but he went along with my mother's desire to maintain a religious household, and that's what we did. We had a religiously observant home. By observant, I mean, we kept strictly kosher, and we kept the Sabbath and all the holidays.

My father was equally observant, but less doctrinal in spirit than my mother was. Here is a story that will give you a sense of how it was. I recall that on one occasion, my father declined an attractive invitation from the Russian-French conductor, Igor Markevitch, to participate in his conductor's workshop, in Mexico City, which Markevitch was directing. My father declined because the programs included performances on the Sabbath. While there were many Jewish émigrés in the Cleveland Orchestra, my impression is that very few—if any—were so religiously observant as my father was.

At the same time, in accord with the Sabbath, no one was permitted to turn electrical switches on or off on the Sabbath. So, we always turned the radio on before the Sabbath in order to hear the live performances of the Metropolitan Opera on Saturday afternoons.

RA: How did you react to your mother's religiosity?

Michael: My feelings about my mother in that regard were complicated. In her practice, she was very observant. But it went beyond religious practice. While I'm sure it gave her strength, she was fundamental in her belief. She was a kind of purist in religion. For me, that felt like a heavy blanket that I wanted to throw off. I again withdrew. I can't remember exactly when I started to go into the closet of my bedroom. I would close the door from the inside, close my eyes, and give myself lectures about such things.

In a way, I felt as if I were having a conversation with my future self. I would reassure myself that in the future, I would get out from under it all. I looked forward to a time when my future self would pick up the conversation with my earlier self, and we would pick up where we'd left off. Actually, it kind of feels as if that has come to pass right now.

RA: What can you tell me about your mother's parents?

Michael: My mother's father, Moritz Strauss, was born in 1876, and died in 1951. In Stuttgart, he was a successful businessman, being the co-owner of a factory that manufactured children's clothing. He was involved in promotion and sales throughout Germany. He drove a Fiat that he used to drive around various parts of Germany to sell his wares. At that time, having a car was a sure sign of prosperity.

My mother's mother, Else, was born in 1887, and died in 1949. Both Moritz and Else sang in a Jewish choir. My grandfather loved the music of Wagner. I remember him as being rather stern, while my grandmother was an extraordinarily kind and loving person. She was a homemaker with a piercing intelligence. During her youth, she had dreamed of becoming a chemist. Alas, given her circumstances, her life didn't allow for that.

In the 1960s, I visited Stuttgart. I tracked down the building in which my grandparents had lived: the address was 93B, Olgastrasse, Stuttgart. It was a lovely stone building with several apartments in it. They lived on the first floor. I could see that it was a comfortable environment.

RA: Did you ever have the opportunity to actually be with your maternal grandparents?

MY EARLY YEARS 17

Michael: Except for two years in New York after our arrival in America, I had no chance to get to know them. But this I do know. My mother's parents had managed to leave Germany just before life for Jews became impossible there. I don't know the exact date, but by the time they got out, they had lost everything. They did manage to get to New York City, and moved into a small apartment at 601 West 156th St, just off Broadway. I remember that address clearly because, when we made our way to New York in 1947, we lived in a really tiny one-bedroom apartment right next-door to theirs. It was so cramped that my mother made her bed on the floor in the kitchen.

Speaking of my grandparents, I still have a vivid memory of meeting them for the first time, when we disembarked from the ship that brought us to New York. Incidentally, that old ship had been a military transport vessel, which had already been deemed unfit for military transport. We were on its last voyage before it burned in the New York harbor. In any case, my grandparents gave us bananas, which seemed huge, but which I later found out were quite standard size for bananas in America. I thought to myself that if they have such huge bananas here, America must be a great country.

RA: So far, you've mentioned your father only in relation to your mother. Where did he come from? What was his early life and career like?

Michael: My father, Laszlo Krausz, was born on April 4, 1903, in Pécs, Hungary.[4] Like my mother, he, too, was an only child. He used to tell me that he would practice his violin in the rear of his father's tailor shop and drive his father's apprentices crazy when he did so.

RA: But I understand that he was very talented.

Michael: Yes, indeed. My father made his first public appearance as a violinist at the age of thirteen. Two years later, he conducted his first orchestra. After finishing high school, he continued his violin studies at the Municipal Music School in Pécs, and then the Budapest State Musical Academy.

From 1923 to 1928, he lived in Vienna, except for the year 1926. During his time in Vienna, starting at the age of twenty, he served as concertmaster of

---

[4] "Laszlo Krausz, Eminent Violist and Sketch Artist," (obituary), *Cleveland Plain Dealer*, May 25, 1979.

a symphony orchestra. In 1926, he studied in Paris at the Institute Modern du Violon where, at the Ecole Normale de Musique, he attended a master class with the renowned Eugène Ysaÿe—to whom Brahms had dedicated his violin concerto.

Back in Vienna, my father joined the master class at the Neues Wiener Konservatorium (New Vienna Conservatory). While in Vienna, he was an occasional member of the Vienna Symphony Orchestra. At the same time, he served as concertmaster with Wilhelm Watzek's Vienna Symphony Orchestra. During that period, he also served briefly as concertmaster in an orchestra in Amsterdam.

In 1929, my father went to Switzerland, where he stayed until 1947. During the first five years of that period, he played with the Basel Orchestral Association, a symphony and opera orchestra, under conductor Felix Weingartner.

At the same time, he completed seven semesters at the Basel University, taking courses in music theory, pedagogy, and philosophy. In addition, he took up the viola and served for several years as first solo violist of the Radio Orchestra in Lausanne. In 1938, he founded and directed the Lausanne String Orchestra.

From 1938 to 1947, my father held the position of first solo violist with the Orchestre de la Suisse Romande under its founder, Ernest Ansermet. He occasionally conducted that orchestra over the National Radio Station Geneva, served as Director of the Ensemble Symphonique de Genève for several years, and was an annual member of the Lucerne Festival Orchestra, an orchestra recruited from the ranks of the finest musicians in Switzerland.

All in all, my father worked with many of the great conductors and musicians of Europe. They included such luminaries as Fritz Busch, Wilhelm Furtwängler, Otto Kleiber, Paul Kletzki, Pietro Mascagni, Charles Munch, Paul Paray, Maurice Ravel, Victor de Sabata, Malcolm Sargent, Carl Schuricht, Richard Strauss, Igor Stravinsky, and Eduard van Beinum. He had played with important musicians, including Pablo Casals, who—after playing chamber music with him—addressed my father as *'cher colleague.'*

RA: Oh my. It sounds as if your father had an extraordinary career in Europe. But do I understand that his trajectory was cut short by Hitler, was it not?

Michael: Yes. After the war, as I've already recounted, our family immigrated to New York, then settled in Cleveland.

RA: You've mentioned that he left New York for Cleveland before your mother followed with you and your brother. So, once in Cleveland, how did things go for your father?

Michael: In addition to his duties with the Cleveland Orchestra, my father headed the String Ensemble Department at the Cleveland Music School Settlement, where he taught chamber music and led the string orchestra. He debuted as a conductor in the United States at a concert at Kent State University, where he conducted what was to become the Cleveland Chamber Orchestra, consisting of members from the Cleveland Orchestra. Later, he was conductor of the Mansfield Symphony, and then, for five years, the Akron Symphony Orchestra. On the occasion of his premier concert with the Akron orchestra, he received congratulatory wishes from Ernest Ansermet, Pablo Casals, Dmitri Mitropoulos, Charles Munch, Eugene Ormandy, Leopold Stokowski, George Szell, and Joseph Szigeti.

But despite his successes, I always had the sense that my father was disappointed. His working relationship with Szell was not wonderful, and he had regarded himself as stuck in Cleveland.

You see, Szell partially reneged on his offer. He had originally offered my father the position of principal of the viola section. Then, after my father arrived in Cleveland, Szell placed him in the third chair. Szell reassured him that that arrangement was only temporary, that the then principal violist, Marcel Dick—also a Hungarian Jew—was very soon to retire. The understanding was that my father would then take his chair. Well, that never happened. You will recall that Dick was also a noted composer, with whom my mother eventually studied.

All told though, despite his disappointment, my father made more than the best of his time in Cleveland.

RA: Your father was also active as an artist. Am I right?

Michael: Yes, he had always made art, ever since his days in Hungary. Then, shortly after he arrived in the United States, he began to sketch his musical colleagues. In Cleveland, he further studied at the Cooper School of Art, where he eventually became a part-time member of its faculty. He also studied at the Cleveland Institute of Art, where he studied painting with Paul Travis. If my recollection is correct, that's also where he got to know Julian Stanczak. He went on to earn a Master of Arts in painting at Western Reserve University.

Then, he was appointed Head of the Experimental Art Studio at the Case Institute of Technology.

He made hundreds of drawings and large paintings. He did many realistic and abstract oils. He had a special gift for portraits, and quickly sketched ink drawings. Later in life, he experimented with abstract shapes and colors inspired by geometric designs from ancient Mesopotamian artifacts. In the end, he also did a series on Hebrew letters, which arose from a growing interest in Kabbalah. He had numerous one-person shows in the United States and abroad, and his drawings were featured in local and national magazines. At first he worked in a small, enclosed porch at the back of our apartment on Middlehurst Road in Cleveland Heights. Then, years later, when my parents bought a house on Blanche Avenue, he converted the back bedroom to a rather ample studio.

A sample of my father's portraits in ink and charcoal is archived in the collection of the Music Division of the Library of Congress in Washington, DC. They include portraits of Pierre Boulez, Robert Casadesus, Leon Fleisher, Paul Kletzki, Frank Martin, Yehudi Menuhin, Paul Paray, Artur Rubinstein, Gunther Schuller, Robert Shaw, George Szell, Leonard Shure, William Steinberg, Arnold Steinhardt, Igor Stravinsky and Joseph Szigeti.

My father pursued his artwork full time after he retired from the Cleveland Orchestra in 1969. He was sixty-six then. He died after suffering a heart attack at the age of seventy-six, on May 25, 1979.

RA: That's an extraordinary career. Or, I should say, careers. We have heard about your mother's parents; what do you know about your father's parents?

Michael: Their names were Simon Krausz, born in August, 1879, and Franceska Spuller Krausz, born in June, 1877. I never met them, but I do know that in May 1944, they were among hundreds of thousands of Jews deported from Hungary to Auschwitz.[5]

RA: Have you had the opportunity to learn more about their life before the Holocaust?

---

5 From May 15 to July 9, 1944, Hungarian officials, under the orders of the German SS, deported around 440,000 Jews from Hungary.

Michael: Of course, my parents spoke of them, and thankfully, my father left the letters from his parents to him.[6] They lived in Pécs, about 130 miles south of Budapest. My grandfather, Simon, was a tailor—by reputation, one of the best in Pécs, known for his craftsmanship and integrity. My grandmother, Franceska, was a homemaker, devoted to my grandfather and utterly so to her only child, my father.

For a period before their deportation—along with the rest of the whole Jewish population in Pécs—they were resettled to a ghetto area very near the Pécs railroad station. This was a time when the end of the war was approaching and the Nazis were particularly keen to murder as many Jews as possible. Then, within the course of several hours, the Jewish community of Pécs was rounded up and loaded in trains. They were all murdered quite soon after arrival.

RA: Have you ever visited Pécs?

Michael: Yes. Several years ago, in 1997. It's an interesting story actually. As part of the Dalai Lama's efforts to elicit the support of parliamentarians from around the world, a meeting at one of the congressional buildings, in Washington, DC, was organized. I was invited to attend one of their sessions as an observer. Parliamentarians were making presentations and discussing proposals. During one of the coffee breaks, I noticed a young man, one Zoltàn Bretter, wearing an identification label indicating that he was a parliamentarian from Hungary. I approached him and asked whether he was familiar with Pécs, explaining that my father was born and grew up in Pécs. He replied, "Of course I know Pécs. As it happens, I represent Pécs in the Hungarian Parliament." Then he looked closely at my identifying name tag and saw that I am a philosopher. Then he added, "Yes, and besides representing Pécs in the Hungarian parliament, I also have a second job. I am on the faculty of the University of Pécs in the Philosophy Department." Needless to say, we quickly fell into an animated discussion and found that we had quite a lot of interests in common. Then he said, "If your travels bring you near Hungary, I would be delighted to host you in Budapest and we could even take a train together to my home in Pécs. I would be happy to show you around." I was taken aback. I then explained

---

6   The letters from Michael Krausz's grandparents to his father, written between 1929 and 1944, have survived. They have been translated from Hungarian into English and are archived in the Laszlo and Susan Krausz manuscript collection at the Western Reserve Historical Society. No letters from Laszlo Krausz to his parents survived. Copies can also be found archived at the United States Holocaust Memorial Museum.

to him that the following year I had an invitation to speak at the University of Vienna and would be delighted on that occasion to extend my trip to visit Budapest and Pécs. That's how that happened.

My trip was memorable. When I visited the memorial for the Jews from Pécs, who had been deported and gassed, I wept inconsolably—hearing myself sounding as if it were not I who was weeping. Perhaps it was the voice of my father, who never had the chance to say the Kaddish for them at that place. Perhaps it was the voice of a still deeper self. I also visited the ghetto area near the train station, including the building where my grandparents were confined just before they were boarded on to the train to Auschwitz. I visited the restored old synagogue where my grandparents' names were inscribed among its members. The synagogue also provided a pamphlet with the names of deported Jews. I visited three possible places where my father might have grown up. Through it all, Bretter consoled me. I shall never forget Bretter's generosity.

RA: Had your father tried to get his parents out of Hungary before the Nazis took over?

Michael: Yes. There is a sad story about that. My father had somehow managed to get false papers for his parents through someone at the El Salvadorian embassy in Geneva I think it was—I cannot be sure. The papers would have allowed them to immigrate to Israel. It had been my father's dream to bring the whole Krausz family together in Israel—including his parents and my mother's parents from Stuttgart. In 1936, he had actually gotten an invitation from Bronislaw Huberman, founder of the newly formed Palestine Symphony Orchestra,[7] to be principal violist. But my mother's parents resisted, and his own parents found the prospect of living in a place as undeveloped and hot as Palestine to be unattractive. Tragically, my father's parents passed up that opportunity.

However, my father was involved with helping to bring numerous others—primarily Hungarians—out of areas occupied by the Nazis. Here's a noteworthy example: The conductor Georg Solti—eventually Sir Georg Solti—needed to get out of Hungary. My father was instrumental in getting him out and helping him get a job at the Geneva Conservatory. Solti was appointed as accompanist for emerging opera singers at the conservatory where my father also taught.

---

7 Founded in 1936, renamed the Israel Philharmonic Orchestra, in 1948, after the creation of the state of Israel.

RA: Did you ever meet Solti?

Michael: Yes. Years later, I saw Solti in Washington, DC, when he was touring with the Chicago Symphony Orchestra. After the concert, Connie and I went backstage to see him. He had an elegant, clear, aristocratic bearing. After the concert, he took his time, and let his many well-wishers wait until he was ready to receive them. Finally, his door opened and the well-wishers were slowly ushered in. He was seated. At an appropriate moment, when it was our turn, I said to him, "Maestro, permit me to introduce myself. My name is Michael Krausz. I am the son of Laszlo Krausz." He got up and bowed deeply.

RA: What was your personal relationship with your father like?

Michael: That's complicated. We were very close. He was my role model, my mentor. He took me everywhere he could. He taught me so much. And in some ways, I think he saw me as his reincarnation. That may be an overstatement, but then again, maybe not.

RA: That's an extraordinary thing to hear. Why do you say that?

Michael: On the one hand, he very much encouraged me. He sustained me, especially during those years of withdrawal, during which I did poorly in school. He never doubted that I would develop into something substantial. He had little regard for my teachers and their disparaging reports about me. His faith in me was unwavering. Later, though, that faith was interwoven with competition and disappointment. Maybe we can talk about that later.

RA: Later, of course. So what was your family's life like when you arrived in New York?

Michael: My mother spoke English quite well, having learned it in school. She had spent some time in England as a student. On the other hand, my father knew very little English in the beginning. As I said, the four of us lived in a one-room apartment—plus tiny kitchen and bath—next to my mother's parents. To make ends meet, my mother taught piano while my father hunted for a job—seeing people, auditioning, trying to make his way as a new immigrant in an unknown new world.

It fell upon my mother to negotiate the family, to help us kids somehow get situated, and to make appointments for my father. Peter was put into a class in a neighborhood public school. I was enrolled at the Yeshiva Soloveichik. They thought they were doing a good thing when they put me there. Soloveichik was a distinguished name in the Orthodox Jewish world.

Peter was about nine years old. He quickly took on a special role. He had a knack for sizing up people and situations. He seemed to understand how this new American scene worked, how to get things done. He became something like the family guide. Peter was my hero. He seemed to adapt, to know everything, to be the good scout. I adored him, as only a younger brother can adore an older brother.

RA: How did your parents feel about America once they got somewhat settled?

Michael: This was a topic of lots of conversation. Of course, America was the Promised Land—where liberty was possible; where being Jewish was not a question of life and death. America was a great gift, full of challenges and opportunities.

At the same time, my parents were somewhat critical of what they found in America. You know the German word, *gebildet* or, *Bildung*? It means something like, 'cultured'—to have a sense of history, of language, a sense of cultivating who you are; that is, to be cultured. In contrast, in America, they found a preoccupation with money. They were taken aback by a kind of materialistic crudeness that would allow one to make money by already having money. So, while America had saved them and they were eternally grateful for that, my parents had ambivalent reactions to America.

RA: That's sounds exactly like Theodor W. Adorno's attempt to apply Marx's critique of commodity fetishism to the mass culture he found in America when he arrived in 1934.[8]

I think a lot of European scholars and artists, who came to America after the war, were discouraged when they encountered a culture of consumerism. This anti-intellectualism sends a message that what intellectuals prize is not what matters in life. What matters to the anti-intellectuals is more pragmatic than intellectual endeavors; they value things that have an immediate impact on their daily lives; things that are more utilitarian than scholarly.

---

8 See Max Horkheimer and Theodor W. Adorno, *Dialectic of Enlightenment*; see also Andreea Deciu Ritivoi, *Intimate Strangers*.

Michael: I think you have captured my parents' sentiments in that regard. At the same time, my parents realized that some of the most so-called *gebildet* people had turned out to have been Nazis or Nazi sympathizers. At home, often times, there were conversations about great musicians, some of whom were Nazi sympathizers—such as soprano Elisabeth Schwarzkopf and conductor Herbert von Karajan. There was talk about whether the conductor Wilhelm Furtwängler was a real Nazi and how much could be blamed on some of them, and so on. These were common discussions.

All of that having been said, I remember when our family became naturalized US citizens, in Cleveland. When we made *shabbas* together on that Friday night, we prayed most thankfully that America had taken us in. It was then, for the first time that I saw my father weep uncontrollably with joy.

RA: I'm puzzled as to why your family left Switzerland after the war was over. After all, they had survived the war in Switzerland.

Michael: There was too much personal and cultural baggage for them there. They had had enough. They just wanted to start a new life for the family. Of course, Europe had been decimated by the war. Among other things, you need to understand how precarious my father's position had been in Switzerland.

RA: What do you mean?

Michael: I remember my father's saying that—even though he was Hungarian born—as a Jewish Hungarian in Switzerland, he suffered from certain measures and negative attitudes directed at Jews. He had identity papers, but that was another matter. On top of that, although he had lived in Switzerland for a total of seventeen years before immigrating to the United States, he never qualified to become a Swiss citizen.

RA: How is that possible?

Michael: In those days, in order to apply for Swiss citizenship, you had to have lived in a single canton for at least ten years. As you know, my father moved from Luzerne to Basel, back to Lausanne, and then, to Geneva—never staying long enough to qualify for the single-canton requirement.

RA: So how did that impact on his daily life?

Michael: Well, during my father's tenure with the Swiss Romande Orchestra, there was a law that allowed any Swiss citizen to challenge the position held by any non-Swiss citizen. In my father's case, that meant that any Swiss violist had the right to demand an instant audition for his position. Quite often, my father had to defend his position without prior notice. Although his relationship with Ansermet was strong, that didn't matter. While no one successfully unseated my father, his position was always precarious.

RA: The challenges they faced in America were hard, weren't they?

Michael: Indeed they were. I think that my father was especially taken aback by that. Here he was, a well-known European musician—with a collection of strong letters of recommendation from world-class names in the European musical world that he had hoped would open doors. He was soon to discover that lots of other accomplished European musicians had their own collections of recommendation letters. He had to compete with all of them.

RA: What more can you tell us about your brother Peter?

Michael: At age sixteen, Peter was the first in our family to learn how to drive. That was a great event. Peter just seemed already to know how to drive. Then there was the issue of a car. From an orchestra colleague, my parents bought a thirteen-year-old, 1941, green Chevy for Peter. I remember that car now with much fondness. Peter would take me for rides in it. His being able to drive changed everything. As I said, Peter really became the deliverer of the new culture, and with that car, he also became independent, complete with dates and all. It was a few years before my parents learned to drive.

In the meantime, while I sang in the Cantors Club at Park Synagogue, Peter was pursuing his own lights. During his teen years, his life and mine took off in different directions. He got more and more involved in Park Synagogue's youth organizations—I think that's where he really first got involved in Zionism—while I was fixated on music.

As I mentioned, Peter was born in Lausanne in 1938, four years before me. By the end of the war, he was already seven years old. He must have been more cognizant of the details of the war and what it meant for our family. That's pertinent to the moral that he eventually drew from the Holocaust generally.

RA: What do you mean?

Michael: Peter was to follow his Jewish identity in the form of a secular Zionism, which later on led him to settle in Israel with his American wife, Judy Grubart. He went on 'Aliyah' in 1970. In Hebrew, *Aliyah* means 'going up' or 'ascending'—in this case, to the Promised Land. Eventually my trajectory with regard to my Jewishness took a different turn. He graduated from Cleveland Heights High School, after which he attended the Jewish Theological Seminary (JTS) Joint Program at Columbia University.[9] During the 1957–1960 academic years at Columbia, Peter supplemented his Jewish and Hebrew studies by living in Jerusalem for five months, where he worked on a kibbutz. While there, he taught Hebrew, math, and English to immigrant children who had recently arrived from Morocco, Tunis, Algiers, Hungary, and Poland. He also had the opportunity to visit many kibbutzim, settlements, cities, Arab villages, army camps, and other Israeli institutions, and he met some of the key people in Israel's political, economic, and social arenas.

In the late 1950s, while at Columbia, Peter served as National Vice-President of the Student Zionist Organization and met with leaders of the Jewish Community in Los Angeles. He was also editor of the *Zionist Collegiate*, which had a student distribution of about 3,500 copies per issue.

Peter became assistant national director of Young Judea, a Zionist youth organization. He settled in Israel, in the town of Ra'anana, with his wife Judy and their young family in 1970. He founded one of the country's first public relations companies, representing such clients as the Ministry of Commerce, Ministry of Tourism, American Professors for Peace in the Middle East, *The Wall Street Journal*, and international trade magazines. He also helped to solicit replacement parts for Israeli army airplanes.

Deeply troubled by 'Prisoners of Zion,' or so-called refuseniks,[10] and Ida Nudel's[11] sixteen-year duel with the Soviets, Peter organized the international campaign to free her from imprisonment and internal exile in the Soviet Union, which ultimately led to her release and arrival in Israel in 1987. Peter

---

9   Since 1954, the Jewish Theological Seminary of America (JTS) and the School of General Studies at Columbia have offered a joint degree program leading to a BA from Columbia University. This program thrives to this day.
10 'Refusenik' is an unofficial term for individuals, who were denied permission to emigrate by the authorities of the former Soviet Union and other countries of the Eastern bloc.
11 Ida Nudel is a Russian born former refusenik and an Israeli activist. She was known as the 'Guardian Angel' for her efforts to help the 'Prisoners of Zion' in the Soviet Union; see Ida Nudel, *A Hand in the Darkness*.

died of cancer on January 31, 1989, at the age of fifty. Ida Nudel delivered one of the eulogies at his funeral. He was survived by his wife Judy and their four children—and now their families: Gilah Krausz-Nevo, Ezra Simon Krausz, Raquel Krausz Goldstein, and Tamar Krausz-Bouille.

I should mention that when Peter began his studies at the Jewish Theological Seminary he intended to become a rabbi. But as it turned out, his Jewish interests led him elsewhere. After a couple of years at the seminary and at Columbia, he realized he was not cut out for the rabbinate. Instead, he concentrated on Zionism. That turned out to be his passion. But it was not mine, and that disappointed him.

RA: How did he show that disappointment?

Michael: There was an episode that I think marked a turn, from us merely going in different directions to me feeling a sense of rejection and disapproval from Peter. During his time, as the president of the Student Zionist Organization, I was at Rutgers. On one occasion, I went to visit Peter in New York; it was one of many times I visited with him and his family. This time, we agreed to meet at the office of the SZO. I went up to his floor in the elevator, and as the door opened, right in front of me, there was Peter in the foyer, engaged in intense conversation with several of his associates. I had come upon an impromptu meeting in front of the elevator. As I approached the group, Peter greeted me, but then continued his conversation with the others. One of their officers had just resigned, and they were discussing what to do about the vacated position. One of the people in the group, who had known me before, spontaneously said, "Hey, Peter! I've got a great idea. Why don't we hire Michael?" At that moment, in a stern and dismissive manner, Peter replied, "Michael? No, we need a Jew for the job."

RA: When Peter said that, implying that you were not a Jew, that must have hurt.

Michael: Yes, it did. Deeply. In a way, it felt as if he were renouncing me. Peter knew that I was philosophically doubtful about the idea of Zionism—at least his definition of Zionism. On numerous occasions, I had pressed him. I wanted to know how he defined Zionism. He would say that Zionism is the view that in virtue of being a Jew, one has a moral obligation to immigrate to Israel, to support others to immigrate to Israel, and generally to support the state of Israel.

RA: What were your doubts about his definition of Zionism?

Michael: I could not see how, in virtue of one's birth as a Jew, one could have a moral obligation to support any political state. Of course, I supported the right of Israel to exist. But I thought Peter's grounds for that support were unjustifiable. I couldn't see that any moral obligations follow from the circumstances of one's birth alone. Peter was unsympathetic about my deviation from his sort of Zionism. That strained our otherwise loving relationship.

I now think that our disagreement was actually generated from a misunderstanding. I still think that the argument that, in virtue of being a Jew, one has a moral obligation to support the policies of the state of Israel, is fallacious. But it is quite another matter to affirm the right of the state to exist altogether. Those are two separate matters. In retrospect, I think that Peter had doubts about my commitment to the legitimacy of the state of Israel, quite apart from the argument that such commitment is entailed by one's birth as a Jew. That was a misunderstanding.

RA: Did you ever overcome your differences with Peter?

Michael: Yes, many years later, Connie and I had been to Oxford, after which we came to Paris to spend a few days with Peter. He was in Paris on business. We met in front of Notre Dame Cathedral. We spent the day talking a lot about our shared early history, about our families, about our dreams and aspirations, about his work and ours, and we talked about his crowning achievement, which was to help liberate Ida Nudel. Over the years, he had often spoken about it, and we were very proud of him. My brother the liberator! Most importantly, we had moments of reconciliation. These were moments of affection. Connie was a wonderful mediator who made that possible.

RA: Going back, then. How did you fare during the time your family lived in New York?

Michael: New York was very hard for me.

RA: Why was that?

Michael: We spoke French and German at home in Geneva. Now, in New York at Yeshiva Soloveichik, I was expected to speak Hebrew in the morning and English in the afternoon. I could speak neither. I couldn't understand the instructions in English. My teacher was an angry, impatient, and dismissive man. He had no patience for me. He would regularly pull my ears very hard. That actually resulted in some damage. I was very unhappy. I was deeply withdrawn and depressed. I just couldn't cope.

RA: What did you do?

Michael: Or not do, would be a better question. I was ashamed and did not tell my parents very much about it. After all, they were so preoccupied just situating themselves. But I did invent my own system of addition—a pretty good one at first, even if, in the end, it didn't work.

RA: Your own system of addition?

Michael: Yes. While I couldn't understand what it meant to add one number to another number, here is how my system worked. Like all first graders, I was presented with a workbook that showed, for example, the following series of numbers:

$$
\begin{array}{cccc}
1 & 2 & 4 & 8 \\
\underline{+1} & \underline{+2} & \underline{+4} & \underline{+8}
\end{array}
$$

Under each problem, I was expected to write the so-called sum of the numbers. That much I got. Yet I hadn't yet quite comprehended what this game was about. But I did notice something rather interesting. That is, the answer to any given problem can be found on the first line of the following problem!

So I would look at the second problem and bring down the first line of the second problem as the solution of the first problem. I saw that 1+ 1 indeed is 2, because that's the number that appears on the first line of the following problem. Then I saw that 2 +2 is 4, because that's the number that appears on the first line of the problem after that one, and so on. This procedure seemed to work quite well, except for two drawbacks. First, there was no problem that followed the last problem from which I otherwise would get an answer. Second, there was no problem that preceded the first problem. The first line of the first problem was unused.

RA: How did you handle that?

Michael: I discovered a way to handle that situation. I would make a closed overall pattern of the series. That is, I would use the first unused first line of the first problem and bring it over as the solution to the last problem. Accordingly,

8+8 would equal 1. According to this pattern, there would be no unused first number of the first problem. Despite the fact that the last problem had no following problem, it did get a solution. That was, after all, the game I thought we were meant to play.

RA: That's fascinating.

Michael: It does have a certain charm, I admit. Not only did the first line of the first problem get to be used, but the fact that there was no problem after the last problem was no longer worrisome. Now this system worked pretty well, or so I thought. I mean, I got passable B's for a while. I didn't much care if I didn't get all my problems right, although I was a bit puzzled as to why I didn't. My system seemed to work well enough for me. I now think of it as my own language game, as Wittgenstein might have called it.

RA: What happened next?

Michael: This went on for some time until all hell broke loose, when, for some reason—incomprehensible to me—all my answers were wrong. As it turns out, the order of the problems had been rearranged. For example, 1+1 was follow by 4 +3 or 6+1. My system completely broke down. Here, after I had been getting B's, suddenly I was getting F's. I was one thoroughly confused child!

RA: Then what happened?

Michael: We moved to Cleveland in 1949, when I was seven years old. Upon our arrival in Cleveland, I was enrolled in the local public school, Coventry Elementary. My parents were called in to see the principal, who told them that I was a backward child, that I had failed first grade, and needed to repeat it. I was put in a class for 'special' (meaning backward) students. I noticed that the others in the class were really challenged. It was only when we were given drums and tambourines to play that they noticed that I was really quite capable. I was then put in the regular first grade class. After that, my school life began to improve. But generally, school was boring for me. My report cards regularly included comments like, "Michael seems unable to concentrate. He daydreams a lot. Perhaps he needs more sleep."

RA: How did your parents react to all of this?

Michael: They were saddened and embarrassed. In any event, my first grade failure affected a great deal of my attitude toward school for many years. My childhood after that was pretty much centered on the family and music. I was pretty much a loner without many school friends—partly because I was kind of different, and partly because I couldn't have friends over to our apartment much, as our household was very Jewish. Many of the kids, while Jewish, weren't kosher or otherwise observant.

My mother had lots of students—often with parents in tow—coming in and out of our second floor apartment. It was a small living space. I'd have to tip-toe my way around the apartment—going between the kitchen and the bedroom via her living room-studio. Of course, I could hear all the music making, sometimes pleasant, sometimes not so pleasant. I got used to it. But there was no getting away from it. On reflection though, I must say that in that environment, I absorbed a good sense of what it means to master an instrument and what it means to make serious music.

RA: Is this when you started to make music?

Michael: Yes. When I was seven, my father started to teach me the violin. Actually, he started both Peter and me at the same time, but Peter didn't take to it. I did.

CHAPTER 2

Music and My Jewish Question

RA: What drew you to the violin over the piano?

Michael: Well, my mother wanted me to play the piano, and my father wanted me to play the violin. I tried to play both for a while, but that was too much for me. My mother was something of a perfectionist, while my father was softer. That may be why I gravitated toward the violin. Over the first five years, I got quite far studying with my father.

Then, in 1954, when I was twelve years old, I heard the first concert of the Akron Symphony Orchestra that my father conducted.[1] The program included Beethoven's Symphony no. 3 in E♭ major, ("Eroica"), as well as Berlioz's *Rákóczi March*. But I was completely blown away by Josef Gingold's performance of Mendelssohn's Violin Concerto in E minor.

After the concert, I announced to my father that I wanted to become a violinist and I wanted to study with Gingold. My father talked with Gingold about it, and he accepted me as a scholarship student. That was the beginning of more serious work with the instrument.

My lessons with Gingold were at the Cleveland Music School Settlement. I had weekly lessons with him. They were supplemented with weekly lessons with Gingold's assistant, Janet Drinkel. As I would walk into his studio, there, in his open case on the sideboard, would be his Stradivarius. I'd glance at it in awe as I walked by it, take out my own student instrument, and have my lesson. Once in a while, he would pick up his instrument and demonstrate a passage for me on it. It was inspiring. Often, my mother would accompany me on the piano at my lessons.

RA: Can you recall any especially memorable moments with Gingold?

Michael: Yes. I recall an extraordinary moment. I was playing Ernest Bloch's Vidui, which is part of his *Baal Shem Suite*. It is a soulful work. In the middle of

---

1 Laszlo Krausz conducted the Akron Symphony Orchestra from 1954–1959, and founded the Akron Youth Orchestra in 1955.

my playing, he stopped me and said, in his heavy Russian-Belgian accent and gravelly voice, "Michael, you know, the notes are fine. But you're not making music." I asked, "What do you mean?" He picked up his instrument from his case. Standing next to him, my head came up to about the height of his shoulder. With his left hand, he placed his violin under his chin. With his right hand, he gently tucked my head under his instrument and placed it so that my right ear connected with the underside of his instrument. Then, with my head cradled upon his forearm, he picked up his bow and played the whole piece with such emotion and finesse! When he finished, he said, "Okay, Michael, now you do it that way." He showed me how to play it. He *showed* me. That was Gingold.

RA: Can you say more about Gingold himself? What was his background?

Michael: Gingold was a student of the great master, Eugène-Auguste Ysaÿe—to whom works by Claude Debussy, Camille Saint-Saens, Cesar Franck, and Ernest Chausson were dedicated. That was Gingold's lineage. In a loving way, he was demanding. He had the highest standards. He was uncompromising, but he was also utterly charming.

Gingold had played under Arturo Toscanini with the NBC Symphony Orchestra in New York. He then became the concertmaster of the Detroit Symphony. Then he became the Concertmaster of the Cleveland Orchestra. Did I mention? After he retired from the Cleveland Orchestra, he became professor of violin at Indiana University. He was famous for being a major violin pedagogue. Some of his students eventually became household names in the music world, including people such as Jaime Laredo and Joshua Bell. By the way, Laredo later was a soloist with my father with the Akron Symphony Orchestra. Many years later still, I connected with Laredo and violist Michael Tree in connection with the Philadelphia Chamber Orchestra (PCO). They served as co-Artistic Directors and I served as Associate Artistic Director of the PCO. But that story will come later.

After a solid foundation from my father, I made significant strides on my instrument with Gingold. I was, of course, honored to be one of his students, and because I was a Gingold student, I was treated specially by music teachers in school. At that time, I was at Roosevelt Junior High School and played in its orchestra, which was then conducted by a Mr. Von Unruh. I was concertmaster. I remember when we played a version of Nikolai Rimsky-Korsakov's *Scheherazade*, which requires a sustained solo part for the concertmaster. For a short while, I worked on it with Gingold. But I sensed that he thought I wasn't up to it. He was right!

Then in 1958, I moved on to Cleveland Heights High School, which had a nationally recognized orchestra. Its conductor, John Farinacci, received me warmly. As it turned out, he was my father's predecessor as conductor of the Akron Symphony Orchestra. But my relationship with Farinacci soured during my senior year, after—as a 'senior officer'—I refused to give out 'demerits' to other students who didn't behave. Demerits were like detentions, where you had to spend time after school doing menial tasks for the orchestra. I just thought that should not be my responsibility, but his. We crossed swords many time.

Perhaps he was something of a foil during my teen years. But here is the good part: He often left me alone to conduct the orchestra. That's when I really learned to conduct. He had tried to coach me with my conducting. But I stubbornly resisted. He urged me to raise my arms higher when I conducted. I replied that that's not how French conductor, Igor Markevitch, does it. He saw that I would not take criticism from him.

RA: So, when did you even begin to think about conducting?

Michael: I was around eleven or twelve when we got our first record player. My mother was working on her Master's degree at Western Reserve University. One of her courses required listening to a long list of pieces on the record player. These included many of the standard classical works. I would listen to them all, and I would pretend to be George Szell and conduct the records, sometimes in front of a long mirror, attempting to imitate Szell, who was famous for his extraordinary baton technique. He was very clear, spare, and elegant. Sometimes I would entertain anyone who cared to watch. Anyway, in my junior year in high school, in 1959, I played in the first violin section along with some other very good players. One day, when Farinacci was absent, one of the senior officers—Peggy Killmeyer—who knew of my background and my itch to conduct, invited me to do so. You should understand that that privilege was usually reserved only for seniors. Yet, after I conducted that first time, Farinacci allowed me to conduct in his absence. His allowing me to do that was a significant exception to the rule.

RA: What did you conduct that first time?

Michael: The orchestra had been rehearsing its part of the "Hallelujah Chorus" of Handel's *Messiah*—without the chorus. I got up on the podium and I conducted like anything. When we ended, there was huge applause from the players. The first cellist, Steve Sindell, told me later how impressed he was with my baton technique. That was my first time. After that, I just had to conduct more. Later, even Gingold said to me, "You know, Michael, I think you're a conductor."

RA: Was studying under Farinacci a good experience for you?

Michael: He was a good conductor. He had attended a conductor's workshop with Pierre Monteux. Farinacci was a bit of a militarist, with whom I had tense moments. But the good thing was that he was often absent from rehearsals, and that allowed me to conduct a lot. That's when I came to be really comfortable on the podium.

RA: During your high school years, did you also get involved in the musical world in Cleveland outside school?

Michael: Yes! I was asked to play in the Cleveland Philharmonic Orchestra, a semi-professional orchestra that rehearsed in one of the rooms at the WHYY radio station in Cleveland. I also went to lots of the concerts of the Cleveland Orchestra. At that time, under Szell, the Cleveland Orchestra was roundly regarded, at least technically, as the best orchestra in the United States.

Interestingly, when David Oistakh, the great Russian violinist, visited Cleveland to give a solo recital, Gingold told me that he had said to Oistrakh, "We have a fine orchestra here in Cleveland." Oistakh responded, "Of course, I know. I have every one of your recordings."

Anyway, before or after a concert, I would hang around the orchestra's locker room where my father would change his clothes. I got to know many of the musicians in the locker room. Several of them—cellist Harry Fuchs, for example—would tease me and joke with me. They treated me as one of the family. I loved it. After concerts, I would join my father in the car pool that would sometimes pick us up and deliver us. My father couldn't drive yet. The musicians would talk about the concert they had just played. They would talk about the program, or the guest conductor, or the soloist and, of course, gossip a lot. Sometimes they would ask for my opinion. I would freely share it. They seemed amused with my forthrightness.

There were such amazing players in that orchestra—especially the first desk players. Besides concertmaster Gingold and associate concertmaster Anshel Brusilow, there were flutist Maurice Sharpe, harpist Alice Chalifoux, piccolo player William Hebert, and so many more.

One more player stands out in my memory. That was timpanist Cloyd Duff. He had the uncanny practice of coming in a fraction of a second before a beat, to frame the sound that would emerge from the rest of the orchestra.

RA: Can you explain what you mean by that?

Michael: Well, when you have an ensemble of ninety or a hundred players—no matter how good—it's mathematically impossible for all of them to come together precisely, say, on the down beat. There has got to be some inexactness even with such a superlative orchestra as the Cleveland. Duff's tiniest anticipation of the beat would clear that up so that an impeccable sound would emerge. That impressed me.

Another orchestra player who impressed me greatly was first cellist William Stokking. How could I know then that years later, when I would conduct the Great Hall Chamber Orchestra, Bill Stokking would be my soloist? And how could I know then that when I conducted the Celebration Chamber Orchestra, David Arben—another fine violinist from the Cleveland Orchestra—would play as my soloist? He would also solo with my Philadelphia Chamber Orchestra.

Still later, I would invite Anshel Brusilow to conduct the PCO. Brusilow had been Associate Concertmaster in Cleveland and shared the first desk with concertmaster Joseph Gingold. He eventually became concertmaster of the Philadelphia Orchestra under Eugene Ormandy. But I'm getting ahead of myself.

RA: Do you recall particular soloists you heard play with the Cleveland Orchestra during that time?

Michael: Oh my. Jascha Heifetz. Isaac Stern. Zino Francescatti. Erica Morini. Rudolf Serkin. I also heard David Oistrakh in a solo recital. The list goes on. I especially cherish my memory of my father's exchange with Zino Francescatti just before his concert. They had known each other in Europe.

My father said to that great violinist, *"Mille fois merde!"*—a traditional French greeting before a concert. It translates into English as, "A thousand times shit!"

RA: And what conductors did you see?

Michael: Of course, I saw Szell often. There was also the Associate Conductor of the Cleveland Orchestra, Luis Lane. He would eventually succeed my father with the Akron Symphony Orchestra. Then there was the well-known choral conductor Robert Shaw. I saw Leopold Stokowski. He was remarkable. Then there was the French conductor Igor Markevitch, whom I liked especially well. Then, of course, there was Ernest Ansermet, who visited us in our home. You will recall that my father had a close relationship with him in Geneva. Carl Schuricht also visited us at our home.

RA: What was so remarkable about Stokowski?

Michael: I recall a story my father told me about Stokowski. He had an extraordinary ear. The background of the story involves the Severance Hall itself. Where you walk into the hall from the mezzanine, a barrier separated the last row of seats from the entranceway. Well, it seems that between Stokowski's first and second visits to Cleveland, a glass panel—no higher than eight inches or so—had been installed on the barrier. When, upon his return, Stokowski began his rehearsal, he stopped the orchestra—and without looking behind him—complained loudly that someone had tampered with the acoustics!

RA: So, what did you do about your yearning to conduct?

Michael: I formed the Youth Chamber Orchestra of Cleveland in 1960. This was an ensemble of about fifteen players, drawn mainly from the Cleveland Heights High School orchestra and a few others from around the city. It included Peggy Killmeyer, whom I already mentioned; violinist, Susan Davenny, daughter of pianist Ward Davenny; violinist, Eric von Magnus; and cellist, Steve Sindell, whom I already mentioned. Later, Steve was to become a lawyer; he argued before the US Supreme Court in the Kent State trial. The orchestra worked very well together.

Our first concert was on February 16, 1960, at the East Cleveland Public Library. The program included the Overture to Handel's *Messiah*, Georg Templeton Strong's "Choral sur un thème de Léo Hassler," and Vivaldi's Concerto Grosso in A minor, with two solo violins. We also premiered a piece called *Lullaby* by Steven Sindell. After that, we had a few more concerts. We even appeared on television. An article about us in the *Cleveland Plain Dealer* referred to me as a 'pink-cheeked maestro.'[2]

Then the Cleveland Musician's Union called me in.

---

2 February 16, 1960.

RA: The union? What was that about?

Michael: They objected to our activities. They summoned me for a meeting with about a half dozen of their officers. They told me that I couldn't go on television anymore because I wasn't a member of the union.

RA: A member of the union? That must have been hard.

Michael: It sure was.

RA: But despite being restricted in your activities by the union, you did continue to conduct that orchestra, didn't you?

Michael: Yes. But there were bumpy rides then too, which involved my father. For example, once, when the orchestra was rehearsing in our crowded living room, my father insinuated himself as a listener, and then, without my inviting him to do so, he gave a critique of what we were doing—what was right and what was wrong. That's when my leadership of the ensemble began to unwind—in part because of some inauspicious decisions on my part.

You see, during that period, my father was the conductor of the Case Institute Chamber Orchestra. It was a nice ensemble, in which I played viola. Well, I had this bright idea. I thought, wouldn't it be nice if we had a concert that would bring together his Case Institute Orchestra and my Youth Chamber Orchestra? My father and I could share the podium. I would conduct Francesco Geminiani's Concerto Grosso in C minor and after the intermission, he would conduct Beethoven's Symphony no. 1 in C major. As I say, I thought that would be nice. But it was not so simple.

Before that concert, the Cleveland Orchestra went on tour. That meant that in my father's absence, I was to rehearse our combined orchestra for the whole program, including the Beethoven Symphony. It was a terrific opportunity for me, and I enjoyed it. When my father returned from his tour and heard the improved ensemble, I asked what he thought. After all, I wanted some credit for what I had done. He gave me none. Even though the concert went off very nicely, I was very disappointed. After that, my leadership of my orchestra dissipated. My father's imposing presence had put me in the shadows.

But I shouldn't give you the impression that my father was never encouraging. For example, when Szell had organized a conductor's workshop with the

Cleveland Orchestra, my father said that my conducting technique was better than most of the participants in that workshop.

RA: You must have learned a lot about conducting from your father too, I'm sure.

Michael: Of course. I went to many of his rehearsals and all of his concerts with the Akron Symphony Orchestra, and at home, I would witness how he prepared his scores.

RA: In the meantime, what was happening with your violin training with Gingold?

Michael: In my junior year I think it was, things with Gingold were beginning to go not so well.

RA: Why? What happened?

Michael: Well, as I was mischievously playing at sword fighting with a classmate—we were using yardsticks—my classmate whacked and broke my right index finger. I had to stop playing violin while my finger healed. For reasons that I still cannot fully reconstruct, when my finger was more or less healed, I just never did call Gingold back to resume my lessons with him.

RA: Am I right to think that you were ambivalent about your violin playing in contrast to your conducting?

Michael: It's true that during the period when I was in high school, my violin playing was at a fairly advanced level. At the same time, when Joe Gingold said to me, "You know Michael, I think you are a conductor," that rang true to me for several reasons. First, I didn't have the inner drive, the fortitude, to practice in the way that would have been necessary to develop into a fine professional violinist. I certainly wasn't of the caliber of Gingold's prodigies, like Carol Sindell.[3] I'm talking about a caliber to play in a professional orchestra. Maybe it was precisely because I knew too much what kind of effort and commitment that would have taken.

---

3 Carol Sindell began studying the violin with Josef Gingold at the age of seven. At the age of eleven, she was the youngest soloist ever to perform with the Cleveland Orchestra, playing the Mendelssohn Violin Concerto under the direction of Robert Shaw.

Anyway, when I was conducting the Heights orchestra on a fairly regular basis, I found that conducting actually satisfied me more. It was a different sort of thing than practicing an instrument. It was more cerebral, yet interactive with other people. I wanted to make something out of many voices at once, to create a unified sound that was communicative in its own way.

Breaking my finger resulted in a kind sabbatical from the violin, during which time, I ruminated a lot about my violin playing. During those weeks, I realized that while I was embarrassed and a little ashamed that I was letting everybody down, I also had to admit to myself that I felt relieved. In any event, for my senior concert with the Heights High Orchestra, I could have chosen to play a solo violin piece with the orchestra or conduct; I chose to conduct the first movement of Beethoven's Symphony no. 1 in C major.

But that's not the end of my violin story. I did continue to play for many decades thereafter, in many situations with many ensembles, but never presuming to have achieved a higher level on the instrument than I did in those days in high school.

RA: But your ambition to conduct remained alive in you?

Michael: Yes.

RA: So while you were intensely occupied with your music during your high school years, did you also continue to wrestle with questions about your religious beliefs during that time?

Michael: Yes. As you know, besides music in the house, religion was the other preoccupation. As a young boy, I attended Park Synagogue—one of the big conservative synagogues of Cleveland Heights. I also went to Hebrew School and had my Bar Mitzvah at Park. That was a good place for me, at least at the start. I was in the Cantor's Club organized by Cantor Simon Bermanis, who had been an opera singer in Europe, and then contracted to sing at the Metropolitan Opera before coming to Park.

I tried to qualify to sing the prayers at my confirmation, but despite my good voice, Bermanis said I could not do that because my Hebrew School grades were not good enough. My grades were as poor in Hebrew School as they were in public school! I was deeply disappointed. But I felt at home at Park—as I say, at least to start with. Rabbi Armond Cohen was very nice to me. Even so,

I began to have philosophical doubts. So much so that in my late teens, I actually declared to my parents that I was an atheist.

That's a day I'll never forget. We were making shabbas—marking the beginning of the Sabbath on a Friday night—with the candles, wine, and bread. It's the custom to make a prayer over the wine before taking a sip from the shared cup and then to make a prayer over the bread before eating a bit of it. After my father recited the prayer over the wine, he passed it on to my mother and then she passed it to me. When it was my turn, I took a sip of the wine without saying the usual prayer. When my mother passed me the bread, I ate it without saying the prayer. Taken aback, my father asked me why I had not said the prayers. I said because I didn't believe in God. I just couldn't make sense of the idea of a personal creator god. How could I pray to such a god? It made no sense to me.

RA: Oh my. How did they react?

Michael: You can imagine. They were silent. They were confused. They were very upset.

My parents saw everything through a Jewish lens. Everything was supposed to have been created by God—our Jewish God. So, I had wondered, are the trees Jewish? Are the flowers Jewish? The idea of a first cause seemed arbitrary. I saw no reason why there couldn't be an infinite series of causes in the past and in the future. For that matter, I couldn't see why the world couldn't be infinite in every direction. My thoughts on this turned out to be close to Bertrand Russell's reasons for rejecting theism, as I later read in his book, *Why I Am Not a Christian*[4]—only his argument applies not uniquely to Christianity. It applies to all the Abrahamic traditions, including Judaism.[5]

I also had difficulty embracing the idea that God necessarily, or inherently, exists. I now see that this idea is what philosophers call essentialism. Essentialism is the view that a thing is what it is—inherently—in virtue of its embodiment of an essence. Anti-essentialism, on the other hand, is the view that holds that the very idea of an essence is uninformative. Consequently, anti-essentialism holds that a thing is what it is in virtue of the purposes and interests that are served in different circumstances.

---

4 Bertrand Russell, *Why I Am Not a Christian*.
5 For a characterization of Jewishness distinct from belief, see Bernard Harrison's *Blaming the Jews*.

RA: It seems that your anti-essentialism would later play an important role in your philosophy.

Michael: Yes. Later on, in a different context, my anti-essentialism was confirmed to me in the teachings of Karl Popper.[6] Later still, the writings of Nelson Goodman were adamant about making no claims of existents beyond what is cognized within some symbol system.[7] And my non-essentialism was confirmed by Joseph Margolis's non-essentialist or non-foundationalist view of human knowledge.[8]

Still later, in a very different context, Tibetan Buddhists confirmed my non-essentialism in its principle of emptiness of inherent existence. They hold that everything, including the human self, is empty of inherent existence. Even Advaitic Hindus[9] agree, at least at the human level, that the human self is conventional. But that story will have to wait.

For now, in retrospect, I can say that when I declared my atheism, I was premature in thinking that all religions assume a personal creator god. And, I was premature in thinking that all notions of divinity are tied to the idea of such a god. I was also premature in assuming that all religious language is descriptive, that is, subject to argumentation as is characteristic of scientific discourse. It may also be hortatory.[10]

RA: What do you say now?

Michael: Now, I say that religiosity starts with mystery and awe and not with the assertion of a creator or personal godhead.

RA: So, is there anyone now with whose views about Divinity you would associate yourself?

Michael: Yes. Ronald Dworkin for instance. I recently read his excellent short book, *Religion Without God*. Despite his essentialism in some respects, Dworkin does countenance numinous experiences as religious in a broad sense. In that

---

6   For Popper's anti-essentialism, see his "Three Views of Human Knowledge."
7   Nelson Goodman, *Ways of Worldmaking*.
8   See Michael Krausz, "Interpretation, Relativism, and Culture: Four Questions for Margolis."
9   Advaita Vedanta is a non-dualistic school of Hinduism.
10 See Hilary Putnam, *Jewish Philosophy as a Guide to Life*.

regard, he associates himself with the views of Benedict Spinoza and Albert Einstein. Here's a short quote from Dworkin with which I resonate:

> When scientists confront the unimaginable vastness of space and the astounding complexity of atomic particles, they have an emotional reaction that matches [Rudolf] Otto's description surprisingly well. Indeed, many of them use the very term 'numinous' to describe what they feel. They find the universe awe-inspiring and deserving of a kind of emotional response that at least borders on trembling.[11]

While I hesitate to speak of the 'religious attitude' in terms of intrinsicality or inherence as Dworkin does in other places, I find it noteworthy that, when speaking about numinous experiences of the vastness, he invokes such terms as reverence, beauty, sublime, and awe. In any case, he emphasizes that the religious attitude need not be tied to or entail a theistic understanding of God. One no longer needs the idea of a personal god to be religious in this broader sense. But, of course, all of that became clearer to me only after my experiences in India.

RA: I can't wait to hear more about that. But it already seems clear to me that your sensitivities about Jewishness and anti-Semitism ran through much of your thinking and being from a very early age.

Michael: Yes. It has always been there. How could it have been otherwise? Dealing with my Jewishness has always been an ongoing project in one way or another. I would be unable to recognize myself without my Jewishness. My understanding of what it is to be Jewish has evolved over the years. Nonetheless, could I recognize myself without my Jewishness? Could I recognize myself in the face of my childhood experiences in regard to the Holocaust and my upbringing? Hardly.[12]

RA: Let's go back to how your parents reacted to your announcement that you were an atheist. Were they afraid that you might forget your Jewishness?

Michael: Yes, indeed. When my father saw that I was philosophically engaged and prepared to take up a different attitude about my Jewishness, one day, he pushed me against the wall and held me there—demanding that I promise

---

11 Ronald Dworkin, *Religion without God*, 20.
12 See Michael Krausz, "On Being Jewish."

him, "Never forget that you are a Jew!" I replied, "Yes, of course. I promise." That uncharacteristic behavior stands out in my memory—and it was psychologically counter-productive. Demands are no way to instill belief. On the other hand, I have come to more fully appreciate what my father's life had been like in the face of the murder of his parents. That's hard for me to fathom.

RA: So, you've described the development of your music as well as the awakening of your philosophical inclinations, which at first were focused on your Jewishness. These were quite serious interests. As your senior year wound down, what were your plans for after graduation?

Michael: I knew I didn't want the musical life that my parents had. I saw struggle and disappointment. My father never reached the kind of stature he had longed for in America, the kind he had already achieved in Europe. As well, while my violin playing was promising—especially in the years with Gingold—I did not come up to the level of Gingold's best students. So, in my senior year, I announced that instead of a conservatory, I wanted to apply to a university. I wanted something different, something bigger. My whole world had been music and being Jewish. While that was a lot, I felt restricted. I wanted something more.

On the other hand, as you know, I had been a poor academic student. Nevertheless, I applied to several universities, including Western Reserve University where, given my parents' associations there, I thought that I just might get some special consideration. No such luck. My grades were mediocre at best and I did not do well on the standardized tests. I was rejected by all of the schools I'd applied to. By any objective standards, there were good reasons for their doing so.

RA: So then what happened?

Michael: Well, during my senior year, my father taught a course in sketching to aspiring engineering students at Case Institute of Technology.

RA: How did that help you?

Michael: Well, my father approached his Division Chair at Case. He said, "I need your advice. I have a son who can't get into college! He's talented, but has not done well in school. What can we do for him?" His chair said, "I think I know who to talk to." He, in turn, talked to his old roommate from his college days at Yale, who eventually became the Vice President of Rutgers University. His name was David Denker. Subsequently, when the Cleveland Orchestra went to New York on one of its tours, I joined my father in New York City. Then, we both went to New Brunswick, New Jersey, to talk with Denker. At the meeting, my father praised me to the skies. He emphasized my abilities despite my poor grades, particularly highlighting my musical abilities that might contribute to the musical life of Rutgers. At the end of the meeting, which went nicely, Denker asked my father, "Laszlo, how are you getting to New York? You have a concert coming up in Carnegie Hall." My father replied, "We're planning to take the train." "Well," Denker answered, "I live in New York and I'm driving to the City. Can I take you?" And so he did. We continued our conversation while driving to New York. By the end of that trip, I was virtually admitted to Rutgers.

RA: What a wonderful opportunity. Perfect!

CHAPTER 3

Rutgers, London School of Economics, Indiana, Toronto, and Oxford

Michael: Perfect, you say! I had no idea what I was in for. I had never really tested my mind in a serious way. Up to that time, I had very little idea of what my real intellectual capabilities were.

RA: Did you also continue to have doubts about entering university rather than a music conservatory at that point?

Michael: Yes, I was regularly questioning whether I had made a big mistake by not applying to Juilliard or some other such conservatory.[1] But I soon got involved with playing quartets at the Douglas College campus of Rutgers, which kept me involved with music to some extent.

RA: And were you also able to remain an observant Jew to some extent as well?

Michael: Yes, I was able to get Kosher meals at Rutgers' Hillel House in New Brunswick.

As regarding my academic challenges, I was most fortunate. There were a couple of professors who took an interest in me. One was my English professor, David Higgins, for whom I wrote weekly papers based on our readings. Also, there was Jacques Marchand, a discussion-leader connected with the required Western Civilization course. He was a Jewish graduate student in the History Department, originally from Luxembourg. We eventually became life-long friends. Later, I also took a political science course that turned out to be a political philosophy course. It was taught by Michael Curtis. He was British, Jewish, and educated at the London School of Economics. He, too, was to become an important figure in my life.

RA: Was the course in political philosophy the gateway for you to study more philosophy?

---

1 It's ironic that starting in 2002, I would begin teaching aesthetics and philosophy of interpretation at the Curtis Institute of Music in Philadelphia.

Michael: Yes, and in my sophomore year, I took an introductory Philosophy course with Herbert Garelick. He was famous on campus for being an outstanding teacher and scholar of Kierkegaard.[2] That's when philosophy really opened up for me. During one of my appointments with him, I expressed skepticism about the entire enterprise of philosophy. Then, he asked me to write a paper about it. I did so. In a subsequent meeting, he said to me, of course, I was expected to do the assigned readings and the weekly papers. But if I wished, he would also give me a supplemental reading list and we could also meet weekly to discuss those works. I jumped at the chance.

One of several books I read at Garelick's suggestion was *Language, Thought, and Reality*, by Benjamin Lee Whorf. It's a book that argues that any given language embeds different ways of looking at and understanding the world. Whorf's chief example was the Hopi language. Many commentators about relativism have used that book to further their arguments.[3] Another significant book for me on Garelick's list was R.G. Collingwood's, *Speculum Mentis*. I loved that book. It's a book about the relationship between art, religion, science, history, and philosophy. He understands these not as domains but as forms of experience. For him, the aesthetic, the religious, the scientific, the historical, and the philosophical are modes of experience. I was impressed with the range and nature of Collingwood's concerns. He wrote in a clear and congenial way. Collingwood's work was to become an enduring touchstone for much of my philosophy that followed.

With Garelick, I was like a duck in water. I discovered that I was adept at philosophical questions and arguments. I loved getting clear about ideas. It was joyous. I enjoyed locating the nerve of an argument. And there was a further advantage for me in doing philosophy.

Reading had always been hard for me. I was incapable of reading quickly. So, when I discovered philosophy, I thought, "This is great! Not only can I only read slowly, but philosophy requires me do so!" My friends, who were taking courses in the English and literature departments, were required to real a lot. In philosophy, any given paragraph is often very thick in content. To understand it, you really do have to read slowly. For that reason too, philosophy suited me. In my sophomore year, I took an art history survey course with another popular

---

2 See Herbert M. Garelick, *The Anti-Christianity of Kierkegaard.*
3 Benjamin Lee Whorf, *Language, Thought, and Reality.*

teacher, Robert Raugh, which was also to inform my later interest in making art.

Also in my sophomore year, Michael Curtis asked me to proofread the manuscript of the second of his two-volume book, *The Great Political Theories*,[4] particularly his own introductory material. He also asked for my opinion of it. In a message to him that I still remember, I wrote, "little wine, lots of water." I had no idea how impertinent that must have sounded. In any case, I began to absorb it all and took it seriously.[5]

It was about then that I decided to major in philosophy. So, I made an appointment with the department chair, Joseph Neyer. As soon as I arrived in his office, I announced to him that I wanted to major in philosophy and that I had come to sign up. He slowed me down. He asked me why I wanted to do so. I can't quite remember what I told him. But I clearly remember what he said to me, "You know, Mr. Krausz, philosophy is like quick sand. If you put one foot into it, you will be fine. But if you put both of your feet into it, you will sink." I was enthralled. I replied, "In that case, please sign me up." I might say that, after Neyer's death many years later, a mutual acquaintance contacted me to say that Neyer had left an instruction: he had gifted me his cane, which I still cherish.

Also in my sophomore year, Curtis suggested that I should study at the London School of Economics and Political Science for my junior year. He was an alumnus of the LSE and offered to recommend me. Of course, the idea excited me. As it happened, he soon had reason to travel to London, and talked with the person responsible for dealing with so-called General Course students. He personally recommended me to her. What a gift that was!

RA: In addition to getting engrossed in philosophical studies, were you active in any other aspects of campus life at Rutgers?

Michael: Oh yes. As a matter of fact, I took an interest in campus politics and was even elected sophomore class President, but I didn't continue in campus politics after I returned to Rutgers.

---

4 Michael Curtis, *The Great Political Theories: 1. From Plato and Aristotle to Locke and Montesquieu*; and *2. From Burke, Rousseau and Kant to Modern Times.*
5 By an extraordinary coincidence, I was recently able to reconnect with Michael Curtis. In 2017, we had a wonderfully gratifying visit at his home in Princeton, New Jersey.

I arrived at LSE in the fall of 1963. My experience at the LSE was to become pivotal in my philosophical trajectory. I arrived at a world-class philosophy department, specifically a department called Philosophy, Logic, and Scientific Method, where the dominant figure was the renowned Karl Popper—later to become Sir Karl. Also, there was Imre Lakatos, Alan Musgrave, John Watkins, and J.O. Wisdom. After a few weeks, Wisdom became my tutor. I developed a fruitful and congenial relationship with him. He was most supportive and encouraging. Of course, Popper was the key figure. There I was, attending lectures, courses, and seminars from all of them. I recall the first time I attended one of Popper's seminars. You must understand what that means. A seminar with Popper included forty or fifty people. In attendance, in addition to LSE faculty members, graduate students, and others like me, were also visiting faculty members from around the world.

Here I was, an undergraduate at the back of this large room, listening to the great Viennese philosopher. Coincidentally, Popper started talking about Benjamin Lee Whorf. You will recall that I had worked on Whorf with Garelik. Something about what Popper was saying about Whorf struck me as not quite right. His characterization of Whorf's position struck me as mistaken.

From the back of the room, I raised my hand. Apparently, this was not something one does, certainly not by someone of my station. After a while, he saw my raised hand. He hesitated. Then he recognized me. I said something like, "Excuse me, Professor Popper, it seems to me that your account of Whorf is not quite as I understand it." I proceeded to lay out my alternative understanding. I finished. He stared at me in utter silence. Then he turned away and looked out of the window. Again, silence. That silence lasted for what felt like a full minute. Then he turned back to the group and carried on as if I had said nothing at all.

At the end of the hour, several of the senior graduate students descended upon me. They said, "We know you're new here. Let us give you some advice. This is Popper's seminar." I said, "Of course, I know it's Popper's seminar." One of them responded, "No, you don't understand. This is *Popper's* seminar."

That introduction turned out to be the beginning of my association with Popper. I saw him privately several times in his room, but he never referred to that first encounter. He was always kind and helpful to me. I went to his lectures and seminars. He signed and gave me several of his unpublished papers. He was a great influence in my philosophical thinking, sometimes as a model, sometimes as a foil.

The parts of Popper's philosophy that captured my enduring interest were his thesis of realism and his anti-essentialism. Of course, he is mostly well known for demarcating science from non-science by characterizing scientific statements as empirically falsifiable rather than being empirically verifiable.

It follows from Popper's logical insight about falsifiability that you can't prove a universal statement—the kind of law-like statements that classical physics, for example, strives for—by providing confirming instances of it. However many confirming instances you produce, won't establish the truth of the universal statement. In contrast—and this is his 'asymmetry' thesis—if you have one or only a few refuting instances, you can be secure in knowing that the universal hypothesis is false. In other words, refuting cases are logically much more powerful than confirming ones. Popper generalized this insight by offering refutability rather than verifiability as the criterion of science. At the same time, as I said, his opposition to essentialism has held enduring interest for me.

RA: What did Popper mean by 'anti-essentialism'?

Michael: My understanding about essentialism first arose in Popper's lectures and his seminal article called "Three Views of Human Knowledge." In that piece, Popper suggests that 'what is?' questions—such as, "What is an x?," "What is science?," "What is intelligence?," "What is art?," "What is music?," and you can add, "What is a self?"—are misguided, that is, if they are understood as asking for the *essence* of the thing in question.

Popper was critical of the view that a thing is what it is in virtue of its embodying an essence. Rather than informing us of the nature of the thing, it stops inquiry by arbitrarily postulating a first cause of the thing. Essentialist explanations are not informative. I found Popper's aversion to essentialism to be correct. And it has informed much my thinking in many ways. This is what he says about it in "Three Views of Human Knowledge":

> My criticism tries to show that whether essences exist or not, the belief in them does not help us in any way and, indeed, is likely to hamper us; so that there is no reason why the scientist should *assume* their existence.

> The belief in essences (whether true or false) is liable to create obstacles to thought—to the posing of new and fruitful problems ... [It is] a creed which is likely to lead to obscurantism.[6]

RA: Since anti-essentialism eventually played such an important role in your work, perhaps you might say a bit more about it.

Michael: OK. As I say, Popper had little tolerance for 'what is?' questions. He liked to use the question, "What is a puppy?" as an example. Consider the answer, "A puppy is a young dog." If you are an essentialist, you will begin by considering what its essence is, that is, what essential properties a dog must have to be a puppy. But if you are an anti-essentialist, you will begin by noting what properties puppies characteristically exhibit and simply label them as 'puppies'—without assuming that they exhibit essential properties. In other words, Popper uses labels to collect the result of our observations, without first assuming that a puppy exhibits essential properties for it to be what it is. Popper's example might seem to be a bit humdrum. But it has significant consequences for the understanding of anything for which you might ask, "What is it?"

As I said, Popper and his philosophy influenced me greatly. His philosophy was to become something of a touchstone for much of my philosophical career.

RA: I can see how his approach can have far-reaching philosophical implications. So how did it differ from that of the logical positivists?

Michael: Popper's philosophy opposes logical positivism—well represented at the time in Oxford by A.J. Ayer.[7] Ayer's philosophy affirmed that hypotheses that couldn't be verified are metaphysical. For him, that meant that they are cognitively meaningless. That was a stark and significant contrast to Popper's view, which held that hypotheses that were un-falsifiable are metaphysical but not on that account cognitively meaningless. Indeed, metaphysical hypotheses have been important in the history of science.

RA: Whom else did you work with at the LSE?

Michael: I was also a student of Imre Lakatos, a Hungarian philosopher of mathematics and science, known for his thesis of the fallibility of mathematics

---

6 See Popper's "Three Views of Human Knowledge," 105, 107.
7 See A.J. Ayer, *Language, Truth, and Logic*.

and its methodology of proofs and refutations.[8] He introduced the concept of 'research programmes' in science and mathematics. Lakatos was brilliant. He had a knack for spotting the nerve of an argument, fixing his attention on it, then demolishing it. His questions in Popper's seminars—especially those he addressed to visiting professors—would initially sound naive. Yet often they were devastating.

My first private encounter with Lakatos was memorable. After a class during which I raised a question, he invited me to his room to continue our conversation. As he opened his door, he stopped me from moving forward. There, on the opposite wall facing us, was a large photograph of Martin Heidegger. Lakatos said, "Before we go in, I want you to promise me one thing." "What is it?" I asked. He continued, "I want you to memorize that face. And I want you to promise me that you will resist everything that man stands for. Only then will I allow you to enter my study." I agreed. What else could I do? In the end, I couldn't always keep that promise, although I still have had an ambivalent attitude toward Heidegger.

RA: So why did Lakatos ask you to make that promise?

Michael: Lakatos thought that as a philosopher, Heidegger was an obscurantist and dangerous. He couldn't stand Heidegger's way of doing philosophy. It's also true that while I have benefitted from the Heideggerian notion of situatedness, and especially from his "The Origin of the Work of Art,"[9] I have never been able to get over his Nazism. Heidegger was a big Nazi. He also served as the Rector of the University of Freiburg and closely associated with Hitler.

But there was still more to it than that. Lakatos had been a significant figure in the Hungarian Communist Party. Then, under the influence of Popper's writings—particularly *The Open Society and Its Enemies*[10]—Lakatos turned against communism. As a result, he was jailed. According to his account, after being in confinement for a year, Lakatos was introduced to a new cellmate, who was a Jesuit priest. The first thing he said to Lakatos was, "In one year I will make you a believer." Lakatos replied, "In one year I'll make you an atheist." In one year, the priest was an atheist. After Lakatos was released—I don't know the circumstances—he made his way to England, where he pursued a doctorate degree in philosophy of mathematics at Cambridge. I think he worked

---

8   See Imre Lakatos, *Proofs and Refutations*.
9   Martin Heidegger, "The Origin of the Work of Art."
10   Karl R. Popper, *The Open Society and Its Enemies*.

under R.B. Braithwaite. And then, he made his way to the LSE as a colleague of Popper. So there they were, Austrian and Hungarian, in Britain.[11]

RA: Whom else did you work with?

Michael: I also took a seminar on Hume with Popper's research assistant, Alan Musgrave. He was perceptive and mild mannered. One day, after I had bought several philosophy books in LSE's *Economist Book Shop*, I went to Musgrave's seminar. Before class began, I placed the books down on the seminar table. Among my new books was James Griffin's, *Wittgenstein's Logical Atomism*.[12] True to the strong anti-Wittgensteinian bias of the LSE department, as Musgrave walked in and glanced at my newly purchased books he quipped, "You Americans. You'll buy anything!"

Toward the end of that academic year, Wisdom and Musgrave urged me to schedule myself for the exam for the MSc degree—their master's degree. They had forgotten that I was an undergraduate at Rutgers. I intended to return to America to finish my BA degree first. What's more, I wanted to avail myself of the long vacation period between the Lent and Summer terms by travelling to the Continent instead of preparing myself for an exam. While they pressed me to take the exam so that I might stay at the LSE and go directly for the MSc. degree, that was a scenario beyond my horizon. It was a path not taken.

RA: Was there more to your decision not to stay at the LSE?

Michael: Well, yes. For all the talk about refutability and criticism in science, there was little concern amongst the Popperians about the place of art and music in Popper's philosophical landscape. I wondered how his philosophy might apply to those areas. I asked about it to my tutor J.O. Wisdom, as well as Alan Musgrave, but they demurred.

It was only later that I found out that Popper explicitly argued against subjectivism in music, particularly the romantic and post-romantic composers. In his autobiography, *Unended Quest*,[13] consistent with his Three Worlds Hypothesis—where he distinguishes between the physical world, the subjective world, and

---

11 For more about Lakatos in Hungary, see Alexander E. Bandy, *Chess and Chocolate*.
12 James Griffin, *Wittgenstein's Logical Atomism*.
13 K.R. Popper, *Unended Quest*.

objective knowledge—he was consistently hostile to subjectivism.[14] That hostility showed itself in his attitudes toward subjectivist music and art. He expressed a strongly anti-expressionist attitude toward art and music.

He would dismiss such composers as Brahms and Wagner for example. It is easy to see why he would be hostile to expressionists in the visual arts and other forms of art that do not see themselves as engaged with solving objective problems. He regarded them as beyond critical evaluation. I couldn't abide that, especially since I was developing a love for Anton Bruckner and later for Gustav Mahler.

RA: But you were unaware of Popper's own interests in music and art while you were at the LSE. Is that right?

Michael: That's right, I learned of it when I read *Unended Quest*, but that wasn't until after I left the LSE. Then I learned even more about it many years later, when I talked with the renowned pianist Rudolf Serkin, then the Director of the Curtis Institute of Music in Philadelphia. Serkin and Popper had known each other during their youth in Vienna. Serkin told me that Popper himself had been an accomplished composer. Both Serkin and Popper had similar musical preferences in that they did not care for the then current music of such a-tonalists such as Arnold Schönberg. It's ironic because Schönberg's music is so very clearly problem situational, what with its twelve tone formulas. As well, it was interesting that the great art historian, Ernst Gombrich did share Popper's objectivist attitude to great effect in his treatment of the history of perspective. Gombrich credited Popper with his 'objectivist' approach to the history of art, as he indicates in his masterwork, *Art and Illusion*.[15]

RA: These were things that you learned after your time at the LSE. What else entered into your decision not to stay at the LSE at the time?

---

14 See K.R. Popper, *Objective Knowledge: An Evolutionary Approach*, which is dedicated to Alfred Tarski. It is ironic that Popper dedicated this book to Tarksi in light of Tarski's resistance to associating his own semantic theory of truth with any particular metaphysics (which would presumably include Popper's objectivism or realism). Here is what Tarski says: "Thus, we may accept the semantic conception of truth without giving up any epistemological attitude we may have had; we may remain naïve realists, critical realists or idealists, empiricists or metaphysicians—whatever we were before. The semantic conception is completely neutral toward all these issues"; see Alfred Tarski, "The Semantic Conception of Truth."
15 E.H. Grombich, *Art and Illusion*.

Michael: Well, I also had reservations about the philosophical environment at LSE. There was a cliquishness about the Popper school, a sense of who was in and who was out. I felt as if I were being groomed to be in. Of course, that was flattering. I heard of others who were in, even if they were at other universities. For example, Joseph Agassi was between Jerusalem and Boston. Ian Jarvie was in Hong Kong and later, at York University in Toronto. William Warren Bartley, too, was elsewhere but mentioned often. There was a closedness about the Popperians, despite the fact that they propounded openness to criticism for the sake of the growth of knowledge. I didn't like that cliquishness. I didn't want to become a 'Popperian.' But still, Popper was the first truly major mind I had encountered. I'd never seen such tenacity and drive to get a philosophical point right, and I resonated with him as a person—coming from Vienna, close enough to Hungary—a victim of the upheaval of Europe. He was an atheist who came from Jewish stock.

Nevertheless, on occasion, I saw Popper behave badly. For example, I didn't like his treatment of a visiting professor from Alexandria in Egypt, and I didn't like his treatment of a graduate student from Hong Kong. In one of Popper's seminars, the Egyptian professor had only just begun to read his paper on Sartre's theories of emotions. He hadn't gotten through his first paragraph when Popper stopped him and gave him a tongue lashing—and I use that phrase advisedly—for even seriously considering a theory of emotions, let alone Sartre's, as a legitimate topic for philosophical discussion in the first place. I'm sure Popper was motivated by his aversion toward 'subjectivist' approaches to knowledge. The guest was devastated. Within days, he left England and returned home to Alexandria. While Popper advocated open and critical discussion, in his practice, sometimes 'critical' turned into bullying. I would not like to have been on the receiving end it.

RA: Were you?

Michael: Fortunately, I never was. In fact, he was kind to me. As the year progressed he received me graciously, offering unpublished papers for me to read.

RA: Still, you said there was another episode that disturbed you.

Michael: Yes. There was a smart sensitive woman, a Master's student from Hong Kong, who had just consulted Popper in his office. By chance, I saw her coming out of his office, in tears. I asked her what the matter was. She said, "That man! That man! He's destroying my God!"

RA: What was your reaction?

Michael: My reaction then was that there are some basic suppositions—they comprise a basic fabric of one's inner life, if I can put it that way—that should be dealt with special care. Criticism of such suppositions should be tempered. They should be treated with sensitivity and compassion and not subject to combative argumentation that might be appropriate in other contexts.

There is more than an issue of civility or good manners here; there is a philosophical point here, which I began only later to appreciate more fully. They concern what Wittgenstein might have called 'hinge' propositions—those central to one's form of life, or, as I like to say, one's fabric of being. Sometimes they include religious beliefs. That episode affected my understanding of what philosophy can or should do, and how one should do it.

Philosophers need to recognize that there is such a thing as a fabric of, or, a form of life—pick your metaphor—by which we can make sense of ourselves to ourselves, so that we can live with ourselves. Of course, we need to attend to it and revise it as needed, in the face of experience. But, as I said, we should deal with such issues with care and humility. In the end, we are dealing with persons—persons who are and have situated themselves within one or another fabric of life—including beliefs and values. That's what allows them to make sense of themselves to themselves. Adjustments in that fabric should be made with care, understanding, and compassion.

RA: It sounds to me as if you are making a general point that goes beyond a philosophy of knowledge, extending to a philosophy of religion.

Michael: Perhaps, but it's not so much a philosophy of religion that I'm talking about as a life-philosophy, a *Lebensphilosophie*. My remarks might sound a bit odd coming from someone who had declared himself an atheist. But my point is larger than religious belief. It goes to the fabric of one's inner life. I am speaking about civility in regard to criticism of basic suppositions that shape one's inner life.

In any case, those episodes contributed to my sense that perhaps, at least in the longer run, LSE was not the place for me. In years that followed, I did wonder whether I had made a mistake by not staying at the LSE. Certainly, my life would have been quite different had I done so.

In any event, my unease with Popperians was born out when I presented a paper in Tel Aviv, in 1978. Joseph Agassi, one of Popper's more aggressive devotees attacked me in such as a manner as to prompt an apology from the presiding department Chair.

RA: Why? What happened?

Michael: In an exploratory way, I had raised doubts about the sharpness of Popper's tripartite distinction between World I (the world of physical states), World 2 (the world of mental or subjective states), and World 3 (the world of objective contents of thought). When I finished, Agassi loudly proclaimed that, in response to my presentation, Popper would have said my treatment was 'immoral.' I asked why Popper would have said such a thing. Agassi replied that Popper would not say why he would say such a thing. In turn, I said to Agassi, "Then you owe me an explanation why you said that Popper would have said that what I said was immoral." Agassi then shouted, "I owe you nothing!" As I say, I received a formal apology from the chair of the department.

RA: In the meantime, you mentioned that that year in London was significant for you in religious ways too. What did you have in mind?

Michael: In a word, I stopped keeping kosher. The fact that I had earlier declared myself an atheist hadn't kept me from keeping kosher until that year in London. I suppose that abandoning the practice was inevitable, but the occasion was unexpected. On a bright sunny day, I had been working at the British Museum. When I walked out of that imposing building, I saw a fairly narrow street ahead of me. I walked down that street and came upon a modest Italian restaurant. I walked in, and sat down in a hard wooden booth. A waitress came by and asked for my order. Without hesitation, I said, "Spaghetti and meatballs, please." A short while later, without a word, the waitress placed an appetizing meal before me. I ate it.

RA: How did it taste?

Michael: Delicious!

RA: As simple as that?

Michael: Yes and no. Over the next days and weeks, I started to feel guilty. My stomach was upset. I was physically uncomfortable.

RUTGERS, LSE, INDIANA, TORONTO, & OXFORD

RA: So then, what did you do?

Michael: There were many Indian students at the LSE, so there was a vegetarian line in the refectory. I would alternate between the vegetarian and non-vegetarian lines. Eventually, I was eating whatever I pleased without difficulty, but it took a while.

RA: You had vacations between the three academic terms at the LSE, did you not?

Michael: Yes indeed. During the break between the first and second term[16] I travelled on the continent, including a visit to Geneva, which as you know, is where I was born. The renowned conductor, Ernest Ansermet, had been such a major figure in the history of our family, I felt as if I already knew him. Indeed, I still have a signed photo, which he dedicated to Peter and me. So, I felt uninhibited about contacting him and asking if I might visit with him. He graciously agreed.

In addition to other things about our family, I wanted to discuss with Ansermet something in his book on music, *Écrits sur La Musique*.[17] In that book, Ansermet disparaged the later works of Stravinsky—his own lifelong friend and professional partner. Those works were composed in the atonal idiom. Ansermet charged that Stravinsky's later works were music no longer. He supported his critique against Stravinsky on essentialist grounds, borrowed from the German philosopher, Edmund Husserl. Music, properly understood, Ansermet argued, must be essentially, inherently, tonal.[18] I took exception with Ansermet's essentialist dismissal of Stravinsky's atonal works.

RA: So how did the maestro receive you?

Michael: He was gracious when speaking about my parents, and he patiently listened to my worries about essentialism. Then he excused himself since he had to rest before his concert later that evening.

---

16   LSE has a three term academic year—Michaelmas Term (MT), during Fall; Lent Term (LT), during Spring; and Summer Term (ST).
17   Ernest Ansermet, *Écrits sur la Musique* (Writings on Music).
18   For a discussion of Ansermet's essentialism in music, see Michael Krausz, "The Tonal and the Foundational."

RA: Remarkable! Are there any other stories you can tell of your travels around Europe that year?

Michael: Among other places I visited during that year, I went to Italy between the Lent and Summer terms in 1964, when I visited Naples, and nearby Pompeii and Vesuvius. At Vesuvius, something extraordinary happened to me, a kind of awakening. I was alone walking on a winding path. I could see Mount Vesuvius in the distance. It was a gorgeous day. As the path turned, I came upon an opening, rather like a crèche. There, before me in the shrubs, were several lambs huddled together. The utter beauty of it all overwhelmed me. That experience was not ordinary. It was powerful and disorienting. I could not fathom what had happened to me. After a while, in my analytic mode, I started asking myself questions such as, "What's happening to me? This is nothing like the way I usually experience things." Of course, by asking such questions of myself I interrupted the experience. Later, I tried to suppress its memory. Still later, though, I recognized that indeed something important had happened to me. I think of it as an aesthetic experience or an awakening.

I might say that many years later, outside Estes Park, Colorado, when Connie and I were hiking in the neighboring Rocky Mountains, I had a similar experience. I was at the foot of a very high constellation. Connie was already some hundred feet higher than I; I was just leaning against a tree. Below me was a gully. I was still. It was then that I experienced another moment as I had had at Vesuvius so many years before.

RA: It sounds as if your experiences at Vesuvius and Estes Park were at odds with the sort of concerns you were pursuing in the philosophy of science at the LSE.

Michael: Yes. From my present vantage point, I might say that those experiences came to be pivotal in my reflections about self-realization. But at those moments, theorizing about such things didn't seem so urgent.

Speaking of urgency, I also had a distantly related episode soon after my travels to Italy, when I visited Israel for the first time.

RA: Distantly related?

Michael: Yes. It involved my going to Marseille and from there I took a freighter to Haifa. Then, I found my way to Jerusalem. At a social gathering involving friends of my brother Peter—namely, with Marvin Wolfe and Eddie Prager—I was introduced to graduate students at the Hebrew University. As it happened, I met a graduate student of Martin Buber. That excited me. I asked if he thought I might meet Professor Buber. After the student made some inquiries on my behalf, he secured Professor Buber's telephone number. I called. A woman answered the phone. I indicated my interest to speak with Professor Buber about philosophical and religious issues. Then she called Buber to the phone. After listening to my introduction and my request to meet and interview him about philosophical and religious matters, he asked in a kindly German accented voice, "Is it urgent?" I paused. He had stopped me. Then I replied, "No, it is not urgent." He then explained that, since he was not well, if I would write him a letter he would reply. Alas, he died a few weeks later on June 13, 1965, before I got a chance to write to him.

I tell the story of that experience, because he did teach me something important during that phone conversation. Certain philosophical or religious questions at certain times can be urgent. As it happened, I was not in such a state of urgency at that time.

RA: Have you returned to Israel since then?

Michael: Yes, indeed. On several occasions, I went to visit with family, as well as to teach for a term in 1978, in the Philosophy Department at the Hebrew University. But I can tell you more about that later.

RA: So, in the meantime, after the spring of 1964, you returned to London from your travels, then you went back to Rutgers for your senior year. Is that right?

Michael: Yes.

RA: What was it like to go back at Rutgers after the heady experiences you had at the LSE and elsewhere?

Michael: My friend and earlier teacher, Jacques Marchand, had introduced me to Michael Greenberg and Gene Lieber—two graduate students in History, who were very involved in community politics. We lived together in a small, shabby apartment at 52 City Alley. The address—in which I took considerable pride—says it all. It was in a depressed black area of New Brunswick. This was an intensely political time, in the throes of the Vietnam War, the Woman's movement, the sexual revolution, and local community action. More than once, I would come home to find a black kid sleeping it off after being bailed out of jail by one of my flat mates.

Michael and Gene were very left-leaning and much taken by the work of the philosopher, Herbert Marcuse. They strongly encouraged me to apply for graduate work at the University of California at San Diego to work with Marcuse.

As you know, Marcuse was a kind of Marxist holist from the Frankfurt school of Critical Theory. I was impressed with the overriding message of his book, *One Dimensional Man*.[19] But I was ambivalent about following his path, partly because I had been impressed with Popper's arguments against holism in favor of individualism, as he had written in his important book, *The Open Society and Its Enemies*.[20]

At the same time, during that year at Rutgers, I took a seminar on Wittgenstein with Amélie Rorty. I must have made a nuisance of myself in that seminar, since I persisted in rehearsing Popper's objections to Wittgenstein.[21] At that time, Amélie was married to Richard Rorty. They lived in Princeton, which is not far from New Brunswick. I also benefitted greatly from other professors in the Philosophy Department at Rutgers, including Fred Schick and Robert Zimmerman.

During that year, Imre Lakatos came from London to Princeton to give some lectures. It was excellent to see him again and to talk with him. Lakatos's own philosophical work on Research Programs was subjected to serious examination and questioning, mostly by inductivists. Chiefly among them was visiting professor Richard Jeffrey—a follower of Rudolph Carnap and Carl Hempel. Carnap and Hempel had been together in the Vienna Circle during the time that Popper was highly critical of the positivists. Hempel himself was now on the Princeton faculty.

At the same time, the philosopher and historian of science, Thomas Kuhn, was also on the faculty at Princeton. But I didn't get to know him personally until many years later, at a National Endowment for the Humanities seminar on interpretation in Santa Cruz, California. Yet, I was well aware of the outlines of his work. My interest in Kuhn's work had already started when I was at the LSE.

---

19   Herbert Marcuse, *One Dimensional Man*.
20   Popper, *The Open Society and Its Enemies*.
21   See K.R. Popper, "The Nature of Philosophical Problems and Their Roots in Science."

In his Three Worlds Hypothesis, Popper insisted upon an objectivist or absolutist ontology in contrast with Kuhn's psychological or sociological approach to the history of science. Kuhn emphasized the human or cultural dimension in contrast to Popper's quasi-Platonic permanentist approach.

With special vigor, in 1963, Popper had attacked Kuhn's then recently published book, *The Structure of Scientific Revolutions*.[22] Popper was vehement in his opposition to it. And when I was back in New Brunswick, I was in touch with Arindam Chakrabarti, who had been a student of Popper's at the LSE and then went to Princeton to write his dissertation under Kuhn.

I started to have still more doubts about Popper's objectivist or absolutist approach to scientific knowledge when I more deeply encountered the work of Kuhn—especially after I attended the International Colloquium in the Philosophy of Science, in 1965, at Bedford College.

RA: Oh. So you went back to London for that now famous conference?

Michael: Yes. And after that, I went to Paris for a holiday where I rented a room close to the Jardin du Luxembourg where I carefully re-read Kuhn's book.

RA: So, what happened at the conference?

Michael: The conference featured a debate on the philosophy of science between Popper and Kuhn. It was quite something.

RA: Who was there? What was that like?

Michael: Oh, my. It included the senior luminaries of that generation of philosophers of science and logicians. Besides Popper and Kuhn, it included Alfred Tarski, Rudoph Carnap, R.B. Braithwaite, Imre Lakatos, John Watkins, J.O. Wisdom, L. Pearce Williams, Stephen Toulmin, Margaret Masterman, Paul Feyerabend, W.V.O. Quine, and others. Sometimes, discussions were quite heated. I was surprised, though, to see how relatively quiet Popper was through it all. Later, the proceedings of that conference were published in an important

---

22 See Thomas S. Kuhn, *The Structure of Scientific Revolutions*.

collection under the title, *Criticism and the Growth of Knowledge*, edited by Lakatos and Musgrave.[23]

RA: What was the central controversy about?

Michael: In a nutshell, it was about Popper's idea that science should to be understood in terms of empirical falsifiability versus Kuhn's idea that science should be understood in terms of normal science, conducted in accord with received paradigms. Kuhn had turned Popper's objectivist question into an historical or sociological question. In different terms, you might say that it was a debate between objectivism and relativism. It became clear to me that the central issue between Popper and Kuhn amounted to a difference in how they interpreted the history of science. More generally, their differences lay in their philosophies of history.

RA: You mentioned that you had some more personal time with Kuhn many years later.

Michael: Yes. Much later in 1988, I had the opportunity to talk at length with Kuhn at that NEH Summer Institute at the University of California in Santa Cruz. Kuhn was one of a star-studded panel of instructors, which included Stanley Cavell, Hubert Dreyfus, Clifford Geertz, David Hoy, Alexander Nehamas, Richard Rorty, and Charles Taylor. They interacted with each other and about twenty of us younger participants. I can talk more about that institute later, but in the meantime, I can tell you that I had a nice relationship with Kuhn. I liked him. He was a sympathetic, open person, very approachable.

During an informal moment with him, I told Kuhn that I was struck by similarities between his view and that of Collingwood—specifically Kuhn's idea of paradigms and Collingwood's idea of absolute presuppositions.[24] I told Kuhn that there seemed to me to be a close relationship between their respective views. I asked him directly whether he had borrowed from Collingwood's idea of absolute presuppositions in formulating his own views about paradigms. He was unguarded and straightforward about it. He said yes, he had. I found this interesting because nowhere in print had I seen that Kuhn had acknowledged Collingwood.

---

23   Imre Lakatos and Alan Musgrave, eds., *Proceedings of the International Colloquium in the Philosophy of Science, 1965*.
24   See R.G. Collingwood, *An Essay on Metaphysics*; see especially "Note to Chapter V," 48.

RA: So, after the summer of 1965, you went to Indiana University?

Michael: That's right. My reasons were both philosophical and financial. There were two separate departments at Indiana University, one in Philosophy and another in History and Philosophy of Science. I could work with excellent people in both. That suited me. As well, a fellowship allowed me to become financially independent of my parents. I was keen not to depend upon their support.

RA: So whom did you work with at Indiana?

Michael: In Philosophy, among my teachers was Alan Donagan, an excellent Australian philosopher and a highly regarded Collingwood scholar. Kenneth Schmitz, a learned Hegel scholar, became my MA thesis director. There was Thomas Langan, a Heidegger enthusiast, and Ernst Manesse, a Holocaust survivor and a visiting scholar in Greek Philosophy from North Carolina Central University. He was personally very encouraging. In the Philosophy of Science, I took courses with Michael Scriven and Wesley Salmon. Scriven was a very quick and intelligent thinker. I learned a lot from him in the area of causation. I was impressed by his idea that a cause is a non-redundant member of a set of jointly sufficient conditions. He presented his idea with wonderful examples. He also raised important questions in other areas. In turn, Salmon was a major contributor to inductive logic and its calculus. While Popper had claimed that inductive logic does not exist, here, in Salmon, was a mild mannered yet penetrating and deeply thoughtful inductive logician! He had been a student of Hans Reichenbach and an associate of Carnap. While I was not disposed to get involved with the formalisms of Salmon's work, he impressed me.[25]

RA: It sounds like that year at Indiana was fruitful.

Michael: It was. Besides my course work, I managed to write much of my MA thesis, "On Method in Metaphysics," which I completed the following summer. I also had a lovely reunion with Josef Gingold.

RA: Gingold, your old violin teacher from Cleveland?

Michael: Yes. When I arrived at Indiana University, I went to its music school to see Gingold. As I mentioned before, he had retired from the Cleveland Orchestra to join the music faculty at Indiana. After I knocked on his door,

---

25   For a collection of Salmon's works, see *Causality and Explanation*.

he opened it. He did not immediately recognize me. I told him that I was Michael Krausz. At that moment, he hugged me and invited me in. It was a lovely reunion.

And years later, I saw Gingold again at the Curtis Institute of Music in Philadelphia where, as a visitor, he gave a Master Class. When Gingold saw me again there, he said without hesitation—as if no time had passed since our earliest days in Cleveland— "Ah, the *Spring Sonata*" (of Beethoven). It was a piece he had coached me on many years earlier in Cleveland. He never forgot. That was Gingold. On that occasion, Gingold told me that despite his age and dwindling technique, he was a better musician then than he had ever been. That puzzled me. But I now think I understand.

RA: What do you think he meant?

Michael: Perhaps it was that after so many years of performing and teaching, he had come to a place where he could more fully understand the larger life context of his music-making. And that understanding allowed him to make music in still more thoughtful, refined, and deepened ways. That is only a surmisal. In any event, his memory continues to inspire me.

I might mention that later still, Gingold wrote me a letter congratulating me on the publication of my edition of *The Interpretation of Music: Philosophical Essays*. My own piece in that book, "Rightness and Reasons in Musical Interpretation," contained the kernel of what was to become a full-blown treatment of interpretation.[26]

RA: In the meantime, it seems that, after Kuhn, your interest in philosophy of science was shifting to the philosophy of history. Am I right?

Michael: Yes, one of the things that became clear to me in Bloomington was that I was getting less interested in the history and philosophy of science and more interested in the philosophy of history more generally—including questions of explanation, understanding, intentionality, reenactment, and the like.

RA: That year in Bloomington must have been intense, doing all your courses and the thesis. What else had been going on during that year in Bloomington?

---

26   Michael Krausz, "Rightness and Reasons in Musical Interpretation."

Michael: I had met Ann Shteir, also called Rusty, when I was a sophomore at Rutgers, and she was a senior at Douglas College, the women's college of Rutgers. She was a year older than I and in her senior year, majoring in German and Comparative Literature. When I came back to New Brunswick from London in the fall of 1964, I resumed my relationship with Rusty. Then, when I did the year at Bloomington, she was already doing her graduate work at Rutgers, working with such figures as Josef Frank, Glauco Cambon, and John McCormack. During that year, we visited each other at our respective locations. After my year in Bloomington, we married in 1966. Our marriage eventually ended in 1972. As in all such things, the reasons were complicated.

In the meantime, of course, there was the question of Vietnam. I was not about to stick around for the draft. No matter what, I was not going to participate in that unjust war. So, I looked northward to Canada. I applied and was accepted with a fellowship at the University of Toronto for my PhD. As it turned out, I was never called up by the draft.

RA: So you were on the move again. What was Toronto like?

Michael: I liked Toronto. I liked Canada. Many like-minded Americans were residing there. The graduate department was and still is, I think, the biggest in North America. At the time, there were about fifty-five full time faculty members. You can imagine the array of sub-fields and orientations represented. When I arrived in Toronto, the head of the graduate program, David Savan—a scholar of pragmatist Charles Sanders Peirce, and himself a wonderful person—called me in to his office. He congratulated me for my admission to the program. Then, he also gave me some disturbing news.

RA: What was it?

Michael: Apparently, coinciding with my arrival at the University of Toronto, the department had instituted a new set of PhD requirements that would go into effect the following year. That meant that the year of my arrival was the last year during which the old-style comprehensive examinations were to be administered. Accordingly, I was expected to take my comprehensive examinations at the end of my very first year in Toronto. Needless to say, I had to work very hard that year of 1966–1967. Besides my course work—and my serving for a while as dormitory supervisor at the Glendon Campus of York University—I had to prepare for the exams in the spring of 1967.

As well, I took a course with J.T. Stevenson who was preoccupied with Edmund Gettier's justified-true-belief account of knowledge. Stevenson was an exceptionally able and clear-minded philosopher. However, I was suspicious about the nature of his philosophical project. My resistance derived from an aversion to what I had inherited from Popper, an aversion to "What is?" questions. Stevenson embraced Gettier's question, "What is knowledge?" in the essentialist way that Popper warned against. The project was to identify the necessary and sufficient conditions for knowledge. Its program entailed an inquiry into the meanings of 'justify,' 'true' and 'belief.' It was an inerentist program. Stevenson's course was excellent of its kind. But it wasn't my kind.

I also worked with American sociologist Lewis Samuel Feuer. He had been a Marxist and later a neo-conservative. He had taught at University of California, Berkeley for many years before coming to Toronto. He was an interesting man. I also became friends with Arnold Rockman, a mature co-member of the Feuer seminar, who was much taken by the work of Marshall McLuhan, who, at that time, was all the rage in Toronto.

RA: How did you fare that year?

Michael: As I say, it was a demanding year, but I did pass my comprehensive exams.

In the meantime, Rusty finally finished her residency at Rutgers the following year, and we moved to an apartment in the center of the city not far from the University of Toronto.

It was during the following year, 1967 or 1968, that I taught a large section of history of philosophy, assisting and supervised by Robert McRay. I much enjoyed the big lecture style. It demanded that I learn a good deal of history of philosophy. I liked performing to a large audience. In the midst of all of that, I also participated in lively discussions with excellent graduate students. I also had excellent philosophical conversations with philosopher Ronald DeSousa, and I started serious work on my dissertation. Not surprisingly, I wrote my dissertation on Collingwood's theory of absolute presuppositions,[27] under the supervision of the noted analytic philosopher of history, William H. Dray. Dray was a key figure in analytic philosophy of history and Collingwood studies, and he

---

27 Michael Krausz, "A Critique of R.G. Collingwood's Theory of Absolute Presuppositions."

was one of the major people in the Toronto department.[28] He was a dream of a supervisor. He would read my drafts carefully and engage in thorough discussions about them. Also, Dray was a proud graduate of Balliol College, Oxford.

But Dray left the University of Toronto for Trent University before I finished my dissertation. In anticipation of his leaving, he said to me, "You know, Michael, you ought to go to Oxford to finish your work on Collingwood." He had in mind for me to finish my dissertation under the supervision of Patrick Gardiner of Magdalen College, Oxford. He offered to help arrange for my acceptance at Oxford through Gilbert Ryle, whom he knew well. At that time, Ryle was Head of the Sub-Faculty of Philosophy at Oxford.

RA: Another happy coincidence in your life?

Michael: I should say so! There is an interesting story about my initial meeting with Ryle when he came to give a much anticipated evening faculty seminar at the University of Toronto. Bill had done all he could to arrange for me to meet Ryle, but there was a snag. There were so many Oxonian philosophers in Toronto, who wanted to talk with Ryle. After repeated efforts, Bill just couldn't manage to bring the two of us together. I was sorely disappointed.

Still, I went to Ryle's seminar. Just as the imposing Ryle entered the large seminar room, I had urgently to relieve myself in the men's room. So I walked out. The seminar room was in a large sterile engineering building. The long corridors were unlit and dark. I started to walk down a long hallway looking for the men's room. Then, I heard footsteps of someone walking behind me. I turned around, and whom did I see? Ryle! He, too, had left the seminar room and was looking for the men's room. As we hunted for the men's room together, I started chatting with him about Bill and his efforts to arrange for me to meet Ryle.

RA: Wow. What happened?

Michael: By the time we returned to the seminar room, I had fully informed him about Bill's intentions and my philosophical background and interests. Ryle assured me that he would do what he could to arrange for a place for me at Linacre College, the newly established Oxford College dedicated exclusively for graduate students.

---

28   See William H. Dray, *Laws and Explanation in History*; *On History and Philosophers of History*; and *History as Re-Enactment*.

RA: That's quite a story. What good fortune!

Michael: I should say so!

RA: How did it go for you at Oxford?

Michael: Contrary to Popper's view of Oxford—he had characterized it as preoccupied with avoiding serious problems of knowledge and had little patience for Wittgensteinian modes of language analysis—I found Oxford to be a refreshingly open place. Ryle had indeed placed me in Linacre College that, at that time, enjoyed a lively coterie of American graduate students, all welcomed by its Fellow in Philosophy, Rom Harré, with whom I still enjoy a cordial relationship. I took several classes with him. We eventually co-authored a book.[29] I also attended classes and seminars and had discussions with Alan Montefiore[30] about emotions, Joseph Raz[31] about ethics, Stephen Lukes[32] about relativism, David Pears about Wittengenstein, and in years that followed, with William Newton-Smith on philosophy of science, and Paul Snowdon on personal identity.

As well, life in the Common Room at Linacre was always lively with philosophical and political discussions. Amongst my graduate student friends were Russell Keat, who eventually landed at the University of Lancaster; Ted Benton, who ended up at Essex; Larry Blum, who teaches at University of Massachusetts in Boston; Rinty Van Straaten, who secured a position at the University of Witwaterstrom; and Michael Teitelman, who went on to a career in medicine.

Patrick Gardiner, with whom Bill had corresponded about my work on Collingwood, was my supervisor at Oxford. He was informed, astute, attentive, and most welcoming. He closely commented on drafts of my thesis. I sat in on many of his classes and seminars, including most notably those in the Philosophy of History, jointly taught by Gardiner and Sir Isaiah Berlin. My time in that seminar was especially rewarding. Gardiner and Berlin asked me to give a presentation on Collingwood, which I gladly did. Berlin thought well of it. That was the first of many associations with him. He became a significant figure in my life.

---

29 Rom Harré and Michael Krausz, *Varieties of Relativism*.
30 Alan Montefiore, now Emeritus Fellow of Balliol College, Oxford University, focused on the theme of emotions in his philosophical research.
31 Joseph Raz is a legal, moral, and political philosopher, with an interest in legal positivism. He is currently at Columbia University Law School.
32 Stephen Lukes is a British political and social theorist.

It turned out that Berlin, himself, knew Collingwood and had high regard for him. In the course of numerous conversations with Berlin that year and others to follow, I learned a lot about Collingwood and much more.

I also attended lectures by A.J. Ayer on the topic of 'facts.' After his first lecture, I introduced myself to him and told him that I was writing a dissertation on Collingwood. Then he said, "Oh yes. [pause] Collingwood. [pause] He was a very intelligent man. [pause] He had a very high opinion of me." According to Oxford philosopher, Peter Hacker, it turned out that despite their philosophical differences, Collingwood had regarded Ayers's *Language, Truth, and Logic* as important.

In any event, Oxford was a wonderful place for me and I did, indeed, nearly finish my dissertation for Toronto under Gardiner. More than that, Gardiner introduced me to Daniel Davin, then head of the Philosophy Division at the Oxford University Press, which eventually published a collection of papers that I edited, entitled, *Critical Essays on the Philosophy of R.G. Collingwood*.[33] When it was published in 1972, it received significant international attention, including a positive front-page review by Ernest Gellner in the *Times Literary Supplement*,[34] with dozens of its copies displayed in the front window of Blackwell's Book Shop on High Street.

During visits to Oxford in following years, I met numerous other Oxford dons and visitors, who included David Novitz from New Zealand—also interested in the theory of interpretation. He became a long-standing philosophical interlocutor of mine. David, in turn, introduced me to Bernard Harrison at Sussex University. That was auspicious, for over the years, Bernard and his wife Dorothy and I became close friends; he was, and continues to be, an exceptional interlocutor. His 'no-ontology ontology'—was especially relevant to me as I later grappled with the relation between ideals of interpretation and the ontologies of objects of interpretation.[35]

Years later, when Jitendra Mohanty—my old friend and colleague from Temple University—was a Visiting Fellow at All Souls College, he introduced me to Bimal Matilal. Matilal was one of the major scholars of Indian philosophy of

---

33 Michael Krausz, ed., *Critical Essays on the Philosophy of R.G. Collingwood*.
34 Ernest Gellner, "Collingwood and the Failure of Realism."
35 See Patricia Hanna and Bernard Harrison, eds. *Word and World*.

his generation.[36] Much of his scholarly career was devoted to discussing the analytic side of Indian philosophy. He and I soon found common philosophical ground. My conversations with him led to his inviting me to join him in presenting a course at All Souls on relativism. Those seminars in 1989 were auspicious. They led to the start of a jointly authored book on relativism, and they led to his facilitating my interest in Indian philosophy, which eventually led to many trips to India. But we will discuss India more fully at a later point in our conversation.

RA: I look forward to that, but for now, why do you say your seminars with Matilal led to the *start* of your relativism book?

Michael: Alas, Bimal suffered an untimely death before that project was finished. I was glad to be able to invite Rom Harré, to replace him as my co-author on that project, which was published as *Varieties of Relativism*.[37]

RA: You mentioned that during your many visits to Oxford, your conversations with Isaiah Berlin were very important to you. Can you expand on that a bit?

Michael: Yes, he was a true mentor to me. We would talk about a range of issues—from Collingwood and philosophy in general to his own history at Oxford. We talked about being Jewish, Zionism, and Israel; anti-Semitism and assimilation; about art and music; about India and mysticism and spirituality. We also talked about self-recognition.

It's interesting that Berlin was one of the quintessential Oxonians of his generation: encyclopedic, erudite, incisive, imaginative, and more. Nevertheless, he told me that, as a Jew at Oxford, he always felt like an outsider. Personally, he was especially encouraging for me to pursue art and music, as well as philosophy. He noted that if Wittgenstein could do architecture and philosophy, so I could do art and music as well as philosophy. When we parted for the last time, he said, "When you come to England again, after you land, go make pee-pee. Then ring me right away." That was the last time we spoke.

RA: Turning back to your conversations with Berlin, you say that you talked a lot with him about Jewish matters too?

---

36   Bimal Krishna Matilal (1935–1991).
37   See Rom Harré and Michael Krausz, eds. *Varieties of Relativism*.

Michael: Yes. We talked quite a lot about his involvement with the state of Israel, its founding, and Theodore Herzl, whom he knew personally. Berlin was also forthcoming about his views about religious and spiritual matters, including about his own Jewishness.

RA: What did he say about those things?

Michael: Although he had a very strong sense of his own Jewishness, he was impatient with religion and spirituality.

As regards anti-Semitism, he said that the only way in which anti-Semitism would end would be if Jews intermarried. In the meantime, Jews should not be overly concerned about anti-Semitism. After all, so much of Christendom is so deeply imbued with assumptions about the supposed sins of the Jews, it is just a mistake to expect the world to love the Jews. But it gets to be a much more serious matter when anti-Semitism becomes institutionalized; that is, when it is sanctioned in an organized and systematic way. That's a much more serious matter.

RA: Berlin must have been an extraordinary person.

Michael: He certainly was. I have a story to tell you about him and Winston Churchill. The story really is quite famous. During World War II, Berlin was stationed in the British Embassy in Washington, DC. He was responsible for monitoring the mood and goings-on in Washington as they related to British affairs. Churchill regularly read Berlin's reports. He was so impressed with their clarity and insightfulness that he asked to meet Berlin. Churchill's staff proceeded to make the arrangements. But they had made a mistake. On the appointed day, a certain Mr. Berlin was ushered into Churchill's chambers. The prime minister complimented him for his good work and proceeded to quiz the gentleman about the Americans in Washington. It seems that Churchill was unimpressed with the responses he heard. He was disappointed and puzzled.

After the meeting, Churchill asked his staff to look into the matter. It seems that the invitation to see the Prime Minister had been issued to the wrong Mr. Berlin. It had been mistakenly issued to the American composer and lyricist, Irving Berlin!

RA: How ironic and funny! In the meantime, did Isaiah Berlin have interesting things to say about music?

Michael: As far as I know, he played no musical instrument. But he was an avid appreciator and very involved in other ways with the musical world. He knew many of the major musicians of his generation, including violinist and conductor Yehudi Menuhin. In fact, it turns out that Berlin was distantly related to Menuhin. There's also an interesting story that Oxford philosopher Alan Ryan told me about Berlin's burial. It seems that upon his death, Berlin had two memorial gatherings, one in Oxford and one in London, where he was buried. There was a revealing episode that happened at the memorial gathering in London.

RA: What was that?

Michael: You know that Berlin was knighted in 1957.

RA: Yes.

Michael: Well, when a knighted person dies, it is customary for the queen to designate another knight as her personal representative to such memorials. In the case of Berlin, the queen's representative was violinist and conductor Yehudi Menuhin. Menuhin had been peered in 1993. At such occasions, upon their arrival, guests are expected to respectfully bow their heads to the queen's representative.

As it happens, Berlin was also close with the world-renowned violinist, Isaac Stern. It seems that when Stern entered and saw Menuhin, he made quite a stir when he clearly announced, "I'm certainly not going to bow down to *that* man!"

RA: What a story! So, going back in time, how did Rusty fare during your time at Oxford during 1968 and 1969?

Michael: Not so well. While the principal of Linacre College, John Bamborough, graciously arranged for her to get supervision from one of Linacre College's Fellows while she was away from Rutgers, it was not a good fit. She also found the general atmosphere at Oxford to be chauvinist.

RA: Did you agree with her perception?

Michael: It was hard for me to tell how much of that was connected with her not being a member of the college and how much of it was a women's issue. Although the number of male and female members of the college was about the same at that time, perhaps she perceived that women were not treated equally.

RA: Then after that initial year at Oxford, you returned to Toronto, didn't you?

Michael: Yes, Rusty and I returned to Toronto in time for the fall semester of 1969. I was hired at Victoria College, one of the colleges of the University of Toronto, to replace the noted aesthetician Francis Sparshott, who was on leave for that year. In fact, I was assigned his office. Sparshott was around enough though to give me some pointers. When he had asked me to replace him I said, "But Francis, I've never taught aesthetics before." He answered, "You'll learn." And that was that.

At the time, I wasn't quite finished with my dissertation for the University of Toronto, so much of the fall was also devoted to putting it in final shape. I defended it in December, 1969. During that year, Bill Dray was the new department chair at Trent University in Peterborough, Ontario, a short train ride from Toronto. He asked me to teach part-time in his department. I was glad to do so, especially since he and I could regularly talk over morning coffee. In the meantime, Rusty had a part-time position at Atkinson College at York University.

RA: How did your defense go?

Michael: There were six or eight examiners. I can't remember how many. Of course, I was nervous! Among my examiners was, of course, Bill Dray. Others included John Canfield and Lewis Feuer. Canfield had put me at ease when I arrived at the tall building that housed the philosophy department. When I got in the elevator, Canfield was already in it. As the elevator went up he said, "There is only one condition under which you will fail this defense." "What is that?" I asked. He replied, "You'll fail only if you have a heart attack right now." That helped a lot. The defense turned out to be a wonderful conversation. Dray later told me it was the most enjoyable defense he had experienced.

RA: What a great story! But may I ask you an awkward question?

Michael: Of course.

RA: With the benefit of hindsight, do you now fully agree with all your central claims in your dissertation?

Michael: That's an interesting question. I now no longer agree with a central thesis I argued then. It concerns the idea of presupposition, which plays a central role in Collingwood's philosophy of questions and answers. Collingwood distinguished between what he called 'relative' presuppositions from 'absolute' presuppositions. He suggested that relative presuppositions are true or false, and are also subject to justifying reasons and arguments. Relative presuppositions answer to prior questions within an inquiry. But absolute presuppositions are different. They answer to no prior questions. They are *just supposed*—not supposed *to be true*. They are the starting point of an inquiry.

It was important to Collingwood that absolute presuppositions should not be assessed in the way that relative presuppositions are. In my dissertation, I was critical of Collingwood's idea of supposing, without supposing to be true. I didn't think that he could sustain that distinction, and without it, neither could he sustain his distinction between relative and absolute presuppositions. I now think I was wrong about that. Now, I am more sympathetic with Collingwood's suggestion. I now think that the idea of supposing without supposing to be true or false is coherent, indeed insightful. That isn't to say that I don't think his label for 'absolute' presuppositions isn't unfortunate. I'd rather call them 'basic' presuppositions. But that's another matter. What matters is that we may *suppose* without supposing *to be true*.[38]

RA: In the meantime, in addition to working on your dissertation, what else were you doing in Toronto that year?

Michael: I was also finishing the editorial work for the Collingwood volume, and I was on the lookout for a tenure track position. I spent much of that year applying for jobs, including places in the United States. Already from Oxford in the previous year, I had initiated correspondence with several institutions that seemed appealing to me, regardless whether they had advertised for applications.

RA: And were you also making music?

Michael: Oh yes. When I was an Instructor in the Department of Philosophy at Victoria College,[39] I organized a concert where I was one of the soloists in Vivaldi's Concerto Grosso in B minor, for four solo violins. Sparshott was

---

38   See Chapter Twelve of this volume.
39   Victoria College is part of University of Toronto.

ecstatic. I also made informal inquiries at the Royal Conservatory of Music of Toronto for further instruction in conducting. But nothing came of that.

RA: So it seems that the question whether you should choose between music and philosophy was still a live one.

Michael: Yes, the question whether to devote myself seriously to one field or more presented itself to me in various forms at numerous times.

RA: How did you make peace with that question?

Michael: As I say, over the years, Berlin was a great help to me in that regard. Eventually, I have developed the ability to actively pursue two things at a time for sustained periods; for example, I can do philosophy and music. And later, I came to see that I can do philosophy and art at the same time. But I cannot do three things at a time. In any event, philosophy is the constant.

CHAPTER 4

Bryn Mawr, Philadelphia, Oxford Again, and Other Places

RA: So, after Toronto, how is it that you landed at Bryn Mawr?

Michael: As I've said, it started while I was still at Oxford in 1969. I knew I was going to be returning to Toronto to finish my dissertation and to teach for the year at Victoria College. I anticipated that in the year that followed my teaching at Vic, I would want to secure a position elsewhere. So, I took it upon myself to make a list of good institutions that would interest me. On that list was Bryn Mawr. So, I wrote letters to the Chairs of those departments, indicating that I was not looking for a position immediately, but that I might be interested to apply if a position might open in the future.

Well, Milton Nahm was the Chair of Bryn Mawr's Department of Philosophy at the time. He was an aesthetician and Kant scholar, and like me, had been partially trained at Oxford. He responded to my letter in an encouraging way. That began correspondence between us. My guess is that he was intrigued by our parallel backgrounds. So, once I returned to Toronto, he asked George Kline—a distinguished member of the Bryn Mawr department and a major contributor to process philosophy and translator of the poetry of Joseph Brodsky—to interview me, when Kline was invited to lecture on Brodsky in Toronto. That's when I met Kline. After that meeting I was invited to come to Bryn Mawr for a formal interview. It went well, and I was offered the position of Assistant Professor. I was to be regarded as Nahm's eventual replacement upon his retirement.

RA: So, who was in the department when you arrived?

Michael: When I arrived, besides Nahm and Kline, there was the Spanish philosopher, José Ferrater Mora.[1] There was also Jean Potter, who taught philosophy of religion and medieval philosophy. Then there was Isabelle Stearns, who taught American philosophy. She was also an expert in the philosophy of Charles Sanders Peirce. In my early years, I had excellent exchanges with

---

1 For full discussion of José Ferrater Mora, see https://tinyurl.com/FerraterMora.

George Weaver, who was a linguistic logician. He was a recent hire to replace the well-known outgoing logician Hughes LeBlanc.

I connected best with Ferrater Mora. He was utterly encyclopedic and brilliant. He was also a prize-winning film maker, and he had a marvelously ironic sense of humor. He became my mentor and much-appreciated advocate in the department. When I arrived for my interview, I also met Pat MacPherson, part-time member of the department, soon to become Dean, and eventually, President of the College. She was to play a large supportive role in my life at Bryn Mawr. Interestingly, she had been a graduate student of Nahm's. Coincidentally, Harris Wofford began his tenure as president of the College when I arrived.

RA: What was Bryn Mawr like when you started to teach there?

Michael: Bryn Mawr was an excellent place—full of eager, bright, well-prepared undergraduates and a fine, if small, PhD program. That interested me greatly.[2] As well, the greater Philadelphia area was rich with fine philosophers at various neighboring institutions. When I arrived at Bryn Mawr, I sought out colleagues at Haverford College. That, I was soon to find out, was—from Nahm's point of view—a mistake.

RA: A mistake? Why?

Michael: It turned out that there was a long-standing feud between Milton Nahm and Richard Bernstein at Haverford. Bernstein was a protégé of Paul Weiss, who had been at Haverford before he was appointed to his position at Yale. It seems that Bernstein had inherited the feud that had existed between Nahm and Weiss. All that contributed to a kind standoff between the two departments. When I arrived, I had naïvely thought that it would be a good thing to introduce myself to Bernstein, whom I had known by reputation to be a serious thinker and effective teacher.

When I did meet Bernstein, he was most cordial and taken aback by the fact that I would reach out to him. In a friendly way, he warned me to be careful about my associations with the Haverford faculty. Dick's warning was well advised, but I did not heed it. This, and other episodes, led to sustained unpleasantness between Nahm and me.

---

2 Alas, its graduate program was phased out along with several others at Bryn Mawr. By 1986, we no longer accepted graduate students.

My difficulties with Nahm were political as well as departmental. Remember, it was 1970—when tear-gassing was routine at peace demonstrations at Columbia University and other campuses around the country. But at that time, Bryn Mawr was a surprisingly apolitical and quiet place. Yet within weeks of my arrival at the college, I was disturbed to learn about the college's practice of releasing private files to the FBI. Nahm strongly advised me not to get involved. I did not head his advice.

RA: What happened?

Michael: Well, within weeks of my arrival at the college, I read an article in the Philadelphia Inquirer that the FBI office in Media, Pennsylvania—in the vicinity of Swarthmore College—had been broken into and a substantial number of files had been stolen and turned over to the newspapers. Those files contained notes and transcriptions of telephone conversations amongst faculty and students who were opposed to the War. It turned out that the Swarthmore College telephone operator was an agent of the FBI and was listening in on their conversations.[3]

I was appalled by this report and made inquiries whether the FBI was engaging in similar practices at Bryn Mawr. I went to the Recorders Office at Bryn Mawr and was told that they, too, cooperated with FBI agents by sharing its files with them. I immediately went to the President's Office to get an appointment with Harris Wofford. When I saw him, I reported to him what I had found out.

RA: What was his reaction?

Michael: Wofford said that this was not a presidential matter. So, I asked, "If this is not a presidential matter, what is? What sort of matter is it?" He advised me that it was a faculty matter and that I should consult with the Secretary of the Faculty.[4] I did so. Remember, I had been on the faculty just a few weeks at this time.

---

3 The Philadelphia Inquirer reported that the Citizen's Commission to Investigate the FBI had been responsible for the break-in, and had delivered the stolen files to several United States newspapers. For expanded discussion of these events, see, "The Complete Collection of Political Documents Ripped-Off from the FBI Office in Media, PA, March 8, 1971," *WIN Magazine*, March 1972, and Betty Medsger, *The Burglary*.
4 The Secretary of the Faculty at Bryn Mawr is a senior elected member of the faculty.

In the end, to guarantee the privacy of faculty and student files, the faculty passed a resolution stating its principled objection to sharing information without the consent of persons involved. It represented a significant victory at that time.

RA: So, how was your initiative received in the department?

Michael: Not well. Nahm advised me not to engage in such political activities. Clearly, I did not heed his advice. I crossed swords with him about numerous departmental matters as well. It's ironic, of course, and more than a little satisfying that in 1991, I was awarded the Milton C. Nahm Professorship in Philosophy.

RA: So, whom else did you connect with at Bryn Mawr, perhaps outside your department?

Michael: Given my interest in the philosophy of history, I also had close associations with members of Bryn Mawr's History Department. These included John Salmon, with whom I joint-taught a senior seminar in the Philosophy of History for history majors. John and his wife Coral Lansbury became friends with Rusty and me, and later with Connie, as did historian Arthur Dudden and wife Adrienne. I also enjoyed friendships with historian Barbara Lane and her husband Jonathan, historian Mary Dunn, and in History of Art, Phyllis Bober, Steven Levine, and David Cast. I felt as much associated with the historians as with the philosophers.

At the University of Pennsylvania, I befriended the historian of science Mark Adams, with whom I taught a graduate seminar at Bryn Mawr. We had a wonderful seminar on the Popper-Kuhn controversy, and we became good friends.[5]

RA: Whom else did you befriend?

Michael: In the early years, between 1970 and 1972—with Rusty, then later with Connie—there was poet and English instructor Tony Litwinko; visiting British scholar Robert Lee; philosopher George Weaver; and social psychologist Philip Lichtenberg. At Haverford, there was Richard Bernstein and his English professor wife Carol at Bryn Mawr; as well as philosophers Mary and Paul Desjardins.

---

5 For more on that controversy, see Imre Lakatos and Alan Musgrave, eds., *Proceedings of the International Colloquium in the Philosophy of Science, 1965*....

In later years at Bryn Mawr, I had personal and academic friendships with Tracy Taft, Christine Koggel, Philip Kilbride, Michael McKenna, Bharath Vallabha, Elizabeth McCormack, and David Cast. At Temple University, there were Joe Margolis and Jiten Mohanty. At Swarthmore College, my friends included Hans Oberdiek, Hugh Lacy, Richard Schuldenfrei, and Richard Eldridge. Jacques Catudal and Richard Burian were at Drexel.

I taught philosophy of science several times with Paul Grobstein, in Biology, and with Guy Blaylock, in Physics, when he was visiting from the university of Massachusetts. We emphasized the question of multiple interpretability of quantum mechanics. Sometimes Liz McCormack, a Bryn Mawr physicist, joined us teaching that course. Then, there was Phil Kilbride, with whom I co-taught a basic course in Cultural Theory, which emphasized questions of cultural and moral relativism. I also taught a graduate course on interpretation in the Art History Department.

RA: And what about your teaching? How did that go for you at Bryn Mawr?

Michael: First, there was a significant difference between my teaching at University of Toronto and at Bryn Mawr. I had already had experience teaching in larger and smaller venues. When I was a Teaching Assistant at the University of Toronto—in tandem with Robert McRae's history of philosophy—I much enjoyed lecturing to large audiences. Then, I taught in smaller environments at Victoria College—one of the colleges within the University of Toronto—and at Trent University. Vic's classes were middle-sized. At Bryn Mawr, my classes were routinely smaller, and certainly, my upper level courses were virtually seminars. Not only did the change in environment change the dynamics of the courses, but it influenced my thoughts about teaching philosophy more generally. I began to realize that my job was to teach my students to slow down! While generally my students were bright, they moved too quickly, not attending to holes in their arguments. I wanted them to identify places in their arguments that were invalid. I took that as one of my primary teaching aims, and, I must say, I loved helping students do that.

RA: Is it fair to say that you were concerned to teach them how to argue, how to engage in critical thinking?

Michael: Yes indeed. And my required assignments reflected that. Characteristically I would ask students to write about one or more of the texts we had discussed in class. I would require that in doing so they follow a pre-set format.

First, they were to offer an exposition of one or more of the leading claims made by the author. I would then have them offer a critique, in which they should rehearse the strongest arguments they could muster against the original claims made. That is, much as a prosecuting attorney might do, they were to offer counter arguments. In turn, much as a defending attorney might do, they were expected to defend the author's initial claims. Such a defense should then be followed by an assessment of the relative strengths and weaknesses of the counterargument and defense, much as a judge might offer. Students then read their presentations in class, which, after discussion, became drafts of fuller papers.

RA: I can see how such a requirement would sharpen their argumentative skills.

Michael: Yes, that's exactly what it was intended to do. I used to enjoy adding that I was less interested in what they believed than in how they argued—rather like prosecutors and defenders. The primary task for them should concern how strongly the arguments hold up.

RA: I'm sure that imparting argumentative skills is a serious aim in itself. But wouldn't you also want to encourage them to think for themselves—to apply their argumentative skills in shaping their own belief systems?

Michael: Yes, indeed. That's why I also asked them to keep a private journal dedicated to discussing how the readings for a given week might apply to their preoccupations, passions, and beliefs. That was voluntary. I would leave time during each session for them to offer their written entries if they so desired. Usually, it would be those entries that evoked the most animated discussions.

RA: I gather your readings were mostly drawn from the analytic Anglo-American literature. So, to what extent did your experiences in India impact upon your teaching?

Michael: Inevitably, they entered into my teaching—mostly as examples, particularly the case of the dead baby in the Ganges in Benares.[6] But I never presumed to give a proper course in Indian Philosophy. I don't regard myself as a scholar in that area.

---

6 See, for example Krausz, "Interpretation and Its Objects."

RA: So, while you were teaching full time at Bryn Mawr, how did you end up teaching at universities in Washington, DC?

Michael: Well, I had met Connie in 1972 at the Haystack Mountain School of Crafts in Dear Isle, Maine, while I was taking a course in printmaking, and she was taking a course in ceramics. Once back at home, we pursued our relationship. We would commute weekly between Bryn Mawr and Washington. We eventually married in 1976. During that time, I had been corresponding with Harold Durfee at American University. He invited me to teach a course there during the academic year of 1973–1974, which I enjoyed.

Then, in 1977, Connie had a solo exhibition at the Phillips Collection in Washington, at about the same time as she took up her post as Assistant Professor in the Art Department at George Washington University. As a consequence of my being in Washington regularly, my professional networking there expanded.

In 1977, I taught a course on relativism at Georgetown. Then, in the summer of 1977, I was a Fellow at the Aspen Institute in Colorado, at which Executive Seminars were presented. Participants included decision-makers from many areas, such as business, government, academia, the arts, and so on. For each of those seminars, Fellows sponsored by the Mellon Foundation would give presentations and contribute to discussions about classical and current philosophical texts and their bearing on current issues of the day. The Executive Seminars were first organized by Mortimer Adler, who originated the Great Books idea.[7]

It was at the Aspen Institute that I met Peter Krogh, the Dean of the Foreign Service School at Georgetown. We agreed that my course at Georgetown in the Philosophy Department would be listed at his Foreign Service School. It was in that context that I got to know Peter back in Washington.

In the meantime, I had been invited by Nathan Rotenstreich, to replace him at the Hebrew University in Jerusalem while he was on sabbatical—to teach his graduate seminar on Collingwood and the Philosophy of History. Earlier on, we had corresponded about his contribution to my volume on Collingwood.

Then something momentous happened in the Middle East. The Camp David Accords were signed in 1978, by Egyptian President Anwar Sadat and Israeli

---

7 Mortimer Jerome Adler, Clifton Fadiman, and Philip W. Goetz, eds. *Great Books of the Western World.*

Prime Minister Menachem Begin, which led to the peace treaty between Egypt and Israel, signed in March 26, 1979. The Camp David Accords gave me an idea. It occurred to me that in this atmosphere of reconciliation, it might be possible for American students to benefit from first-hand experiences in both Egypt and Israel, with the thought that future generations might gain from mutual understanding. I thought, wouldn't it be wonderful if—under the auspices of Georgetown University—a program might be instituted whereby students could spend a semester at the American University in Cairo and a semester at the Hebrew University of Jerusalem? As it happened, Georgetown already had cordial relations with the American University in Cairo.

I proposed to Krogh that Georgetown should sponsor a year-long program in which students would study in Cairo for a semester and then in Jerusalem for a semester. Gretchen Carroll, head of foreign programs at Georgetown, would be central to the effort. In short, it worked—at least, for a few years.

Lots of converging conditions made it possible. As it happened, I was in a position to make this proposal, since Rotenstreich and I had had earlier correspondences about Collingwood and his contribution to my volume on Collingwood.[8] As well, Rotenstreich headed up the Central Committee for all universities in Israel. Before I spoke to the President of Hebrew University, I consulted with Rotenstreich. He was helpful. But an interesting back-story will show that I had extra help besides Rotenstreich's. It involved the Cleveland Orchestra in the Soviet Union and my father!

In 1965, the Cleveland Orchestra had toured the Soviet Union. But there was a snag that had to be overcome before that could be possible. As I've already mentioned, many members of the orchestra were Jewish. While the management of the orchestra was planning its tour with the State Department, it became clear that the orchestra would be expected to be in Moscow during the first day of Passover. My father was an outspoken member of a group in the orchestra, which insisted that its members must be allowed to observe Passover with a Seder. Without a Seder, the group argued, there would be no tour. Unfortunately, the Soviet Union had mandated that Seders were illegal!

RA: So, how was the impasse resolved?

---

8   See Nathan Rotenstreich, "Metaphysics and Historicism."

Michael: Someone had to be found who could negotiate the situation. As far as I can reconstruct the chronology, it fell upon a young Israeli diplomat, Abraham Harman. At that time, Harman was the Israeli consul-general in New York. He was born in England, graduated with a law degree from Oxford, and emigrated to Israel in 1938. I don't know the details, but Harman managed to get the American embassy in Moscow to sponsor the Seder for the members of the Cleveland Orchestra. And you know what? It was perfectly legal, because the embassy was immune from Soviet restrictions.

RA: Great story, but what did that have to do with your proposed Middle East program?

Michael: Well, during Harman's negotiations, he consulted with members of the orchestra about what was to be done. And, as was my father's way, he made a very fine portrait of Harman. That portrait was stored in Cleveland amongst lots of other artworks he made.

RA: What's the significance of that?

Michael: Harman went on to have a distinguished diplomatic career—including becoming the Israeli Ambassador to the United States. He eventually became President of the Hebrew University in Jerusalem in 1968. And whom did I need to see in Jerusalem, in 1978? The very same Abraham Harman.

RA: That's quite a coincidence. So how does that portrait enter the story?

Michael: Well, before I left for the Middle East, I visited Cleveland and asked my mother if I might have the portrait of Harman to give to him upon my arrival in Jerusalem. She agreed.

RA: How did all of that turn out in Jerusalem?

Michael: Of course, before my arrival, Harman's office had received all necessary background materials including the Georgetown proposal for the Middle East program. Of course, he was aware that I was about to teach a graduate seminar in the Philosophy of History in his Philosophy Department.

RA: So how did it go?

Michael: When I was ushered into his room, the first thing I did was to convey good wishes from my mother and present him with the gift of his own portrait, done by my father. Harman melted. He loved it. It's hard to say how much of that really entered into his welcome of the proposal, but I like to think it helped.

RA: So how did it go on the Egyptian side?

Michael: Since Georgetown already had good relations with the American University in Cairo (AUC), the ear of its president, Richard Pederson, and his administration was open. But nothing is Egypt is simple. By that I mean that everything that goes on in a place like AUC is monitored by the Egyptian intelligence, and one of its representatives was quietly present at my first meeting with numerous university administrators.

RA: That must have been somewhat delicate. How did you handle that, given your Jewish background?

Michael: That's a good question. As it happened, the evening before I left Jerusalem for Cairo, I was invited to a dinner at which academic and government people were present—including Rotenstreich. At one point in the evening, a senior gentlemen, who was introduced to me as an Israeli diplomat, asked to speak with me privately in order to offer some advice. Of course, I was eager to hear what he had to say. He advised that before I even begin to raise matters of substance with administrators at AUC, I should take my time and fully introduce myself. That is, I should tell them everything about my personal history, my background and interests, including the activities of my family, what brought me to Jerusalem in the first place, and so on. I should hold nothing back. When I asked him why I should be so candid, he said, "If you don't tell them, they will find it out for themselves and they will hold it against you." I did as he suggested, and it turned out to be excellent advice.

RA: Why do you say that?

Michael: Because when I arrived at the AUC, I was treated formally and respectfully. Then, when President Pederson invited me to set out the terms of the Georgetown proposal, I said that I would first like to introduce myself. I did so fully. The atmosphere of the room gradually changed. Everyone became more informal and cordial. The discussion that ensued went smoothly—including the conversation about their one condition that there could be no direct communication between them and the Israelis. I assured them that that would not be necessary. The two parts of the program could be kept separate, and all communications about curricula and related matters could be negotiated through Georgetown. I stayed on for a few days to talk to many constituencies of the university. And finally, Pederson agreed to the proposal. And in the process, I had made some very good friends, including the then Director of External Relations, Carl Shieren, and his future wife, Afaf Mahfouz. She was professor of law at Cairo University. Carl and Afaf now live in New York. They remain close friends.

In fact, such a good connection had been established between AUC administrators and academic staff that Connie and I were invited as Distinguished Visiting Professors to AUC, in 1980. Later, a friendship had developed with Richard and Nelda Pederson.

RA: Wow. So what happened when you returned to Jerusalem?

Michael: When I told Harman that the Egyptians had agreed he was surprised and delighted. After numerous follow-up meetings with faculty members and administrators at Hebrew University, the program was approved. Under the guidance of Gretchen Carroll of Georgetown, it was an effective program for several years until the relations between the two countries chilled again.

RA: You mentioned before that, as a Jew, you often felt out of place. Do I presume correctly that that was not an issue when you visited Israel in 1978, or at other times?

Michael: I have visited Israel several times, some in relation to Peter and his family as well as in relation to academic commitments. When in Israel I felt 'at home,' or, as one among family so to say. As a Jew, I did not feel like an outsider as I did in European countries or even in America. But, it was not so simple even in Israel because, like many families, Israel felt fractured—between the secularists and religionists, between the Sephardic Jews and the Ashkenazim, between the left leaning Peace Now movement and the right-leaning supporters of settlements on the West Bank, between those interested in genuine dialogue between Israelis and Palestinians, and those who were not interested.

RA: Moving ahead, then, what challenges and opportunities arose for you at Bryn Mawr over the years?

Michael: They were numerous—both at Bryn Mawr and elsewhere. For example, Phyllis Bober, art historian and Dean of Bryn Mawr's graduate school, was most helpful to me. She was a great supporter of my philosophical and artistic work. She urged me to apply to the Ossabaw Island Foundation—a small thriving artist-writers retreat—in Georgia, for a Resident Fellowship. I was accepted. I attended the foundation for a summer session in 1978, then again in 1980. The first time, I worked on my art, and the second time, on my philosophy. Both were special times for me.

RA: How so?

Michael: Phyllis had already mentioned the name, Roman Jakobson, to me but I did not recognize it. She explained that he was a regular visitor at Ossabaw Island and a member of its Board. As it turned out, he was there during both of my sessions. Our meeting in 1978 was friendly. But I had not really registered who he really was. I found him to be brilliant and most engaging. We would sit together during meals, during which he inquired about my philosophical and artistic work. Only then, from others, did I realize with whom I was really dealing. He was a historically significant linguist and literary theorist at Harvard. But more than that, he was the founder of the Prague School of Linguistics. I soon recognized that I had struck up a conversational relationship with a major mind. He had a kind of razor-edged intelligence, with encyclopedic knowledge. When I think of Jakobson, I think of an enormous intellectual space, the kind of space that I had experienced in the Carlsbad Caverns in southeast New Mexico—only several times bigger—if I may be allowed that comparison.

RA: What did you talk about with Jakobson?

Michael: Actually, that was at a time when I was preoccupied with the idea of a personal program as it arose for me while thinking about creativity, particularly my personal program concerning my art. I recall my questions about personal programs triggered his talking about inner dialogue or inner speech. Those conversations reinforced my sense of the importance of personal programs.[9]

RA: Did Jakobson say anything about his personal life?

Michael: Among other things, he told the story about his escape from the Nazis. It was from Sweden that he embarked on a cargo ship for New York in 1941. Also, on that ship, was none other than the philosopher Ernst Cassirer. The details were astonishing. It seems that once the ship was on its way out from the coast, a Nazi helicopter spotted it, stopped the vessel, and called down to have the passengers identify themselves. The information about the passengers was relayed to the helicopter. That information was radioed to Berlin. After the OK

---

9 See Michael Krausz, "Creativity and Self-Transformation," 192–194.

was sent back, the soldiers sent word down to the ship to warn them that the whole area was full of mines. They then offered to escort the ship through the mines. That's what they did until the ship would no longer be in danger. Thus, the Nazis actually helped save Jakobson!

RA: How extraordinary! So, how were you fairing at Bryn Mawr and in Philadelphia during this time?[10]

Michael: Concurrent influences were at work. One was a growing frustration on my part that—given the small size of our department—I wanted to establish a larger coterie of conversational partners. As well, my growing interest in the theory of interpretation led me to sit in on seminars at Temple University given by Joseph Margolis and later by Jitendra Mohanty.

I knew of Joe's outstanding work in aesthetics and related areas, and I asked him whether I might sit in on one of his graduate seminars. He agreed. As well, Joe and I had a series of conversations—one of which hatched the idea of a consortium of institutions to bring together a coterie of philosophers.

I had been struck by the fact that there were so many strong philosophers in the Philadelphia area. So, I thought, wouldn't it be a good thing if they could be brought together in a consortium to meet and sponsor conferences, and pool intellectual and financial resources?

Joe and I came up with the idea of organizing a consortium that would bring in significant philosophical figures from around the world in conferences dedicated to the theme of philosophy of the human studies. With considerable effort, we founded the Greater Philadelphia Philosophy Consortium (GPPC) in 1980, which would come to make a distinctive contribution to the field.[11] The original four founding members were area institutions, which offered graduate philosophy programs. Those four were represented by Joe Margolis from Temple, Paul Geyer from the University of Pennsylvania, John D. Caputo from Villinova, and myself, representing Bryn Mawr College. I served as its Chair from 1988 until 1992, and then as Co-Chair from 1992 until 1994.

---

10 For a history of the Bryn Mawr Philosophy Department, see https://tinyurl.com/BrynMawrHistory.

11 An early compendium that issued from our work was published as Margolis, Krausz, and Burian, eds., *Rationality, Relativism, and the Human Sciences*.

We had a very strong run during the first few years, being sponsored by major foundations such as the Ford Foundation and the Pew Charitable Trust. Eventually, the financial sponsorship fell to the member institutions. World-class philosophers such as Jürgen Habermas, Richard Rorty, and Anthony Kenny have presented papers at our conferences. I worked closely with Joe for several years on getting GPPC launched. As well, I owe him a great intellectual debt for our conversations, particularly about his 'robust relativism' and interpretation theory. From the start, Philosophy of Human Studies was a core theme of GPPC.

RA: Can you say more fully how you helped to begin the organization?

Michael: Well, as I said, at that time, there were four institutions in the Philadelphia area that offered graduate degrees in philosophy. Besides Bryn Mawr, there was University of Pennsylvania, Temple University, and Villanova University. We began with those institutions. Joe and I consulted with departmental representatives from each of them. The idea was that each school would make a contribution—both philosophical and financial. It made good sense for everyone. It would provide a forum for serious and sustained philosophical dialogue as well as provide an economical way for all of us to benefit from interaction with world-class figures that would otherwise have been too expensive for any given institution to sponsor alone. Of course, we had to interest appropriate administrators at higher levels as well. I very much enjoyed working with Joe in that capacity. And over the years, many more than four institutions joined the consortium, and it now has fifteen member institutions. The GPPC turned out to be a significant addition to the philosophical life of the community.[12] I was most closely involved with the consortium for the first eight or ten years. I take great pleasure in seeing what has emerged from it since then. I personally benefited from in the philosophical resources of the GPPC, which expanded the resources available at Bryn Mawr.

To my disappointment, as I already mentioned, along with other graduate departments at Bryn Mawr, our graduate program in philosophy was eventually discontinued for financial reasons. We accepted no more graduate students

---

12 There are now fifteen colleges and universities in the greater Philadelphia area that comprise the GPPC. They include Bryn Mawr College, Drexel University, Haverford College, La Salle University, Pennsylvania State University, Rosemont College, St. Joseph's University, Swarthmore College, Temple University, the College of New Jersey, University of Delaware, University of Pennsylvania, Ursinus College, Villanova University, and West Chester University; see www.thegppc.org.

after 1986. That, for me, changed the teaching atmosphere of the place. In time though, what I lost at Bryn Mawr, I more than gained by the GPPC. Yet, in the end, Bryn Mawr turned out to be an excellent place for me, what with its support of my efforts with the GPPC and my pursuits in art and music in addition to my philosophical work. I even had a couple of art exhibitions at Bryn Mawr, and later, the college hosted the Great Hall Chamber Orchestra concerts. But that's another story. The college also encouraged and sponsored numerous teaching appointments overseas, including one to Nairobi in 1986.

RA: So, how did it happen that you went to Kenya?

Michael: Odera Oruka–or more fully, Henry Odera Oruka—an important Kenyan philosopher,[13] whom I met when he was guest professor at Haverford College, had invited me to give some lectures and seminars in his department at the University of Nairobi. He was Chair of his department. Given our shared interests in cultural diversity and cross-cultural dialogue, we hit it off. It turns out that Odera was a major figure in African philosophy, especially sagacious or Sage Philosophy, and the philosophy of indigenous communities. He invited me to be a guest in his department in 1985. I might also mention that I would occasionally teach a course on cultural analysis with Phil Kilbride in the Bryn Mawr Anthropology Department. Phil was an Africanist who had a research project in Eldoret, about 160 miles northwest of Nairobi. So, it all fell into place. I gave some lectures in Nairobi and visited with Phil in Eldoret.

RA: What was Kenya like for you?

Michael: Well once I got settled at the university's guest facility, I made my way to Eldoret to visit with Phil. My first visit with Phil was both unfortunate and auspicious.

RA: How's that?

Michael: Well, soon after my arrival in Eldoret, Phil took me to the bush country where we were to visit Kikuyu communities. Unfortunately, I got sick to my stomach. I went to an area with shrubbery, where I vomited. As I did so, I caught sight of a couple of dozen tribes-people making a big circle around me with expressions of curiosity. Once I gained my composure, I called out to Phil and asked what is going on? He said, "Michael, you are a white man. They have

---

13   See, for example, Henry Odera Oruka, *Practical Philosophy*.

never seen a white man get sick. They don't think of white people getting sick." But then something very touching happened. A woman, who turned out to be a medicine woman, took me by my hand and led me to a small, primitive hut. It contained a bed which took up most of the space. She bade me to lie down. Then, she picked up some rattles. In hushed tones, she began to chant and shake her rattles while I lay quietly. In time, I did feel quite a lot better. She had performed some rite of witchcraft.

RA: That's very interesting. Were there other episodes like that when you were in Kenya?

Michael: Actually, as I mentioned already, Odera Oruku was a great expert about Sage Philosophy. He used to interview many witch doctors as part of his effort to record tribal philosophies. He invited me to join him on one of those interviews.

RA: What an extraordinary opportunity.

Michael: Yes it was. Odera asked if I would like to conduct one of the interviews, with Tago Athieno, a Luo medicine man well known to Odera and his family. Odera offered to translate from Swahili. I was delighted. After we got settled in Tago's hut, Tago chanted for about five minutes. When I expressed interest in the rattle he had used while chanting, he showed me other instruments too, including small drums and single and double stringed instruments made of rudimentary materials. Then he asked if I had questions, after which the interview began.[14] We talked about whether being a witch doctor can be taught, and about a class of moral sins, or '*Kira*,' as he called them. They include incest and homosexuality. He said engaging in such things cause mental and sometimes physical disturbances that damage the community. Such sins have to be cured. That's what the witch doctor can do.

RA: What other experiences in Kenya struck you in regard to cultural differences?

Michael: Well, one cultural difference within academia comes to mind. When I arrived at the university, I was received most cordially. After my first lecture, I was shown great courtesy. No seriously challenging questions were put to me. Similarly, after my second lecture, questions were carefully and courteously

---

14 See Michael Krausz, Appendix, "From an Interview with a Luo Medicineman."

raised. Then in the third and fourth sessions, I sensed a significant shift. Questions were more challenging and incisive. The philosophers questioned the cultural presuppositions from which I was speaking. I had never experienced such intelligent interventions that challenged presuppositions of my work. I asked Odera what had happened over those weeks. He explained to me that in the Kenyan culture, it's important first to establish a personal relationship with the person with whom you're discussing serious matters. Mutual respect for such efforts needs first to be established. This is the ground rule for serious philosophical discussion. It was matter of civility. I enjoyed my stay there tremendously.

RA: And what about your Jewishness in Kenya? How did you experience that?

Michael: Aside from wonderfully varied experiences in Africa, I sensed a relief. Being Jewish seemed not to be on the African radar. The question of Jewishness came up only once, and I raised it myself. At a dinner party, I asked the gathering, "What does it mean to you when you hear that someone is Jewish?" Upon reflection, one person replied, "Well, I guess that's connected with Israel, and I guess what I know about Israelis is that they're pretty good fighters." That was the extent of the conversations about what it meant to be Jewish. Although the majority of Kenya's population is Christian, I didn't experience myself as a Jew in a Gentile world, as one 'other' than Christian. I was in a place where I did not feel the heaviness of the Holocaust or its legacy. Of course, as a white man, I was one 'other' than Luo or Kikuyu, or Massai.

RA: If you'll permit me to digress from your account of your trip to Kenya for a moment, may I ask whether you felt the heaviness of your Jewishness when you went to Germany, in 1995?

Michael: Oh. You're referring to when I was invited to present some seminars in the Anthropology Department at the University of Ulm in Germany, in 1995. Until then, I had resisted the very idea of going to Germany at all. After all, I came from a family that would refuse even to buy any goods made in Germany. But my actual experience there was different from what I had expected. That trip afforded me the opportunity to interact informally with anthropology researchers and students. We openly discussed the Holocaust.

I asked my newfound German colleagues about their feelings about the Holocaust, and how they were dealing with the legacy that they had inherited. I was somewhat surprised at how preoccupied they were to redress their collective past. They shared stories about family members during the war—both resisters and those who were complicit with Hitler's project of eliminating the Jews. I was struck by the measure of their understanding. I had not expected it. When I shared my own family's history—that I am the grandson of victims of the Holocaust—they regarded me with care and compassion. I just hope that those sentiments continue in our present day, as recently, there seems to be such a resurgence of anti-Semitism across Europe, England, and elsewhere.[15]

RA: How did it happen that you were invited to Ulm in the first place?

Michael: It was quite fortuitous really. I had met a distinguished German anthropologist, Ina Rösing, in the Delhi airport, while we were both waiting for a plane to Leh, which is the Capital of Ladakh. Her primary academic interests focus on cultural anthropology and transcultural research, including traditional healing in Ladakh. She was en route to one of her research sites. We quickly found areas of common interest, including transcultural understanding and relativism. Our common interests led her to invite me to Ulm.

RA: Thank you for that. So now, returning to your Kenya story, what else was memorable there?

Michael: Again, talk about serendipity. While in Nairobi, quite by coincidence, I met the distinguished philosopher, Georg Henrik von Wright, at a reception held at the Finnish embassy, which he had hosted for philosophers in Nairobi. He was a close associate of Wittgenstein and responsible for editing much of Wittgenstein's works. He was the leading philosopher of Finland, and he succeeded Wittgenstein at Cambridge.

RA: What was his connection to the Finnish embassy?

Michael: Well, as it turned out, Von Wright was the father-in-law of the Swedish ambassador to Kenya. Our meeting in Nairobi led Von Wright to invite me to the University of Helsinki to give a paper, which I did, in 1986, on the occasion of a conference celebrating his retirement. Numerous excellent philosophers came to that conference, including Thomas Nagel, who had been a student of Von Wright at Cornell. My meeting Von Wright led to his publishing

---

15   Bernard Harrison, *The Resurgence of Anti-Semitism*.

a book in my series with Brill Publishers, entitled *The Tree of Knowledge and Other Essays*.

RA: You have had the good fortune of having known some outstanding philosophical figures.

Michael: Yes. One especially outstanding occasion comes to mind, which I've already mentioned, that Summer Institute at the University of California at Santa Cruz in 1988, sponsored by NEH. Its theme was Interpretation in the Sciences and Humanities. Those instructors were some of the leading voices in philosophy at that time. Over the course of several weeks, besides the daily lecturers and discussions that followed, I had the opportunity to engage in good exchanges with nearly all of them. I much enjoyed Geertz. He was a leading anthropologist at the Institute for Advanced Study at Princeton. He had a dry sense of humor; he was a warm person. I had occasion to talk with him about his piece, "Anti Anti-Relativism." At the time, I was editing *Relativism: Interpretation and Confrontation*, and had asked his permission to include it in my edition. I was sympathetic with his piece. The title says it all. In it, he embraced neither relativism nor absolutism but challenged those who, like many, seem to have a knee-jerk reaction against relativism without carefully considering the possibility that some forms for relativism do not prohibit the possibility of communication.

Then there was Richard Rorty. He, too, turned out to have a piece—entitled, "Solidarity or Objectivity?"—in that same volume. In his laconic way, like some relativists, he denied the viability of grounding pertinent claims in ahistorical, acultural, or absolutist terms. But he preferred to call his view 'pragmatist' rather than relativist. He came under heavy criticism, however, from members of the seminar in regard to a key suggestion he made in his defining book, *Philosophy and the Mirror of Nature*, to the effect that, in light of the radical historical nature of all culture—including the sciences as well as the humanities—one should reconcile with the fact that pertinent commitments arise from what edifies. Of course, he was asked—rather often I might say—what he meant by edification. Numerous participants asked for an analytic account of edification. His answer would be, "Of course, you know what edification is. Of course, you know what edifies you." His dismissive attitude toward the question did not satisfy many in the group.

Then there was Tom Kuhn. As you know, Kuhn had already played a significant role in my intellectual development; I enjoyed Tom. He was a friendly, warm person, who had a fresh enthusiasm for philosophical dialogue. His book, *The Structure of Scientific Revolutions*, had become a staple in the philosophy of science and the humanities as well. As a matter of fact, *Progress in Art*, by Suzi Gablik, had made an impression on me as well.[16] She had attempted to apply Kuhn's idea of paradigms to the history of art. Moreover, since my days at the LSE, when I had adopted Popper as something of a foil, here was Kuhn, who had become one of Popper's most influential opponents, and whose work had influenced me. Indeed, their disagreement had become a staple in my teaching. I was so pleased to have the chance to talk with Tom in a relaxed way. It was then that I asked him whether he had been influenced by Collingwood's idea of an absolute presupposition. What I found fascinating about *The Structure of Scientific Revolutions*, and in his writings afterward, was his resistance to the idea of being called a relativist. He rejected the term. But Kuhn's relativism is what Popper could not abide. In contrast, I thought that more work should be done on the idea of relativism in order to dissociate it from an entrenched construal of it that would entail irrationality.[17]

I thought that relativism need not foreclose the possibly of informed conversation between enquirers embracing different frames of reference or paradigms. Popper has insisted on the possibility of such conversation, as had I, and ironically so had Kuhn. Maybe that was why, in his more reconciliatory moments Kuhn insisted how much he agreed with Popper. In any event, much of my own work later on was to concentrate on the possibility of rational dialogue between inquirers who assume different reference frames.

Then there was Charles Taylor, a man of stately bearing, a devoted Canadian of exceptional intelligence. He had an irenic philosophical temperament. By that I mean he impressed me as one who would bring together different philosophical traditions in fruitful ways. I had heard Taylor in Oxford already and was impressed with the ease with which he would draw upon Hegel for example, to inform his analytic concerns. His writing, especially about his idea of the 'language of perspicuous contrast' as he called it, was clear and insightful. It was concerned with overcoming barriers to communication between disparate communities and traditions. Alas, ultimately I found it unconvincing. For

---

16   Suzi Gablik, *Progress in* Art.
17   My conviction was enforced earlier in my career by Jack Meiland, of the University of Michigan. Indeed, our correspondence led to our jointly editing, *Relativism: Cognitive and Moral*.

I could see how his idea of language of perspicuous contrast could be regarded as a reference frame, thus ultimately, consistent with relativism.

RA: What about Stanley Cavell?

Michael: My conversations with Cavell were of a different order. They were more personal. He was a very curious and empathetic being. He shared with me his sense that he felt himself to be something of an outsider, both at Harvard and in the profession. Perhaps that was because his range was enormous. He was not easily categorized. Besides philosophy it included music, film, literature and criticism. But we didn't talk much about his work. I was deeply touched by his interest in my efforts somehow to manage three lives in philosophy, art, and music. His encouragement was pivotal.

RA: And Alexander Nehamas?

Michael: Nehamas had recently published his important book on Nietzsche[18] and had made serious contributions to the theory of interpretation. His article, "The Postulated Author: Critical Monism as a Regulative Ideal," would play a significant role in my own reflections about ideals of interpretation and my introduction of the ideas of singularism, multiplism, and their relation to the metaphysics of objects of interpretation. Our time together in Santa Cruz began some fruitful discussions between us.

RA: And Dreyfus and Hoy?

Michael: Bert Dreyfus and David Hoy were the organizers of the whole institute. Dreyfus was near the end of writing his much-anticipated important book, *Being-in-the-World*. He shared portions of his manuscript with us. I must confess, I was not completely engaged by those discussions, because of what may or not be a reasonable bias against Heidegger to start with. If you recall, Lakatos had really set me against Heidegger.

Finally, David Hoy shared with me his interests in the metaphysics of interpretation. He did so from the point of view of post-structuralism. His eventual article, "One What? Relativism and Poststructuralism" appears in my edition of *Relativism: A Contemporary Anthology*.

RA: That institute in Santa Cruz must have been significant for you.

---

18   Alexander Nehamas, *Nietzsche: Life as Literature*.

Michael: Indeed it was, and several of its participants went on to pursue noteworthy careers. I am honored to have been part of it.

RA: Over the years, you've returned to Oxford, haven't you?

Michael: Yes, on multiple occasions. As you know, I was a fairly regular Visiting Senior Member at Linacre College, for several years running. During those earlier years, after my spring semesters at Bryn Mawr, I would go to Oxford for portions of their Trinity Term, which usually started at the end of April. I visited annually from 1986 to 1990, and then again in 1997 and 1999, and again, in 2016 and 2017.

RA: What did you do while in Oxford during all those trips?

Michael: Of course, we're talking about a number of years. Over those years, in addition to those I've already mentioned, such as Lukes and Montefiore, I also had continuing conversations with scholars such as Joe Raz and Peter Hacker.[19] In connection with my edition on Collingwood, I consulted with Stephen Toulmin[20] and, in connection with my edition on relativism, with Indian economist and philosopher, Amartya Sen, and ethicist, Martha Nussbaum.[21]

I also saw Jerry Cohen[22] periodically at All Souls College. For several years in the 1980s, Jerry, together with three other stellar thinkers—Sen, Derek Parfit,[23] and Ronald Dworkin[24]—presented a seminar in moral and political philosophy at All Souls, which some dubbed the 'Star Wars Seminar.' It was an extraordinary series to have witnessed.

In any event, it was also during one of those stays at Oxford that, with Bojan Bujic of the sub-faculty of music that I helped organize a seminar on the philosophy of music. Some of the papers presented there—including one by

---

19   Please see Chapter Three, n31.
20   A British philosopher, Peter Hacker's expertise is in the philosophy of mind and philosophy of language. Hacker is a major interpreter of Wittgenstein.
21   Stephen Toulmin was a British philosopher. Influenced by Wittgenstein, Toulmin devoted his works to the analysis of moral reasoning.
22   Gerald Allan 'Jerry' Cohen was a Marxist political philosopher who held positions at the University College London and All Souls College, Oxford University.
23   Derek Antony Parfit was a Marxist political philosopher who held the positions of Quain Professor of Jurisprudence, University College London and Chichele Professor of Social and Political Theory, All Souls College, Oxford.
24   Ronald Dworkin was an American philosopher and jurist.

London philosopher Francis Berenson—eventually made their way into my edition, *The Interpretation of Music*.

Others with whom I consulted while visiting Oxford included pianist and theorist Charles Rosen; historian of early music, Margaret Bent; and philosopher Bryan Magee. I had found Magee's book on Wagner noteworthy for his cultural and historical treatment of anti-Semitism in contrast with opposing innatist treatments.[25] Magee did not regard the Jews as inherently chosen, but saw their exceptional creativity during certain historical periods—such as can be seen in the late nineteenth and twentieth centuries—as a consequence of their having been emancipated from closed societies.

In addition, as I've already mentioned, I met Bimal Matilal at All Souls. A most important thing that arose from my association with him was his strong suggestion that given my enduring interest in relativism, I should go to India. That suggestion would start a new chapter in my life, starting in 1992. Matilal's close association with Jiten Mohanty opened numerous doors in Indian philosophy departments, starting with my appointment in 1992, as Visiting Fellow at the Indian Institute of Advanced Study in Shimla. It was during that first visit to India, in 1992, that I would meet Swami Shyamacharan Srivastava and the Dalai Lama. Several notable events in India would follow. In 2001, Delhi University would sponsor a three-day international conference on my work. The papers at that conference would become the basis for a volume dedicated to my work, published in 2003.[26]

Also, in 2003, the Indian Council of Philosophical Research awarded me a grant to visit numerous Indian universities, where I would lecture. After many visits to India, I returned to Oxford, starting in 2017, to organize the Linacre Philosophy Seminars. I am now Adjunct Fellow at Linacre College.

---

25 Bryan Magee, "Jews—Not Least in Music."
26 Andreea Ritivoi, ed. *Interpretation and Its Objects*.

CHAPTER 5

My Epiphany and Art

RA: So far, you have not said much about your art-making.

Michael: That will bring us back in time—to 1971. It all began rather suddenly. You must understand that I had not been particularly visually sensitive in my youth. It came upon me suddenly. As I mentioned briefly during our last session, in the fall of 1971, I experienced an epiphany.

I had gone to New York and visited with my artist friend, Leah Rhodes, in her large studio in SoHo. She brought out and hung huge, shaped canvases for me to see what she was doing. As I gazed at one particular piece, something quite extraordinary happened to me. Suddenly, rather than looking *at* the work, I experienced myself as being at-one—*in* the space of the painting. As well, suddenly, I became extremely visually sensitive—to spatial relations, to colors, and more. I started seeing in a rather different way.[1] After that, I just *needed* to paint. I needed to be *in* the space that I would forge. I needed to place myself in it. And paint I did—obsessively! It was a matter of inner necessity.

When I returned to Bryn Mawr, I immediately went to a local art supply store and bought basic supplies—including canvases, stretchers, acrylic paints, brushes, masking tape, and so on. I had a rudimentary knowledge about art supplies, since, as you know, my father was an artist, and I was acquainted with his materials in his studio as I grew up.

RA: What did you paint?

Michael: I started making simple geometric paintings that pointed toward a very distant horizon. I worked like a demon. The whole thing overtook me. I painted most of every day in our dining room, hardly preparing for my classes at Bryn Mawr. After making larger kinds of paintings, I then made shaped canvasses along the lines of Ellsworth Kelly and other minimalist artists. I had soon outgrown my dining room as a workspace.

---

1 I later came to think of this experience as what Dewey called a 'consummatory experience'; see Dewey's *Art as Experience*, LW: 25; see generally, Chap. 3, "Having an Experience."

I was much encouraged in all of this by my friend, a fine Austrian artist and printmaker, Fritz Janschka, who was on the faculty of the Art Department at the college. At the time, I had no idea how distinguished an artist he was.[2] He arranged for me to set up a studio in the back room of an unused gymnasium, very close to our apartment on campus. I worked there compulsively, and with joy. At the end of the year, I had my first one-person show at the local bank, the Provident National Bank, in Bryn Mawr. Since then, I've had thirty-five solo art exhibitions across the United States, the UK, and India.

RA: How extraordinary. What was in that first show?

Michael: Paintings, silk screens, and small, shaped canvases. In time, the shaped canvases grew in size, some as large as ten feet across. One of those pieces, entitled, *Opposition*—spiky and monochromatic—still hangs in the lobby of the Annenberg Center for Performing Arts in Philadelphia. My interest in art-making informed my work on creativity, which we can discuss later.

RA: I'm really curious to hear about how your preoccupation with art informed your philosophical work on creativity. But for now, can you say how it affected your relationship with Rusty?

Michael: Rusty couldn't fathom what had happened to me. She, as well as some of our friends and colleagues, was mystified by what was possessing me. She could not have known how seriously involved I would eventually become with my art. She had a hard time taking my new life in art seriously.

At the same time, she was a leading figure in her woman's consciousness raising group, which regularly met in our apartment. It was composed of a group of about twenty women—several of whose marriages broke up during that period. Our own marriage was strained. We eventually parted ways in 1972, when she left for Toronto to take a tenure track position at York University.

RA: So, how did your art epiphany affect your teaching?

Michael: After my epiphany and initial intense period of studio work, I wanted to better understand what was happening to me. What kind of experience had

---

2 Fritz Janschka (1919–2016) was an Austrian artist who was a founding member of the Viennese painting school of Fantastic Realism.

I undergone? What, after all, was it that I was doing when I painted? I started to pursue these questions with my students in my aesthetics class at Bryn Mawr. Unlike the more standard aesthetics class, which I had taught at Victoria College, this time, my serious interest in aesthetics arose from my own experience as a painter.

Criteriological questions—such as, "How do we distinguish art from non-art?" or "Is there a criterion between them?"—gave way to other questions concerning aesthetic experience, the nature of creativity and personal programs in art. I also started asking questions about the theory of interpretation in art. Suzi Gablik's *Progress in Art*, which relies heavily upon Kuhn's idea of a paradigm, was helpful. She understood the history of art as basically one paradigm after another, with revolutionary moments in between. In fact, it seemed to me that Kuhn's idea of paradigm shifts better reflects the history of art than it does the history of science.

RA: Can you say more about your art itself?

Michael: As I mentioned earlier, I was influenced by the minimalist work of Ellsworth Kelly as well as the reliefs of Ben Nicholson. Then came the stage of monochromatic shaped canvases.[3] Then I tried silk screening. But I found the colors of silk-screening to be too opaque. I wanted more shading. And I wanted something more spontaneous. After that, I tried spraying acrylic paint on large canvases. They were about 5' × 7'. Those paintings were reminiscent of Carlos Castaneda's novels. They afforded me a good measure of recognition. But I wanted something more personal.

What has emerged is a kind of automatic writing or 'ciphers' on color fields. For color fields—reminiscent of Mark Rothko's work—I burnish powdered pigment on museum board. Then, with wetted pigment, I apply my ciphers. My ciphers are somewhat reminiscent of Mark Tobey's work, which was inspired by Asian calligraphy. Once dry, I smear them to affect a sense of their motion. I then spray the surface with fixative. Sometimes I add a final coat composed of finely crumbled Japanese rice paper, and spray again.[4]

---

3   My work, *Opposition*, still hangs in the Annenberg Center in Philadelphia.
4   For a video of Michael Krausz discussing his art, see https://tinyurl.com/y8lnps68; see also https://tinyurl.com/yboxxbfq.

RA: Can you name others whose works have influenced you?

Michael: Adolph Gottlieb, Franz Kline, Robert Motherwell, Jackson Pollock, and Ad Reinhardt, Agnes Martin. And, of course, over some forty-five years, I have been influenced by Connie. She, after all, is a highly accomplished artist, with extensive experience as an artist and art educator. She has works in major museums like the Phillips Collection, the Hirshhorn Museum and other museums.

RA: What is her work like?

Michael: If you need a label—which she would resist—you might characterize her work as metaphysical surrealistic. Her 'inscapes' evoke quietly sensual infinite spaces, fashioned with meticulously layered graphite. She has come to characterize her work as being about the 'presence of the unseen.'

RA: Do your ciphers have any literal significance?

Michael: Some viewers have seen them as characters in Chinese, Arabic, or Hebrew, but they have no literal significance.

RA: Lacking literal significance, is there some motivating theme in regard to their content?

Michael: The paintings emerge as I go. But I can say this much. I have had shows entitled, for instance, *Between Lines, Beyond Words*. They are motivated by my preoccupation with spaces between veils of language. So, one theme concerns limits of language. One of my favorite paintings is called *End of Texts*. In it, I take some of those ciphers as marks of the effable in relation to the beyond. More recently, I have been pursuing a series called, *Beyond Between*. I wonder about the space beyond individual elements.

RA: That sounds like a paradox. Even to say that there is a space beyond what you call individual elements, is to indicate a relation. I don't see how you can get away from relationships.

Michael: Of course that's a paradox. Actually, it's a paradox that I find in Advaitic philosophy, which we can discuss later. I think of my work as indicating a meditative space, where individual elements are left behind.

MY EPIPHANY AND ART

RA: It sounds to me as if, in your art, you are doing philosophy. Maybe in your philosophy, you might be doing art.

Michael: You're right about the first part of what you just said. In my art, I am doing philosophy. I'm not sure that in my philosophy I am doing art though. But that's another matter. Often, when I have had enough with words—as when I write and teach a lot—I am happy to return to my art. It's as if another world always waits.

RA: Are you regularly involved with other artists?

Michael: Yes. I'm a member of the Artists Exchange of Delaware.[5] It is a group of a dozen or so professional artists. We meet once a month. We critique each other's works—sometimes works in progress, and sometimes finished pieces. Sometimes we have shows together at one or another gallery.

RA: When you meet with your colleagues at the Artists' Exchange to talk about your works, what sorts of issues do you generally raise with each other?

Michael: We may find a particular painting puzzling and ask questions such as, "Why did you do this rather than that?"; "What were you intending to do with this piece?"; "What is the challenge you set for yourself?"; or, we might react to the piece in relation to a larger project that the artist is engaged with. Sometimes, we praise the artist because the piece 'works.' Sometimes we say, "Don't do anything more to it! Don't overdo it!" Sometimes, the artist gets gifts, as when the work overshoots the artist's goal. The piece might be more interesting than the artist originally intended.

RA: Do you get involved with more general questions about one's direction and motivation?

Michael: Yes, indeed. For example, there's a highly trained realist painter in our group. He can paint still life with photographic perfection. For example, sometimes we may ask, "Why are you doing this?" "What interest do you have in doing yet another reproductive rendering of oranges?" An artist may be

---

5 See https://www.artistsexchangede.org/michael-krausz

struggling with the work, seeing that it has become stale. Then we talk about such dilemmas, and ask why we paint in the first place. Sometimes we ask one another whether our work is improving, and whether such questions even make sense. Our discussions sometimes get rather philosophical in that way. But more often than not, we make concrete suggestions about how a particular work might be improved, or how it might serve as a springboard for a subsequent piece.

RA: Am I right that you are self-taught? You have done all this without formal art training?

Michael: In the main, you are right. Yet during the summer of 1972, I did take a course in printmaking at the Haystack Mountain School of Crafts. At that time, I was experimenting with silk screening, in addition to my painting. As I mentioned, I eventually found that medium to be unsatisfying. It wouldn't give me the sort of shading I wanted. Nevertheless, it was a great chance to work with excellent artists such as the Canadian etcher, Jennifer Dickson, and New York painter, Herbert Perr. Later, I also took courses with Walter Lubar at the Philadelphia College of Art—now called the University of the Arts. He was most helpful and encouraging. We became friends.

However, when I raised the question of formal training, Connie was dubious about academic training for me. It was clear to her that I was already on my individualized path. All I really needed was to find the materials and techniques for the path I was already pursuing.[6]

RA: You mentioned the question why you paint. Why *do* you paint?

Michael: I paint because I *have* to. I cannot *not* paint. If I don't paint for an extended period, I feel out of sorts—out of tune with myself.

RA: It sounds as if you developed something like a personal agenda.

Michael: Yes. I call it a personal program. Actually, I have developed the idea of a personal program in my philosophy of creativity. If you recall, I talked with Roman Jakobson about the idea of a personal program when we were both at Ossabaw.

---

6 Twice, in 2009 and 2015, Michael Krausz has been awarded the title, 'Master,' by Delaware by Hand, currently sponsored by the Biggs Museum of American Art, Dover, Delaware; see https://tinyurl.com/y73kqz49.

RA: Can you say something about your personal program?

Michael: Sure. I understand my creative work to include more than 'thingly' products. It includes process as well as product, verb as well as noun, doing as well as what is done. It recognizes non-dualistic experiences as benchmarks of a creative life path. It allows for unintended by-products when combining media with spontaneous movement.

My personal program differs from that of Larry Briskman, a follower of Karl Popper. He and I had numerous fruitful exchanges at Bryn Mawr and in Edinburgh that resulted in several published works by both of us.[7]

The spirit of my process-centered program agrees with that of M.C. Richards, as expressed in her book, *Centering in Pottery, Poetry, and the Person.* She had taught at Black Mountain College along with John Cage. I was fortunate to have met her at one of my follow-up stays at Haystack. Connie and I still prize one of M.C.'s pots, which she gave us for our wedding.

RA: You say you met Connie at Haystack in 1972.

Michael: Yes. She had just returned to the United States after visiting friends in Romania. I had signed up for printmaking. She had signed up for ceramics. We met on the first evening of that session at a dance in the print studio. I just went up to her and asked if she would like to dance. That's how it started.

RA: How did Connie strike you?

Michael: She was and is tall, beautiful, very smart, sensitive and so deeply artistic and spiritual in a Nordic sort of way.

RA: How did it unfold after that?

Michael: I guess Connie began to take more notice of me in connection with a couple of instructors at Haystack.

---

[7] See my "A Painter's View of Self-Development and Creativity," 143–145; Rejoinders to David Carrier, Larry Briskman, John Broyer, James Munz, and Joan Novosel-Beitel; "On a Painter's View of Self-Development and Creativity"; and "Creativity and Self-Transformation."

RA: Who were they?

Michael: Peter and Ritzi Jacobi were distinguished instructors in the weaving studio. They had just defected from Romania. The Jacobi's were internationally recognized textile sculptors. Their enormous pieces were featured in major museums throughout the world. As a sign of protest, rather than allow the Romanian authorities to appropriate their work after they defected from Romania, they took their own remaining works in the street and burned them. Peter and Ritzi had just arrived in the United States, and spoke very little English. With my medium-good German, I helped them along. Connie and I got to know each other better in that context. It didn't hurt my standing with Connie that Ernest Gellner's review of my Collingwood edition had recently been featured on the front page of the *Times Literary Supplement* just before my trip to Haystack.

That was the start of many years of commuting between Bryn Mawr and Washington DC, where Connie was doing a lot of art teaching, including at the Smithsonian Institution, and later at the George Washington University Art Department. With such an extraordinary background, and being an established artist, she was a popular teacher.

RA: It sounds as if a lot was going on in your life around 1972 and 1973.

Michael: Indeed, a lot was! And it was fortunate that I was able to take a Junior Research Leave in 1973–1974; for that academic year, I moved to Frederick, Maryland.

RA: What was Frederick like for you?

Michael: Frederick is about fifty miles from Washington DC, where I rented the first floor of a house, part of which I converted into a studio. Besides doing my philosophical work, it was then that I did my surrealistic landscapes reminiscent of Castaneda's novels. I knew a number of artists in Frederick, including H.I. and Elaine Gates, and John and Harriet Wise. That lasted for a year. Then I returned to Bryn Mawr.

RA: Again, to commute between Bryn Mawr and Washington?

Michael: Yes. I really had fallen in love with Connie. I knew that if my relationship with her was to mature, we would marry; and indeed, in May 1976, we did marry—on the beach at Cape Henlopen State Park in Lewes, Delaware—after we had our civic ceremony in the City Hall in Philadelphia in the chambers of Judge Ned Spaeth, then Chair of the Board of Bryn Mawr College.

RA: But Connie was not Jewish.

Michael: That's right. I knew that marrying her would mean that, for my parents, heaven would fall. And it did!

RA: Did they try to stop you from marrying Connie?

Michael: Yes, indeed. My father wrote me a very long, hand-written letter. It must have been ten or twelve pages long. In it, he rehearsed how important it was for me not to forget that I am a Jew, and that his parents had been murdered by the Nazis only because they were Jews, and that I had a responsibility to Jewish history and culture—and to them—that I not marry a non-Jewish person. It was a devastating letter.

RA: What did you do with that?

Michael: I decided that there was no purpose in my answering his letter point-by-point. I folded his long letter, attached a short covering note, put them both in an envelope, and returned it to him.

RA: What did you say in the note?

Michael: I wrote that I loved Connie and that if he really meant for me not to pursue my happiness, would he please resend his original letter back to me.

RA: And?

Michael: He never sent it back to me.

RA: And Peter? How did he receive the news?

Michael: Surprisingly, it was Peter who supported me. He urged me to follow my heart. As for Connie's not being Jewish, he had only one question: Did she support Israel? Of course, many non-Jews support Israel. Was Connie one of them? That was the most important question for Peter. In fact, over the years, Peter and Connie got to be good friends.

RA: How did it all turn out with your parents?

Michael: Over time, my father grew to like Connie quite a lot as well. Years later, my mother indicated to me that Connie was good for me. I might add that Connie and I recently celebrated our forty-second wedding anniversary. She continues to make me a happy man. And, I have not forgotten that I am a Jew.

CHAPTER 6

My Music Again

RA: You mentioned how you began to conduct during your teen years in Cleveland and then again at Rutgers in 1964.

Michael: Yes, but after that, it was not until years later that I had the opportunity to conduct again. In the meantime, I remained fairly active with my violin. I participated in several orchestras. I played with the Bryn Mawr College Orchestra for a while. When visiting Connie in Washington, I would play with the Arlington Symphony Orchestra. When in Oxford, I played in an Oxford community orchestra. In Philadelphia, I played in a quartet that included colleagues from Temple University. I also took violin lessons from Yumi Scott, who was in the Philadelphia Orchestra and taught at the Curtis Institute of Music.

Later, I took lessons from David Arben. You'll remember Arben, who used to play in the Cleveland Orchestra. He then joined the Philadelphia Orchestra. All of that was satisfying. But I longed to conduct again. Of course, I would go to orchestral concerts. But I was often frustrated about not conducting myself. I would come out after concerts with growing unease. I just needed to conduct again. In any event, David suggested I play with a fine semi-professional repertory orchestra in Philadelphia conducted by Luis Biava. At that time, Luis was the principal of the second violin section of the Philadelphia Orchestra. He also served as the orchestra's Resident Conductor. He would eventually coach me in conducting. But I'm getting ahead of myself.

RA: How did the opportunity to conduct again present itself?

Michael: It was not until 1982 that I would return to conducting. As my fortieth birthday was approaching, I wanted to give myself a gift—to conduct. I talked about it with a good friend, Richard Burian, a very fine cellist and philosopher at Drexel University. In fact, we had collaborated on projects with the Greater Philadelphia Philosophy Consortium, including a co-edited volume.[1] He helped me form a chamber orchestra of about twenty players. I called it the Celebration Chamber Orchestra. We held a concert at the Ethical Society Hall on Rittenhouse Square in Philadelphia. The hall has excellent acoustics.

---

[1] Margolis, Krausz, and Burian, eds., *Rationality, Relativism, and the Human Sciences*.

We opened with the Overture to Handel's *Messiah*. Violin soloists Linda Burian, Min-Soo Chang, Joy Friday, and Kijai Kim were featured in Vivaldi's Concerto Grosso in B minor, for four solo violins. Then James Winn was a featured flute soloist for Bach's Suite no. 2 in B minor. Then, after we played Francesco Geminiani's Concerto Grosso in E minor, David Arben joined us as violin soloist in Bach's Violin Concerto in E major. By the way, James is a dear friend, whom I'd met at the Aspen Institute in 1977. We were both Mellon Fellows at the Institute. In any event, for that concert, we had a full house, which included many friends. The players performed extremely well, and I was delighted with the results. My mother came from Cleveland to hear it. She was surprised and impressed with the high level of music making that she heard. I knew then that I had to conduct more.

RA: You say you also studied violin with Arben?

Michael: Yes. David had been a colleague of my father's when they both were in the Cleveland Orchestra, as well as a soloist with my father with the Akron Symphony Orchestra. I wanted to improve my violin playing and musicianship. So, I asked David for lessons in exchange for paintings. He was obliging. Lessons were mixed with good conversation. David and I made a real connection. In fact, some of our discussions led to our hatching the idea of putting together the Philadelphia Chamber Orchestra (PCO)—comprising some of the best players from the Philadelphia Orchestra.

RA: How did it turn out with the PCO?

Michael: However short-lived, the PCO was one of the finest ensembles of its kind that I've ever heard. I managed to get the violinist-conductor Jaime Laredo and noted violist, Michael Tree, to serve as Co-Artistic Directors. I formed the board, helped raise funds, and generally oversaw the operation. I was President of the Board and Associate Artistic Director. Did I mention that Laredo was a student of Josef Gingold in Cleveland? He also was soloist with my father in Akron. The first guest conductor of the PCO was Lawrence Leighton Smith, the fine conductor of the Louisville Symphony.

RA: What did they play?

Michael: The premier concert was on April 27, 1986 in the Church of the Holy Trinity on Rittenhouse Square. It was a full house. Packed. The anticipation was palpable.

They began with Haydn's Symphony no. 68 in B♭ major. The performance was transcendent. Then they performed David Diamond's Rounds for String Orchestra, which is an energetic contemporary piece, technically demanding. They pulled it off with verve. Then violist Michael Tree—Co-Artistic Director of the PCO and violist with the Guarneri Quartet—soloed in Hindemith's *Trauermusik*, for viola and strings. Michael was a master of his instrument. For the final piece, Michael joined David Arben in Mozart's Sinfonia Concertante in E♭ major.

As president, my role was primarily administrative, but I did play a role during the final rehearsal. While David was playing on a Stradivarius violin, the volume of his instrument was overpowered by that of Michael Tree's Busan viola. I convinced Michael to stand further back on the stage and allow David to stand forward on the stage to effect the right balance between them. All in all, the concert was a smashing success. At the reception that followed—including Laredo—everyone was excited about the prospect of the orchestra's future.

RA: I assume you had to do a lot of administrative work to launch the PCO, including work with the administration of the Philadelphia Orchestra, since members of the Philadelphia Orchestra comprised the PCO.

Michael: Yes. And that gives rise to an interesting story. It so happened that the Executive Director of the Philadelphia Orchestra at that time was Stephen Sell. Coincidentally, Steve was an old friend from my college days at Rutgers. Both of us had worked with Julius Bloom. During that time, Bloom was head of the concert programs at Rutgers as well as Executive Director of Carnegie Hall. In fact, he was largely responsible for encouraging Vladamir Horowitz to make his historic return to the concert hall in 1965. Steve and I were part of a coterie of students who helped Bloom with concerts at Rutgers. That's how I got to know Steve. As well, Bloom was most encouraging in my formation of the Ensemble Symphonique at Rutgers, in 1963, which was a small orchestra and choir comprising Rutgers students.

Anyway, before coming to Philadelphia, Steve had worked as an administrator of the Cleveland Orchestra. Steve eventually became Executive Director of the Philadelphia Orchestra. My history with Steve became important as I organized the PCO, because we had to have the blessings of the Philadelphia Orchestra—or if not its blessings, then at least its tacit approval. Steve managed to get its assent from Maestro Riccardo Muti.

RA: So how did the second concert of the PCO go?

Michael: Our second concert, held on October 25, 1987, at the Shubert Theatre at the University of the Arts, in Philadelphia, was also its last. Anshel Brusilow was the guest conductor.

Brusilow had been associate concertmaster with the Cleveland Orchestra under George Szell—seated next to Joe Gingold. He had also been a soloist with my father in Akron. After Cleveland, he moved to the post of concertmaster of the Philadelphia Orchestra under Eugene Ormandy. Brusilow was also a conductor. Earlier, he founded the Philadelphia Chamber Symphony, composed of members of the Philadelphia Orchestra, but without the encouragement of Ormandy. That orchestra was short-lived too. Deteriorating relations between Brusilow and Ormandy led to Brusilow's eventual departure from Philadelphia to take a position heading the orchestra program at Southern Methodist University in Texas.

The PCO program of the second concert included Mozart's Symphony no. 29 in A major; Ermanno Wolf-Ferrari's Suite-Concertino in F major, for bassoon and orchestra, with solo bassoonist Bernard Garfield; and Mozart's Symphony no. 41 in C major ("Jupiter").

RA: You said that the PCO had only two concerts. What happened?

Michael: The location had been moved to the Schubert Theatre, which was not so acoustically responsive. Other things also led to the PCO's demise. First of all, there already existed a good chamber orchestra in Philadelphia then, founded and led by Marc Mostovoy in 1964, called the Concerto Soloists.[2] The Chair of its board—and this was told to me by Steve Sell—systematically approached our major funders to discredit our efforts. He complained to them all that it was unfair that Philadelphia Orchestra musicians, who were already well paid, should get still more money from the PCO—money that he believed should go to his Concerto Soloists. The contest was very uncomfortable. We lost.

---

2 It was renamed "The Chamber Orchestra of Philadelphia" in 2000. This organization is still in existence; see https://chamberorchestra.org/.

In addition, my administrative responsibilities with the PCO intensified to such a degree that it began to infringe upon my academic work. I had to turn the leadership over to another board member, whose leadership was not effective. Finally, my efforts to establish the PCO—as *The Philadelphia Inquirer* music critic Daniel Webster pointed out—followed numerous other such efforts involving players of the Philadelphia Orchestra. But without the robust institutional sponsorship of the Philadelphia Orchestra, it would be unlikely that the PCO could sustain itself. As Webster said, "Until [the Philadelphia Orchestra's sponsorship] happens, each new ad hoc chamber orchestra rising from its ranks represents a promise that cannot be kept, a hope that is doomed to fade."[3] I now see that Webster was right.

RA: Yet it seems that you learned a lot though.

Michael: Yes indeed. I learned a lot about administration and orchestra management. I learned a lot about the music world. I also learned about my own ambitions to conduct. It's one thing to administer an orchestra—however outstanding. It's something else to make music oneself.

RA: It sounds like your love for conducting eventually dominated.

Michael: Yes. Even before we launched the PCO, it had become clear to me that I would need to study conducting more. As it turned out, my friend Marty Moskof had a friend who was on the staff of the Aspen Music Festival and Music School. She arranged for me to audit one of Murray Sidlin's conducting workshops in 1983. He coached me informally, and with the conductor's orchestra, I conducted the beginning of the last movement of Brahms's Symphony no. 4 in E minor. Informally, I was also asked by a group of students to conduct a pickup ensemble. We played Dvořák's Serenade for Wind Instruments in D minor. That was fun. As well, I started associating with really talented young conducting students at Aspen. From them, I heard that an amazing conducting pedagogue was in Baltimore—just the sort of person I could talk with. He was the Director of Conducting Programs at the Peabody Conservatory. Besides having conducted major orchestras, I learned that he would be somebody who would be intellectually alive. That advice turned out to be solid. His name was

---

3 Daniel Webster, "What does the Future Hold for Philadelphia Chamber Orchestra?," *Philadelphia Inquirer*, May 11, 1986.

Frederik Prausnitz. Prausnitz had recently published an important book for conductors entitled *Score and Podium*.

I corresponded with Prausnitz, after which he invited me to see him at his room at Peabody. I told him that I had met several of his graduate students at Aspen and wanted to pursue the possibility of studying with him. I told him about my family, my past experience as a conductor and organizer of orchestras, and my need to conduct—all the while of course continuing my philosophical and teaching career at Bryn Mawr. He took me on as a private student, allowing me to attend his conducting classes and orchestral rehearsals at Peabody. Mostly, I worked with him at his home privately for a couple of years between 1983 and 1985, and beyond.

RA: What work did you do with him?

Michael: Mostly Mozart, Beethoven, Brahms, Schubert, Dvořák. We would talk about their performance challenges. It was just what I needed. We also became friends. In fact, before he retired from Peabody, he and his wife Margaret visited us in Lewes. When he did retire, they moved to Lewes, and we continued our warm friendship. I helped him too. I was instrumental in connecting him with editors at Oxford University Press, which eventually published his book on Roger Sessions.[4]

RA: What did Prausnitz think about your conducting?

Michael: He thought I was exceptionally gifted. He said to me: "You have everything—except repertoire." He thought I needed exposure. But he was reluctant to facilitate opportunities.

RA: So, how did your next opportunity present itself?

Michael: Actually, it was Fred's wife, Margaret who presented it. She noticed a flyer on Fred's desk announcing conducting possibilities with professional orchestras in Bulgaria. One thing led to the next. That's when things really changed for me. For several years running, I conducted professional orchestras

---

4 Prausnitz, *Sessions: How a 'Difficult' Composer Got that Way*. Prausznitz died on November 12, 2004. His obituary can be found in *The Guardian*; see also Donald Mitchell, "Frederick Prausnitz: Conductor-Teacher with a Passion for Contemporary Music," 1 December 2004; available at https://tinyurl.com/ybfhwqoq.

in Bulgaria. They included the Pleven Symphony Orchestra, the Vratsa Philharmonic Orchestra, and the Plovdiv Philharmonic Orchestra. The Pleven Symphony Orchestra was the first big professional orchestra I had conducted.

RA: So, how did the first rehearsal with the Pleven orchestra go?

Michael: At the first rehearsal with the Pleven orchestra, on May 18, 1999, I began with Mozart's Overture to *The Marriage of Figaro*. When it ended, there was thunderous applause from the orchestra's players. I was ecstatic. The program also included Mendelsohn's exciting Symphony no. 4 in A major ("Italian") The night of the concert, May 20, 1999, was particularly memorable because it happened to fall on my father's *Yahrzeit*—the 21st anniversary of his death. He had died in 1979 at the age of 76. Remember, our relationship had been extraordinary in that there had been this mutual identification. To give you an idea, while rehearsing in Pleven, I caught sight of my bare right conducting arm. It looked to me as if it were my father's! His influence had always been something that I had to deal with—one way or another—for most of my life.

So, that evening of the concert, in one of the rooms of the apartment that had been provided for me, I lit the *Yahrzeit* candle and recited the prayer for my father. I added, "Please excuse me, Daddy, but I'm going to have to close the door on you. I have to do this without you!" It was a big moment for me. That first concert was most satisfying in many ways, despite an odd episode that followed it.

RA: What was that?

Michael: After that concert, a tall, stern, well dressed Bulgarian came backstage and asked me directly, "*Sie sind ein Juden, nein? Nicht wahr?*"—You are a Jew are you not?—I snapped back, "*Aber naturlich!*"—Of course I am. I felt threatened and liberated to shout back at him, to register the obvious in the face of my triumph.

RA: And you returned to Pleven the following year, didn't you?

Michael: Yes, I did. I had a second performance with the Pleven orchestra on June 1, 2000. We opened with Beethoven's Coriolan Overture, followed by Beethoven's Piano Concerto no. 4 in G major, with British pianist, Mark Hooper, as soloist. There's a back story about that, too. When I was at Oxford in the spring of 1999, I attended a concert at the Jacqueline Dupre Hall to hear a recital by Mark, who impressed me enormously. For a long time, I'd wanted to perform that Beethoven Piano Concerto, with a suitable soloist. So I asked Mark if he would join me the following year in Pleven to do so. He agreed. What a work that is, especially its second movement, *Andante con moto*. We did it together in Bulgaria for that second concert. I know of no musical work that so dramatically contrasts bestial force with transcendent tenderness—finally resolving itself in a reconciliation of tranquility.

Also on that occasion, we performed Beethoven's Symphony no. 3 in E♭ major ("Eroica"). Its second movement, *Marcia Funebre—Adagio Assai* ("Funeral March"), touches my soul.

RA: And the following year?

Michael: The following year, June 14, 2001, I conducted the Vratsa Philharmonic Orchestra. I recall that we performed Beethoven's Symphony no. 8 in F major—a beautiful work. I also conducted Brahms's Symphony no. 4. at that concert, as I would later, with the Plovdiv Philharmonic.

RA: When did your concerts in Plovdiv start?

Michael: On March 14, 2002. I again opened the concert with Beethoven's Coriolan Overture, and again I did Brahms's Symphony no. 4. A wonderful Bulgarian violinist, Micho Dimitrov, performed.[5] He was the concertmaster of the Hilversum Radio Symphony Orchestra in Holland, returning to his hometown of Plovdiv. We did Beethoven's Violin Concerto in D major. He played beautifully, and the orchestra was so responsive!

RA: Of course, you were still teaching at Bryn Mawr during the time you were conducting in Bulgaria, correct? So, what else was happening there?

Michael: At this point, I should mention that in the fall of 2002, along with my teaching at Bryn Mawr, I began teaching Aesthetics at the Curtis Institute of Music in Philadelphia. The arrangement was that I would do so once every second year in their liberal arts program. It was in that context that I met harpsichordist, Lionel Party. I mention him because he played a significant role in

---

5   Dimitrov won "Musician of the Year 2013" at a ceremony held on June 5, 2013 in Sofia, Bulgaria; https://tinyurl.com/yb8xjkvu.

my experience at Curtis, as well as with the Great Hall Chamber Orchestra (GHCO). But I'll get to that later.

In any event, I returned to Plovdiv for another concert on April 15, 2004. As I review my diary entry from the day after the concert, I am reminded that things don't always go evenly:

> The concert last night was great in many ways. This was despite the fact that we had a challenging rehearsal when the orchestra was restive.... Still, the Rossini Overture—*La gazza ladra*—went well. The Bulgarian pianist Dimo Dimov was superb in the Mozart Piano Concerto no. 24 in C minor. He played with such finesse![6]

Then, the first movement of Brahms's Symphony no. 4 went well. But in the second movement, the orchestra was not responding to my tempos. While the third movement was acceptable, the last movement brought some moments of sheer ecstasy.

RA: After your orchestral experiences in Bulgaria, how did it go musically for you at Bryn Mawr?

Michael: At the college, I asked colleagues whether funds might be available for a concert that I would bill as an "East-West Concert." For the 'West' part, I would present the 'Conservatory Symphony Orchestra,' named after conservatory musicians gathered from area conservatories. The personnel was managed by Michael Johns, who had been recommended by Luis Biava.

The Conservatory Symphony Orchestra had its only concert on February 18, 2003. The first half of the program was to have been presented by the Peabody Percussion Group, under Robert van Sice—then on the faculty at Peabody, now on the faculty at Curtis. The percussion group was to play music inspired by Asian themes. The second half of the program was to have featured the Conservatory Symphony Orchestra.

---

6 Dimo Dimov graduated from the Bulgarian State Academy of Music. In 1970, he won 1st prize at the Sv. Obretenov National Competition, and in 1979, 1st prize at Maria Callas Piano Competition in Athens.

RA: Why do you say *was* to have?

Michael: Unfortunately, due to a terrible snowstorm, the truck with the percussion instruments got stuck in Baltimore. The ensemble had to cancel. At the last minute, to substitute for them, Biava arranged for the distinguished pianist Charles Abramovic to substitute for the percussion group. He delivered a fine performance. During the second half, we performed Beethoven's Coriolan Overture and Symphony no. 7 in A major.

RA: What was it like for you to be conducting in the Great Hall at the college, in contrast to Bulgaria?

Michael: While the orchestras in Bulgaria were excellent and the audiences were enthusiastic, very few of my friends at home could attend. As well, the Great Hall has wonderful acoustics. So, it was a great gift when, after hearing me conduct the East-West concert, our friend, Anne Sclufer, offered to underwrite much of the cost of the next concerts. That's how the Conservatory Symphony Orchestra was able to morph into the Great Hall Chamber Orchestra.

RA: You say that Biava coached you.

Michael: Yes. From the beginning of my involvement with the Great Hall Chamber Orchestra, Biava offered much encouragement and assistance. We would discuss questions of tempos, touchy entrances, and matters of baton technique. But it was much more than that. Luis was an inspiration. Besides practical matters, we talked a lot about what is means to make music. He also helped me to identify people such as Michael Johns—who himself was a highly accomplished horn player and administrator—as well as Colleen Hood, who was a most effective personnel manager for many years. At Curtis, my friend, Mary-Jean Haydn, was most encouraging also.

RA: So, when was the premier of the GHCO? And how did you get your soloists?

Michael: The first concert of the Great Hall Chamber Orchestra took place on Saturday April 2, 2005. We were careful not to schedule it as early as mid-February when we were less likely to be snowed in! It was a festive occasion. The orchestra of thirty-three young professionals—which eventually expanded to forty-four—played as well as the orchestras I conducted in Bulgaria. It included recent and present students from Temple University's Boyer Conservatory and the Curtis Institute of Music. The first concert was the first of nine annual concerts from 2005 until 2014, skipping only 2013.

RA: What was the program of the first concert?

Michael: It included Mozart's spirited Symphony no. 35 in D major ("Haffner"). Then, harpsichordist Lionel Party was soloist in Bach's Piano Concerto no. 1 in D minor. I got to know Lionel at Curtis where he was on the faculty. He was the harpsichordist of the New York Philharmonic. Finally, the GHCO played Mendelssohn's "Italian."

RA: Do tell more about the GHCO concerts that followed.

Michael: By all means. The program for March 17, 2006, included the Overture to Mozart's *The Marriage of Figaro*, Saint-Saëns's Cello Concerto no. 1 in A minor, and Beethoven's "Eroica."

RA: So who was your cello soloist for the Saint-Saëns?

Michael: It was William Stokking—a fabulous cellist. For many years, he was the principal cellist of the Philadelphia Orchestra. He also was on the faculty at Curtis. He, too, had been a colleague of my father's with the Cleveland Orchestra and a soloist with the Akron Symphony Orchestra. It was a delight to work with him. In our many conversations, he would bemoan the tendency of many musicians to over intellectualize music making at the expense of the sheer joy of making music. Our performance of the Saint-Saëns reflected his joyfulness. We also had very satisfying social moments together with Connie and his wife Nancy Leichner Stokking, also a cellist.

RA: It seems that you came to know several musicians who had moved to Philadelphia from the Cleveland, starting with Arben and Brusilow, then Stokking.

Michael: Yes, and each in his own way was generous in giving me encouragement and guidance.

RA: How about the following year, 2007?

Michael: That concert, on March 31, 2007, included Mozart's Symphony no. 38 in D major ("Prague Symphony"), followed by Max Bruch's Violin Concerto no. 1 in G minor, and Beethoven's Symphony no. 8.

RA: And who was your soloist for the Bruch concerto?

Michael: It was the wonderful violinist Kimberly Fisher. She was the principal of the second violin section of the Philadelphia Orchestra. Coincidentally, she was Biava's successor in that post. With the GHCO, she was energetic and highly communicative.

RA: So let's move on to your 2008 concert. What was on its program?

Michael: On April 5, 2008 we performed the Overture to Mozart's *La Clemenza di Tito*. Then we did the fabulous Brahms Double Concerto in A minor, for violin and cello, and the towering Beethoven's Symphony no. 5 in C minor. What a night that was!

RA: And who were your soloists?

Michael: José Blumenschein on the violin, and Nicholas Canellakis on the cello. José—straight out of Curtis as concertmaster of the Curtis Orchestra—was a new Associate Concertmaster of the Philadelphia Orchestra, and Nick, the principal cellist of the Curtis orchestra, was a regular collaborator of José's. Both have gone on to distinguished international careers. In fact, I heard that José had been appointed Concertmaster of the Vienna Philharmonic and the Vienna State Opera.[7]

Actually, there's an interesting story behind my engaging them. It happened at one of the weekly teas at Curtis. I was speaking with the head of the violin department, Ida Kavafian, and asked for her advice. I explained that I was keen to do the Brahms Double Concerto and asked if she had a suggestion about appropriate soloists. As it happened, José was in the crowd. She beckoned him to come over to us. After Ida introduced us, José and I went off and had a conversation, after which he agreed and suggested that Nick should join us in the Brahms. And so it was.

RA: What serendipity. OK. Let's move forward with this wonderful list.

Michael: By our concert of March 28, 2009, the orchestra had grown to forty players. We performed the Overture to Luigi Cherubini's *Médée*, Beethoven's

---

[7] "José Maria Blumenschein Appointed Vienna Philharmonic Concertmaster," *The Strad*, December 16, 2015; available at https://tinyurl.com/y8j9anc6.

beloved Violin Concerto in D major, and Robert Schumann's Symphony no. 4 in D minor.

RA: So this time, who was your soloist in the violin concerto?

Michael: José Blumenschein. This time he was well established as Associate Concertmaster of the Philadelphia Orchestra. And what a performance it was!

RA: It seems that you were developing a special partnership with José.

Michael: I think so, and there's more. On March 26, 2010, I conducted the Overture to Carl Maria von Weber's *Silvana*, and Schubert's Symphony no. 9 in C major ("Great"). What a demanding piece that is! But more to the point, we also performed Beethoven's Concerto in C major, for violin, cello, and piano ("Triple Concerto"). The three soloists were José and his close associates, cellist Efe Baltacigil, and pianist Benjamin Hochman—all Curtis people. Efe was the Associate Principal Cellist of the Philadelphia Orchestra, later to solo with the Berlin Philharmonic under Simon Rattle and later still to become the principal cellist of the Seattle Symphony. Benjie was to become an internationally acclaimed soloist. What a joy it was to play with them.

RA: Did you ever get the opportunity to perform with them again?

Michael: Yes, indeed. On April 1, 2011, The GHCO opened with Christoph Willibald Gluck's opera, *Iphigénia in Aulis*. Then Efe Baltacigil soloed in Haydn's Cello Concerto no. 1 in C major, and Gabriel Fauré's *Élégie*. His renditions were memorable. Then we concluded with Beethoven's Symphony no. 7 in A major. After sitting in on my rehearsal of the Beethoven Symphony, Efe said to me, "It just doesn't get any better than that!"

RA: What a tribute to you!

Michael: It certainly was. Much buoyed, we moved on to plan the next concert. But it turned out to be a bittersweet occasion.

RA: Why do you say that?

Michael: The next concert was scheduled for March 30, 2012. Our dear friend, Anne Sclufer, had died suddenly on March 1, 2012. That was a blow in so many ways. Until then, she had been a steadfast and devoted benefactor of the GHCO. We dedicated the March 2012 concert to her memory. We opened with the Overture to Mozart's *Idomeneo*, followed by Beethoven's Piano Concerto no. 4 in G major. Amy Yang was our soloist. Amy is a magnificent artist currently on the Curtis faculty. She also had been a student of mine in my Aesthetics class. It was a pleasure working with her in this different capacity. Then we closed with Brahms's Symphony no. 4 in E minor. I had come to have had a special relationship with that towering piece.

Alas, on account of financial difficulties, we played no concert in 2013. Our last was to be in March 28, 2014. For our final concert, we opened with the Overture to Mozart's *The Marriage of Figaro*. Benjamin Hochman played Mendelssohn's Piano Concerto no. 2 in D minor. His performance was truly memorable. His musical sensitivity was breathtaking. Then we closed with Beethoven's "Eroica." I had dedicated its second movement—"Funeral March"—to Anne's memory.

RA: I've often wondered what it's like to conduct.

Michael: For me, that's a big question. But generally, I can say this much. Just standing on the podium communicating with musicians by gestures and words in the midst of glorious sound is one of the most thrilling experiences I can have. Clearly, there are many challenges. But when it works—and I emphasize, *when* it works—there's nothing like it. It brings me utter joy.

RA: Do say something about how you prepare.

Michael: First, I need to make the music my own. By that I mean, besides mastering the scores to the best of my ability, I need to allow it to sink into my consciousness in such a way that it becomes second nature to me. I am reminded that in his book, Gunther Schuller reports what the great conductor Bruno Walter said about conducting. It's worth considering Walter's own words about 'assimilating' the intentions of another:

> For the criterion of our talent as reproductive musicians lies exactly in our capacity for assimilating the intentions of another so completely that not only are the demands of the work no burden to us, but that we feel them to be our own demands. Only thus shall we feel free within the limits of the laws imposed on the work by the author, and only thus will our music-making sound spontaneous, since we now are free to follow the

bent of our own heart which has learnt to beat in unison with that of the composer.[8]

Once on the podium, I am a coordinator, an instructor, a coach. Sometimes I need to be a gentle umpire. As well, I am a conjurer and cheerleader. I'll do what it takes to get the best out of my musicians in order to deliver an authentic and alive musical experience for the players and the audience. The performance should not just be a mechanical rendering of a score.

RA: How do you prepare for your first rehearsal?

Michael: Actually, whenever possible, I would have preparatory sessions with my concertmaster—to get more acquainted and to indicate broad outlines of my conception of the works we will play. As you may know, the concertmaster plays a distinctive role to help translate the conductor's intentions to the rest of the ensemble. Often, the concertmaster will be in a position to make useful technical and musical suggestions. I would regularly have such preparatory sessions with soloists as well. For the GHCO, for example, I would have such sessions in one of the rooms at the Curtis Institute of Music in Philadelphia.

RA: So what usually happens at the first rehearsals?

Michael: I generally begin by running through the entire movement or piece from start to finish without interruption. My primary concern when I run through the piece is for us all to get to know each other musically speaking, to give us all a sense of the sound that might be expected from strings, the woodwinds, the brasses, the percussion. I think of the first run-through as a way of making ourselves known to one another. It's also an occasion for the players to get to know me—or at least update their sense of me as a communicator. Of course, in the process, we all become aware of the rough spots that will need attention later on. As well, I become aware of what I need to explain to the group by way of the interpretive nuances that I will want to perfect.

Of course, when I'm dealing with an orchestra that I worked with before, that will be a matter of re-introduction. Even then, certain personnel changes will have been made since the last time we worked together. So, it really is a matter

---

8 See Gunther Schuller, *The Compleat Conductor*, 92. Schuller's father was a violinist in the New York Philharmonic and a great friend of my father.

of re-acquaintance. You'd be surprised how different a given orchestra can feel and sound on different occasions. Then, of course, comes the more detailed work. After the first run-through a range of questions may arise—though not in this order—such as questions of tempo, dynamics, balance, and coordination. Then come rather more distinctive questions that bear on shaping the performance in accord with what general conception I might have about the piece.

RA: Can you give a couple of examples how this might go in particular pieces?

Michael: OK. Consider the question of tempo in Beethoven's Marcia Funebre: Adagio Assai, the second movement of Eroica Symphony.

As you know, I conducted that symphony on several occasions with different orchestras. The tempo of that second movement was especially challenging for me. I asked myself how slowly I should take it. Of course, a funeral march should be slow. But how slow is slow? Beethoven's marking, 'adagio assai,' didn't tell me all that much. After all, as maestro Riccardo Muti once pointed out to me, 'adagio'—or in Italian, '*ad-agio*'—is not so much a matter of tempo as one of disposition.[9] That is, it means, "with-comfort." In other words, the music should be played "with comfort." Further, the word '*assai*' in Italian means 'very.' So, how very is 'very?' Add to that, it is widely accepted that Beethoven's metronome may have been defective.[10] So, his own tempo markings—one eighth note to 80 beats per minute—cannot be taken with certainty to accurately reflect Beethoven's intentions.

RA: So what sorts of cues did you depend on?

Michael: I listened to recordings, notably those of the great German conductor Wilhelm Furtwängler, who fostered a tradition of taking the movement extremely slowly. It is a tradition that has been imprinted in the psyches of so many musicians. Yet, I judged that the extreme slowness of Furtwängler's tempo threatens to make the movement not just somber, but even ponderous.

---

9 Interview at the American Society for Aesthetics, April 21, 1989.
10 See, for example, Sture Forsén, Harry B. Gray, L.K. Olof Lindgren, and Shirley B. Gray, "Was Something Wrong with Beethoven's Metronome?."

RA: So how did you decide to take the tempo?

Michael: Actually there was a further musical consideration I wanted to take into account. Within the development section—starting from bars number 114 until letter E—there follows some of the most glorious orchestral sound that I have heard. Now if there is to be a consistent relationship between the tempo of that material and that which started the movement, the starting tempo must be taken faster than that set by Furtwängler! I explained all of this to my musicians of the GHCO. Yet it took quite a lot of effort to get them to play the movement at my tempo. The Furtwängler tempo seemed to have been sedimented into their bones, or at least in their minds' ears. Finally, they relented. They even enjoyed the faster tempo. And what a performance that was—one of the very best I have conducted.[11]

RA: Obviously, you gave a lot of thought to this!

Michael: Yes. But even with a lot of forethought, conducting is a cooperative enterprise. To a certain extent, each player has anticipations of how they expect to play the piece with you. The sound that comes out of this collective body is always somewhat different from what the conductor may anticipate. Sometimes there are unintended results—sometimes welcome, sometimes not.

Many of the musicians will have played some of the pieces before, with different conductors, and they bring those memories with them. They have built-in musical expectations. Sometimes those expectations don't agree with each other, and some of them won't agree with what I will want to draw out of them in the end. All that becomes the material out of which I will shape an interpretation. As you see, it's a cooperative effort. That fact both challenges and excites me.

RA: How does all of that manifest itself in your conducting technique?

Michael: One issue concerns the temporal disparity between my conductorial gestures and the actual sound of the orchestra. What I have in mind, for example, is how much time there must be between a beat and when the sound is

---

11 David Zinman's recording of Beethoven's *Marcia Funebre—Adagio Assai*, much to my liking, takes the tempo of that movement noticeably faster than Furtwängler.

expected to arise. If this issue is not established with the orchestra fairly soon, then there will be difficulties between the conductor and the players.

Andrea: What do you mean?

Michael: Like all conductors, I must have a preconception of what I wish the sound to be like. In other words, in my head, I must be ahead of the orchestra. Without that, I will not be able to lead the orchestra. A conductor who is consistently behind the orchestra is no leader, but a follower. The players sense this immediately.

RA: Can you give an example of how the sound from the orchestra actually caused you to alter the tempo?

Michael: OK. In the spring of 2000, I conducted Beethoven's "Eroica" with the Pleven Symphony Orchestra. This time, before the first rehearsal of the first movement, I had a clear conception of how I would conduct the tempo. It was motivated by the thought that, if the opening dramatic chords of the work were taken too slowly, the rest of the movement would be ponderous. If played too quickly, the first theme would resemble an unwanted waltz.

However, when I actually heard the orchestra begin to play, I discovered that with these particular musicians, I would lose an unexpected, but welcome, sonority by taking the tempo as fast as I first intended. So, I relaxed the tempo somewhat, still within the limits of the score and the spirit of the work. The revised tempo, with the fine sonority, turned out not to be ponderous after all. In collaboration with the players, I found the right tempo. Again, the point is that orchestra playing is—to a degree—a collaborative effort.

RA: To a degree?

Michael: Yes. Ultimately, it is the conductor who must take responsibility.

RA: Still, I guess there's considerable latitude for interpretations above and beyond what is demanded in the score.

Michael: Yes. But sometimes it is not easy to articulate what is demanded by the score.

RA: Can you say a little about how that is?

Michael: Sure. I think of musical scores as characteristically incomplete, in the sense that composers cannot fully specify all pertinent aspects of interpretation. By that, I mean that scores can't specify every little detail about how the piece should be performed. Every composer knows that. In fact, composers count on it—leaving room for performers to make something of the score. They know that what they commit to paper amounts to a more or less rough set of instructions. The players will need to fill in details.[12]

RA: I guess that's where the multiplism, as you call it, comes in. Different musicians may interpret the same piece differently.

Michael: Right. Different interpreters bring different interests and concerns to bear when they perform the work. They will hear it in their mind's ear differently. Also, these will arise from different traditions of music making. They may shape phrases differently, for example. They may emphasize certain notes differently. They may emphasize certain passages more or less loudly or softly. They may handle ornamentation differently. They may want to express somewhat different emotions.

I am reminded what philosopher and musical commentator Bryan Magee says about performances of the Brahms symphonies by Arturo Toscanini and Bruno Walter:

> Under Toscanini they are played with almost demonic ferocity and drive, and are deeply disturbing. Under Walter, they have a glowing, autumnal relaxation and warmth, and are deeply consoling. Neither conductor transgresses the letter of the scores, nor their spirit. Yet the sum of what they bring out in them could not possibly be combined in a single performance. The acidity and cutting edge of the one entirely precludes the loving embrace of the other.[13]

RA: But I would imagine that some conductors think there is one and only one way to interpret a piece—and it is their way! After all, some conductors have the reputation of being tyrannical in that way.

Michael: Here I need to distinguish between what I call a singularist and a bully. The singularist is one who believes that for any object of interpretation,

---

12   For an elaboration of these ideas, see Michael Krausz, "Making Music: Beyond Intentions."
13   Bryan Magee, *Aspects of Wagner*, 89.

one and only one interpretation of it exists. A bully is one who is dictatorial in forcing the players to play as demanded.

RA: So are you suggesting that a multiplist could be a bully, and a singularist might still not act as a bully?

Michael: Indeed. The distinction between bully and non-bully does not line up with the distinction between singularist and multiplist. For example, I would say that conductor Simon Rattle is a multiplist and not a bully. That, for me is ideal.

But you can imagine the case where someone may be a multiplist by conceding that—in the abstract—more than one interpretation may be admissible, but still bully others into accepting his point of view.

Actually, that reminds me of a memorable encounter I had with Maestro Simon Rattle. It was very nice, really. When Rattle was in Philadelphia to conduct the Philadelphia Orchestra, he also conducted the Curtis Orchestra in a reading of the Brahms Symphony no. 4. I was present at that reading. As it happened, it was an especially rainy day. After the session, many people gathered at the exit, waiting their turn to leave the building. Coincidentally, Rattle and I exited together. As we left the building, it was clear that he was headed across Rittenhouse Square. I offered him shelter under my umbrella. We started to talk as we walked. I said that I had recently been in Bulgaria to conduct the Pleven Philharmonic in Brahms 4. To offer a compliment, I said, "You know, Maestro, your Brahms 4 is quite different from the Brahms 4 I did in Bulgaria." Then, he quipped, "Is that a good thing or a bad thing?"

RA: That's lovely. Now what lesson did you draw from his remark?

Michael: I guess it was just a given for him that two conductors will inevitably conduct the same piece differently. I also learned that he has a wry sense of humor. But, more to the point, you must allow that there is a difference between a characteristically incomplete score and admissible interpretations of it. A score underdetermines an admissible interpretation of a work. Yet the score indicates the work's 'essentialities,' which an interpretation must—within limits—embody if it is to be considered a performance of that given work. Such reflections about musical interpretation—it really goes back to hearing my mother's reactions to her lessons with Leonard Shure who seemed to insist that his way was the only way—have led me to formulate the distinction between singularism and multiplism. But we can talk about that distinction later.

RA: Am I right that your distinction gives rise to question about the intentions of the composer?

Michael: Of course, but keep in mind what Bruno Walter says. One should respect the intentions of the composer as much as possible, but there are constraints there as well. For one thing, one may not have full access to or knowledge of what a composer's intentions were. Or, the intentions themselves might be ambiguous or ambivalent. In fact, the score might come to contain features that the composer did not intend at all. In any case, where possible, I believe that the composer's intentions should be respected.

Yet—and I am indebted to Biava for emphasizing this point—once one settles upon an interpretation, one should be *decisive* about executing it. One should urge players to perform it as convincingly as possible, even if they had qualms about it to start with. Otherwise, the performance will lack conviction.

RA: I guess you mean to emphasize that even if we don't have conclusive reasons for our interpretations, sometimes, we're forced to act in a decisive way.

Michael: That's right. Actually, I think that this dictum of decisiveness without conclusiveness applies not only in the case of music performance, but in life generally. It applies to many of life's consequential decisions. Choices of a life partner, choices of profession, choices of religion or life-philosophy—all these require actions typically in the absence of conclusiveness of reasons, and arguments. The contingencies of life characteristically require decisiveness.

Others may contest this view by holding that decisiveness should be keyed to conclusiveness, that decisiveness should not over-reach conclusiveness. It is best, they may say, to be tentative in the face of inconclusiveness. Perhaps this alternative attitude may be appropriate in some contexts, but not the concert hall.

RA: Michael, you've mentioned that in your art, you think of your ciphers as being in a space of silence. Does anything similar appear in your music?

Michael: I guess you're asking how silence enters into my music. Yes! I've become sensitive to the difference between sound and silence. This is a persistent preoccupation in my music making. For example, Schubert's "Great"—a big work, about fifty minutes long—has passages where there are breaks; these are significant pauses, significant breaks. When I performed it, I started looking at the score as a whole in terms of the silences between the parts, between phrases, between notes, the 'between-ness.' I think of the silence in relation to sound in much the way, for example, that I think of negative space in relation to positive space. Silence is as important as sound, in much the same way that negative space is as important to positive space.

RA: You've been talking about the interactive relationships between composer, conductor, and players. Does it ever happen, in your opinion, that any such distinctions just evaporate?

Michael: I suppose you're talking about such experiences as when musicians experience themselves as one, or, when the ensemble and audience experience themselves as one. It's what chamber musicians Leonard Matczynski and Michael Kelley have called the '5th element.'[14]

In that regard, I find that psychoanalyst Anthony Storr's talk of 'oceanic' experiences is useful. He says, "The oceanic feeling is usually compared with states of mind described by the mystics, when the subject feels at one with the world and with its self."[15]

RA: This sounds like we are entering into a religious dimension.

Michael: I'm not sure what you include in the idea of a 'religious' dimension. But it's interesting that John Dewey describes something like it when he talks about having 'an' experience, that is, where:

> We are, as it were, introduced into a world beyond this world which is nevertheless the deeper reality of the world in which we live in our ordinary experiences. We are carried out beyond ourselves to find ourselves … the work of art operates to deepen and to raise to great clarity that sense of an enveloping undefined whole that accompanies every normal experience. This whole is then felt as an expansion of ourselves … Where egotism is not made the measure of reality and value, we are citizens of this vast world beyond ourselves, and any intense realization of

---

14 Personal conversations at the Apple Hill Chamber Music Center, New Hampshire in 2015 and 2016.
15 Storr, *Music and the Mind*, 95–96.

its presence with and in us brings a peculiarly satisfying sense of unity in itself and with ourselves.[16]

I take it that the sense of unity, which Dewey is describing in such experiences, applies to music as well as art. It is an epiphanic experience of oneness.

RA: Do you know of musicians who have reported such experiences?

Michael: Yes. For example, Riccardo Muti reported that once, while conducting Bach's Mass in B minor, a sense of oneness descended upon him, his musicians, and, on all accounts, upon all present in the hall. When I pressed him about his report of feeling such a sense of oneness, he said:

> It happened two or three times in ten years, and not for an entire performance but just for a few minutes. You feel that you, the orchestra, and the public are having the same exact experience with the same exact feelings. Then the hall becomes something like a temple, and something electric and magical keeps everybody together. You feel physically that you, the orchestra and the public are one unity, that we are one soul. The audience, the orchestra, the entire hall breathes like one ... I have experienced this two times, and just for a few moments. And then it disappears. It goes, because it is something that is so magical that you cannot keep it. The moment that you become aware of this thing it goes.[17]

Biava also reported similar cases of such experiences. They include moments in Philadelphia Orchestra performances of Verdi's *Requiem*, conducted by Eugene Ormandy, and Mahler's Symphony no. 9 in D major, conducted by Leonard Bernstein. Luis spoke of such experiences, fleeting they may be, as trance-like, in which there is something like a felt suspension of dualistic consciousness.

And here is yet another such example of epiphanic experience or oceanic feeling. My father told me this story. At the end of a European tour in the 1950s, the Cleveland Orchestra, under its conductor Szell, visited Basel, Switzerland. Since the musicians were already exhausted from a grueling touring schedule, Szell had canceled the rehearsal scheduled for the evening's performance of

---

16   Dewey, *Art as Experience*, LW: 199.
17   From transcript of my interview with Muti when I was the Program Chair for the Eastern Division of the American Society for Aesthetics, which occurred during "An Evening with Riccardo Muti" at the Barclay Hotel on April 21, 1989.

Beethoven's Symphony no. 6 in F major ("Pastoral"). At the concert, as soon as the orchestra began the piece, there descended a sense of oneness encompassing the music, conductor, orchestra, and audience that many later described in religious terms. Afterwards, several musicians spoke of a visceral nausea from the intensity of the experience.

RA: I'm wondering whether, during the epiphanic moments you speak about, the more usual dualistic or controlled attitudes drop out and the epiphanic moments take over. That is, do you think that the more usual judgments cease to operate?

Michael: That's an interesting question. I would think that dualistic judgments need to be there at some level—perhaps at an automatic level—in order to sustain a minimal level of control. After all, even if automatic, the musicians draw upon embedded practices that have become second nature for them. I don't think such second natures can simply drop out. Otherwise, how could they continue to play their instruments at such moments? So I don't think epiphanic experiences simply replace intentional activity. Rather, they can occur concurrently with intentional activity.

It's interesting that epiphanic experiences have been reported by both artists and musicians. They can also be experienced more generally, as reported by Hindus and Buddhists.

RA: I'm looking forward to our discussions about them.

CHAPTER 7

My India

RA: Well! You've already described how, inspired by your interest in relativism, Bimal Matilal suggested that you would benefit by visiting India. Can you say more how your travels to India actually came to pass?

Michael: Sure, I'd be glad to! When Bimal made the suggestion, I replied, "That sounds interesting. I'd like to do that. Can you perhaps arrange for an invitation?" And so he did, by arranging for an invitation for me, for a few weeks, at the Indian Institute of Advanced Study in Shimla and other places in 1992. That's how I got to go to India for the first time.

As well, close personal and philosophical connections between Matilal, Mohanty, and D.P. Chattopadhyaya, in Calcutta, later issued in my being received well in Indian academic circles, including at Jadavpur University, where I met Chhanda Gupta—whom Hilary Putnam had described as one of the best analytic philosophers in India.

It turned out that Matilal was right. Besides affording me the possibility of meeting interesting people, and, in some cases, making wonderful friends among informed Indian philosophers in diverse settings, it provided experiences that enriched my philosophy.

My first trip to India was for about six weeks. I did a lot of traveling around India visiting various universities. They included Jadavpur University in Calcutta, Utkal University in Bhubaneshwar, and University of Bombay. By the way, on the way to India for the first time, I lectured at Hong Kong University; and after my trip to India, I lectured at Chiang Mai University in Thailand.

RA: I'd like to back up just a bit. Why was it so obvious to Matilal that given your interest in relativism, you should go to India?

Michael: I expect that what he had in mind was that India's diversity of human practices and belief systems is so different from the West that it would enrich my repertoire of cases of cultural differences. That diversity might help to elaborate questions having to do with relativism. After all, relativism begins with the anthropological fact of extraordinary diversity. Of course, that diversity, in itself, does not entail relativism.

RA: Am I right that during that first trip to India, among those whom you met was the Dalai Lama? How did that come about?

Michael: That's an interesting story. Again, my friend in New York, Marty Moskof—whom I had met years earlier at Haystack—had mentioned to me that a friend of his had just been to Dharamsala as part of a Jewish delegation to meet with the Dalai Lama. It seems that the Dalai Lama had been impressed with the success that Jews have had in keeping its people together in its Diaspora. It had sustained its culture over many centuries without a homeland. So, he sponsored a session in Dharamsala on the Jewish Diaspora to learn what lessons he could to apply to the Tibetan Diaspora.

Marty suggested that his friend might provide the information necessary to communicate with the Dalai Lama's office. I corresponded with them, and after some backing-and-forthing—to establish my credentials and serious interest—they decided that I might see him if nothing in the last minute would override any arrangements. No firm commitment could be made though. In any event, that possibility was there before I went to India.

RA: Ok, then. How did the trip unfold before you saw the Dalai Lama?

Michael: At the end of my cycle of lectures, after a month of demanding travel and lecturing, I was on a plane from Banaras to Delhi. Seated next to me was a woman who turned out to be an off-duty flight attendant for Air India. As we chatted, I mentioned how tired I was. She suggested I go to Manali, known to be a restful tourist retreat, to take a break. She suggested that I fly from Delhi to Kullu, and from Kullu, I could hire a car to Manali. That sounded good to me. So, that's what I did.

RA: How far is Manali from the Kullu airport?

Michael: It's about a two-hour trip by car, through beautiful terrain at the foot of the Himalayan Mountains. So, I took a small plane that was destined for Bunthar, the airport for Kullu-Manali. Seated next to me on that flight was a man who turned out to be a Canadian doctor. His name was Gary Miller, or Guarav, in Hindi, as he explained. He had just finished a stint as a doctor in

Saudi Arabia on his way to his home and family at an ashram in Kullu. He started talking to me about meditation, self-realization, and oneness. I told him that I really wasn't so interested in such things, that I was an analytic philosopher, and that I was tired from my lecture tour. Still, he invited me to visit his ashram and to introduce me to his swami. I thanked Guarav for his kind invitation, but explained that I was not disposed to pursuing his suggestion. Nevertheless, he persisted, reminding me that once my visit to Manali was over, I would have to pass through Kullu, again. He explained that the ashram was open to invited guests on Sundays. If I found myself in Kullu on a Sunday, I would be welcome. Why not stop by the ashram?

RA: What happened after your rest in Manali?

Michael: Well, after a few days of relaxation in Manali, and after stopping to see the Roerich Hall Estate in Nagar—a village en route between Manali and Kullu, where Nicholas Roerich, the important Russian painter and explorer, lived and worked for many years in the early part of the twentieth century—I did, indeed, find myself in Kullu, in the vicinity of the ashram that Guarav had spoken about. There, in the street in front of the ashram, I happened across him! I asked, "What are you doing here?" He replied, "I'm waiting for you."

RA: What happened next?

Michael: It was a brilliant sunny day. Guarav accompanied me up some stairs to a veranda, where about 200 people were gathered, listening intently to the guru,[1] who was seated under a large, brightly colored umbrella, addressing a group of Western and Indian devotees. They appeared to be intelligent and engaged—which I hadn't expected. I stood well behind the gathering, taking it all in.

While listening to the guru's message—which I could not quite understand—I heard such words as, 'visitor' and 'philosopher.' Before long, I was asked to sit next to him. I did so. Then he turned to me and said, "Say something." I was speechless. Here I was, in an altogether unfamiliar environment, being asked by this venerated person to say something, presumably relevant to my being

---

1 Shyamacharan Srivastava also known as Swami Shyam, hereafter referred to as Swamiji.

there in the first place or relevant to what he had been saying to the gathering. But I couldn't make sense of what he had been saying.

RA: So, what did you say?

Michael: Slowly, I said something like this. "I find that I am beginning this sentence without a clear idea of how it will end." That was it.

RA: And then what?

Michael: He replied, "You are mistaken." Then I replied, "How can I be mistaken when I say that I don't know how my sentence will end?" He smiled and proceeded to give me an exposition—and I was taken aback by what he said!

RA: Which was?

Michael: He said that I would be mistaken if I thought that it was I who was speaking. Then I asked, "If it is not I who is speaking, who is speaking?" He replied, "It is the One who is speaking." This, I thought, was incomprehensible. As I questioned and challenged him, the gathering occasionally would, at unpredictable moments, burst out in laughter. I could not understand why they would do that at what I thought were such inappropriate moments. At least I thought they were.

RA: How did you react to all of this?

Michael: On the one hand, I found what Swamiji was saying to be farfetched. It sounded outlandish. On the other hand, I much enjoyed our banter. It had the quality of a Greek dialogue. Mostly, I was attracted to his presence. He was joyous, effervescent, lovable, and effulgent. Apparently, he, too, was enjoying our exchange, since he asked whether I would like to join him and others to continue our conversation after lunch—at, where else?—the Roerich Hall Estate in Nagar, where I had just been! I jumped at the chance. That's how it all started.

RA: That's quite a beginning.

Michael: Yes, but it was just the beginning. After lunch, about two dozen devotees commandeered several taxis to make the forty minute drive back to

Nagar. We settled in and talked for much of the rest of the day. It was there that Swamiji really began to elaborate upon his vision of Oneness.

RA: Can you say more about Swamiji's message?

Michael: Of course. His message was embodied in the Advaitic declaration "Thou art That," which means that all individual beings, including all individual persons, are manifestations of the Supreme Self, the One. The One is birthless and deathless. The One is 'pure, free, forever.'

Swamiji expressed that vision in his special mantra, "Amaram Hum, Madhuram Hum." For him, that utterance means, "I am eternal, I am bliss." He affirmed that realizing oneself by recognizing this truth will free us from human suffering, especially from our fears and anxieties about our inevitable decline and death.

RA: His message must have sounded foreign for someone who had been educated and trained in Western analytic philosophy.

Michael: Foreign and, at first, incomprehensible. But I have come to understand him better over time. We will examine these ideas more fully in our discussion of self-realization.

RA: I look forward to that! For now, may I ask, how long did you visit with Swamiji during that first visit?

Michael: Our conversations continued for two or three days, as did those with several of the devotees, whom I came to see as compassionate, informed, and eager to share their experiences with me. I was quite moved by them. At the end of my stay, Swamiji bestowed upon me the Hindi name, Gyaan Swaroop, which means, knower, or lover, of the way of things. In the meantime, I started to turn my attention to my upcoming trip to Dharamsala and the Dalai Lama's residence.

RA: Did you mention to him that you were scheduled soon to see the Dalai Lama?

Michael: Yes, indeed. During my first encounter with Swamiji, I asked him whether it is the case that the Hindu and the Buddhist are talking about the same thing. He said, "Yes, we are talking about the same thing. And the Buddhist is wrong."

RA: Wrong?

Michael: Yes. He was clear and straightforward about it. I was taken aback by the antipathy that he expressed toward Buddhism, which, in later conversations, he softened.

RA: So, in the meantime, was it finalized that you would meet with the Dalai Lama?

Michael: As finalized as it could be under the circumstances. A few days after my time with Swamiji, a driver took me from Kullu to Dharamsala. The drive took the better part of a day. After getting settled in my quarters, very near the residence of the Dalai Lama, I checked in with his office. They assured me that my appointment was still on, and that I should wait for a message to be delivered on the morning of the appointed day. As hoped, the message came and I went to the residence as instructed. After going through security procedures, and waiting my turn in a reception area, which contained a series of accolades displayed—including the Nobel Prize—I was ushered into the Dalai Lama's room. We were alone except for a translator sitting in a distant corner.

RA: How was the Dalai Lama's English?

Michael: As it turned out, we didn't need the translator. The Dalai Lama's English is quite good. Out of respect, I did not begin the conversation. We were sitting rather close to each other. He was seated in a deep chair. I was at the end of a couch just next to him. I looked at him. He looked at me. I just sat quietly. We continued to look at each other. Then he started to giggle. I started to giggle. Then, we both started to giggle, and the level of giggling rose. Then he started to laugh. I started to laugh. Soon, both of us were howling with laughter. Finally, we both settled down. Then he asked, "What bring you to India?" That's how it began.

RA: And then?

Michael: Over the course of our wide-ranging conversation, we talked quite a bit about Buddhism and Judaism, about the Buddhist principle of emptiness—which resonated with my anti-essentialism—about emotions, about his feelings about the Chinese, about his own spiritual path, and more. He was very clear that all religious traditions deal with the same basic human needs—to be mutually helpful to one another. He was not interested in converting anybody. He emphasized that one should stay in one's own tradition and pursue it. Then the discussion turned to the same question that I had asked Swamiji. "Is it the case that the Hindu and the Buddhist are talking about the same thing?" He said, "No, they are not talking about the same thing."

RA: How did that strike you?

Michael: The issue about sameness was already pressing in my mind. My encounters with Swamiji and the Dalai Lama confirmed my thought that in order to have a disagreement, the parties must be talking about the same thing. If they are not talking about the same thing, they are just talking past each other. As simple as this point might seem, it secured a presupposition in my theory of interpretation, this time to be applied to the case of religion. The conflicting answers to my question—whether the Advaitic Hindu and the Tibetan Buddhist are talking about the same thing—effectively exemplified their disagreement about whether they could be disagreeing! In other words, they were disagreeing about whether they were disagreeing!

RA: That seems like such an important insight. What else did you talk about with Dalai Lama?

Michael: As our discussion continued, I asked His Holiness about his feelings about the Chinese: "After all," I said, "they killed so many of your people and destroyed so many of your temples and monasteries." He replied, "Oh, the Chinese. They are my greatest gurus."

I was flabbergasted to hear him say this. I said that I did not understand. "After all that has happened, how can you regard them as your gurus?" He replied, "They provide my greatest opportunity to develop compassion."[2]

---

[2] Tens of thousands of Tibetans had been killed during uprisings, and the Chinese had destroyed about a thousand Buddhist temples and monasteries during the 'cultural revolution' in 1959.

RA: What did you think of that?

Michael: As His Holiness says, it is causes and conditions that give rise to people's bad behavior; that evil is not lodged inherently in individuals; that anger toward persons is not only destructive to those at whom it is directed but also to the one who is angry; that in all cases, ego-centrism is destructive. All this showed me another way to regard my own anger and grief about the Holocaust and the murder of my grandparents. The Dalai Lama's example was a great gift.

RA: Did you ask him about his own spiritual journey?

Michael: I was hesitant to ask, but I did. I asked him about his own path toward realization. He replied that he had been pursuing his path for much of his life and that he still had a long way to go. At that time, he was fifty-seven years old. I also asked him whether it is true that he is the embodiment of the Buddha. He smiled and replied, "Some people say so." I was surprised by his candor as well as his modesty.

RA: What an experience that must have been. So how did your meeting with the Dalai Lama go from there?

Michael: Well, I had brought photographs of Connie's artwork and mine to show him. He was eager to see them. After taking his time looking at them separately, then together, he exclaimed, "It fits! It fits!" That, too, was a great gift.

RA: How did it all end?

Michael: Well, as we both got up, I didn't want to turn my back on him. So I moved backward toward the sliding glass door that opened on to his garden. As I did so, in child-like way, he waved back at me, and I waved at him. We kept waiving at each other until we were out of each other's sight. Then, as I walked across the square in front to the Dalai Lama's residence, many of the monks who had been practicing their Buddhist dialectical exercises paused and smiled broadly at me.

RA: So, did the Buddhist thought that persons are empty of inherent existence have a palliative effect on you?

Michael: Yes. It helped lift a burden that I had—and still carry to some extent.

I came to realize that in their own ways, Hinduism and Buddhism both share the premise that individuals—like tables and chairs as well as individual persons—are not *ultimately* or *inherently* real. On this point, the Buddhist and the Hindu agree, and that is that individuals are empty of inherent existence, because they ultimately do not exist. Hindus go still further though, to assert that only the One, the Atman, ultimately and inherently exists. That is how I understand it.

RA: That's interesting. So do I understand it correctly that the Advaitic view holds that the only thing that ultimately or inherently exists is the One?

Michael: Yes. That's the main point that separates them. But the non-inherent existence of human individuals is what unites them.

RA: Is it fair to say, that after those initial experiences in meeting with Swamiji and the Dalai Lama, you faced something of a choice?

Michael: Yes and no. They started me thinking about the similarities and the differences between the Advaitic approach and the Tibetan Buddhist approach at a philosophical level. They also started me thinking about how each might edify me—that is, how each might provide me with healing and solace.

RA: So you were left with a tension between what you might find philosophically compelling, and what you find edifying. Is that right?

Michael: Yes. That's it.

RA: How did you deal with that tension?

Michael: Well, that turns out to be an ongoing story. On the one hand, it involved many more trips to India, some to Mcleodganz for a second visit with the Dalai Lama, and then several tutorials with other Buddhist scholars—including Geshe Lobsang Gyatso and conversations with Ngawang Samten in Sarnath. And on the other hand, regular visits with Swamiji in Kullu.[3]

---

[3] My visits to Kullu were pretty much annual until Swamiji's death on February 15, 2017. He was reported to be ninety three years old at the time of his death.

RA: You say you had a second meeting with the Dalai Lama?

Michael: Yes. That was in 1995. I had lingering questions for him. His office was kind enough to arrange a second meeting.

RA: What was that like?

Michael: Well, certainly what we discussed changed; it was more centered on the Buddhist idea of emptiness of inherent existence. Also, by that time, I had gotten more involved in the Tibetan community. We talked about the Tibetan Children's Village and the possibility of his visiting Bryn Mawr and the Philadelphia area in connection with the Greater Philadelphia Philosophy Consortium, which at that time, I chaired. The Dalai Lama was amenable to such a visit. Alas, that never worked out. But what was deeply moving for me was that at the end of our second meeting, the Dalai Lama placed his forehead against mine and held it there for quite some time. I was later told by a monk that he was blessing me. As we parted, he said, "Stay in touch."

RA: Why didn't his trip to Philadelphia work out?

Michael: The security arrangements for such an event would have been overwhelming. It was beyond my capability to arrange. As well, I even got some resistance from my own board of the GPDC. My Vice-Chair objected that the Dalai Lama was not an academic. He had no earned PhD. It seems that his having received the Nobel Prize was not enough. Can you imagine such an absurd thing?

RA: So how did you get more involved with the Tibetan community?

Michael: For a few years, Connie and I financially sponsored two Tibetan biological brothers. I also got involved with organizing a couple of exhibitions of Tibetan children's art—one exhibition in Paris with the help of two Parisian friends I had met in Dharamsala—artist Victor Laks and Priya (Françoise) Cossery. The other exhibition took place in Philadelphia at the Please Touch Museum. Amongst the Tibetans, a wonderful people, I encountered such compassion, clarity of faith, and peacefulness. There's something serene about the Tibetans. I regret not having been more involved with them in more recent years.

RA: I remain fascinated by the question of how you dealt with the tension between Buddhism and Hinduism. In your mind's eye, how did Swamiji's vision compare with that of the Dalai Lama? What was your attitude with regard to both of these thinkers?

Michael: I came to be fascinated by the philosophical tension between their two traditions. In the early years—when I interviewed them both—my attitude was more one of a fascinated philosophical anthropologist, leaving my own position somewhere in the background. In time, though, I began to wrestle with their differences as a basis for understanding my own self-realization, as well as help with other personal problems—not just mine, but my mother's also. For example, Swamiji was most helpful to my mother, in correspondence, when she was experiencing intense death anxiety.

RA: How so?

Michael: In his correspondence with my mother, he wrote, "Death is not for you." She was much relieved. In reply, she wrote a piano composition, entitled, "Amaram Hum, Madhuram Hum," recorded it, and sent the recording to him. And he was so helpful to me when she did die, in 2008.

Also, after I married Connie, in 1976, my father could no longer look at me directly in my eyes with the tender, loving, kindness and warmth that he once had. That caused me great pain for many years. But then, in February 2011, Swamiji looked at me with such an intense, searing light of love. It was electric. It reached me so deeply that the emotional scars that had built up somewhere in me were gone.

RA: That is no small thing.

Michael: Indeed not. When I return to the West, and sometimes friends inquire about my trips to visit Swamiji, I say that I saved myself a lot of fees for therapy.

RA: So, why couldn't all of that have happened in a Buddhist environment?

Michael: I don't say that it couldn't have. It just didn't. Would I be helped more in one environment rather than another? I cannot say. In any event, the Dalai Lama's presence on the world stage was fully established and still growing. It would be most unlikely that he himself would have the time or inclination for me, personally. And I certainly did not want to insinuate myself into his schedule, even if I could.

RA: Still, you mentioned that you had tutorials with Lobsang Gyatso. What was that like?

Michael: Yes, I had wonderfully instructive sessions with Lobsang Gyatso, who then headed the Institute for Buddhist Dialectics in Dharamsala. He taught me a lot about the Buddhist principle of emptiness, emotions, and detachment.[4] He was a teacher and associate of the Dalai Lama. I saw him for private tutorials in the course of two or three years until his brutal assassination in 1997.[5] I have not been disposed to return to Dharamsala since then.

I also have had a long history with Geshe Ngawang Samten, who eventually became Vice Chancellor of the Central University for Tibetan Studies in Sarnath. I originally met him at Hampshire College in Massachusetts, in 1996, when Connie and I had a show at their wonderful gallery.

RA: But you gravitated toward the Advaitic attitude toward Oneness. Am I right?

Michael: I was, and am, ambivalent about that. One of the reasons why I eventually spent more time in the Advaitic tradition is that, given my Jewish sensibility, I resonate more with its Oneness. That is not to say that I find the Advaitic view more philosophically compelling than the Buddhist view. Perhaps later, we can talk more about that, but, in a general way, I can say that the ashram at Kullu feels like home—and that includes the community of devotees, many of whom were present on that fateful day on the veranda in 1992, when Swamiji said to me, "Say something."

RA: It sounds as if your introduction to India was a significant turning point in your life.

Michael: Yes it was, and at various levels. But it was not as if I had been trained and pursued a career in Western analytic philosophy and then just abruptly turned to edificatory matters. My analytic philosophy was actually nurtured by my Indian experiences, just as my analytic philosophy informed my edificatory pursuits. In turn, my analytic work about edificatory matters turned from a private affair to a philosophical preoccupation.

---

4   See Lobsang Gyatso, *The Harmony of Emptiness and Dependent-Arising*.
5   "Murder in Dharamsala," *In the News*, Summer 1997, https://tinyurl.com/ydgfmt8g.

RA: That's helpful, Michael. Earlier in our conversations, you mentioned that in Kenya, you sensed a feeling of relief regarding your Jewishness, that being Jewish seemed not to be 'on the radar' as you put it. In India, your focus was, of course, on Hinduism and Buddhism. But did you experience any particular feelings regarding your Jewishness while you were in India?

Michael: In India, at least initially, I experienced a kind of relief similar to the one that I felt in Kenya. India does have a history of the Jews that goes back to the Inquisition from Spain in 1492, when many Jews emigrated there. Close to Cochin, in Goa, there is a small village called Jewtown. But today the presence of Jews remains insignificant. As well, the percentage of Christians in India is about 2 percent.

RA: Say more how your spiritual instincts were affected by those trips to India.

Michael: As you know, I had rejected the idea of a personal first cause, creator god many years before those trips. But that left room for a wider sense of Divinity, a sense of a 'numinous beyondness.' I hadn't revisited the question of my religiosity very much before my trips to India. My first trip was motivated by the prospect of a great adventure, which of course it was. But it turned out to be much more than that.

RA: What happened that made it so much more?

Michael: When I first arrived in India, I was struck by how much religion was everywhere—in the streets, the shops, on the dashboards of taxis. The place was imbued with religion of some sort or other. But many were not religions that assume a first cause creator god. It struck me that I had been mistaken to equate religiosity—divinity is perhaps a better word—with the idea of a creator god. On top of that, I found Hinduism and Buddhism were deeply concerned with self-realization. That is something that I had not encountered so much in my experience of Judaism. Of course, I had been primed for it by my epiphany in relation to art.

CHAPTER 8

Trajectories and Transitions

RA: What has struck me in our conversations so far are the formative encounters you have had with eminent scholars, philosophers, musicians, artists, and religious leaders. I am also struck by your many transitions between places and practices.

Michael: I guess you have identified something consistent in my life so far. As I think of it, I have experienced numerous 'betweens' and 'beyonds.'

RA: That's interesting. And it seems that in the course of your betweens and beyonds, you've gotten involved with different communities. You seem to be at home in them all—in America, Canada, England, Israel, Egypt, Kenya, and India, as well as in music, in philosophy, and in art. How do they all go together? Or don't they? I mean, are some of those communities at odds?

Michael: That's an interesting question. You might as well ask whether it's the same Michael Krausz, who exhibits different aspects of himself in each of those disparate communities, or whether it's actually a different Michael Krausz in each of those communities, or, whether the question about sameness even matters.

RA: Okay, then. Consider yourself asked!

Michael: Consider this. I have a history of trying to find a philosophically comfortable Jewish community. As you know, I helped found the Seaside Jewish Community (SJC) in Rehoboth. I'm happy to be part of that community, despite the inevitable growing pains of any emerging institution. I am also a member of the larger Jewish community in its Diaspora. At the same time, I have ambivalent feelings about key Israeli policies. Still, I find that, in a removed way, Israel is *a* home to me.

RA: The question of your identity and your place in various communities—especially Jewish communities—seems to have been a persistent one. Perhaps you might say a bit more about that.

Michael: All right. I guess my question has been, if I am neither an observant Jew, nor especially Zionist, in what sense am I a Jew? I deeply recognize myself as a Jew. But articulating what that is is not easy. It's an enduring question for me. Of course, I have recognized that being a Jew—a Levite at that—is part of my history. But in the past, that didn't seem to be enough of an answer. So, I talked to a lot of people in my situation. They were broadly reconstructionist or somehow connected with a movement called New Jewish Agenda. I asked them, "Do you regard me as a Jew?" I'd get different answers. "Of course you're Jewish. The fact that it's a live question for you is sufficient for you to be Jewish. You are struggling with questions about your Jewish identity."[1] I talked with Rabbi Arthur Waskow, for example, who has now become something of a grandfather figure to the New Jewish Agenda.[2] He answered me that way. He was associated with the Jewish sage, Rabbi Zalman Schachter-Shalomi.

RA: What else did you do with regard to the question of your Jewishness?

Michael: I thought that maybe this kind of question is also an academic one. So I asked myself, "Why don't I put together a book collecting the views of mostly Jewish philosophers?" That's what I edited with David Goldberg, which became *Jewish Identity*.

That was an effort to see how mostly philosophers in my situation would deal with this question. We all offered different accounts about how we understood Jewishness. Of course, that was an occasion for me to write my own statement as I best saw it at the time. I confess that remains an open question to this day.

RA: Did you want to join a congregation at all?

Michael: After leaving Toronto for Bryn Mawr, I looked into a couple of congregations in Philadelphia and Swarthmore.

RA: I expect that you had been looking for a community that would fully accept that you had married Connie.

Michael: Yes, that was a big part of it. As it happens, my mother lived in Cleveland Heights close to Taylor Road, an old orthodox Jewish community. Now, if a Jew marries a non-Jew, in the orthodox community, it is customary to regard that Jew as dead. Sometimes Shiva—the prayer for the dead—is said for that person even when they are still alive. I do not know if Shiva was said for me by anyone in my mother's orthodox community. Certainly, my mother did not do

---

1 See Michael Krausz, "On Being Jewish."
2 See Arthur Ocean Waskow, *Godwrestling*; and *Godwrestling—Round 2*.

so. But when I would visit her regularly, I would be well aware of the fact that in the eyes of some of her neighbors I was a non-person. That was hurtful. I am still saddened that my parents did not want to come to our wedding.

In any event, I continued my search for a community with which to identify myself. That didn't work out until 1997, when I helped to found the Seaside Jewish Community.[3] The first few years was engaging and inspiring. SJC is now a thriving, open congregation, which welcomes GLBT and interfaith marriages and partnerships. Many of them hold a wide range of political and religious views—including those about Israel. It is also open to a kind of meditative spirituality.

RA: There seems to be an incompatibility among various Jewish communities. Yet, at the same time, there seems to be a bond as well. I'm reminded of an anecdote that you have related, when you visited Bucharest and met a Romanian Rabbi in front of a synagogue—an elderly gentleman. He did not know you, yet, he grabbed you by your shoulders and the two of you started walking down the street speaking to each in an animated manner, using a combination of Yiddish, German, and French. The two of you quickly acted like old friends. How did that instant closeness come about?

Michael: He was one of mine. This means we shared a history and we shared a cultural past.

RA: Would you say that you shared a common morality?

Michael: I'm not sure I would call it a morality. I guess it's more a matter of temperament, perhaps more a matter of a shared understanding of how the other one is in his conceptual or religious space. Maybe it's a matter of common recognition. Maybe it comes from a space of pre-understanding. Sometimes we meet people and have a sense that we really know them at a depth that belies the shortness of time we had spent with them. Maybe it's like instantly seeing oneself in the other.

RA: How else have you dealt with your understanding yourself as a Jew?

Michael: Interestingly, I got a degree of resolution when addressing the question of my own burial. I found myself having a strong need to respect the

---

3   For information about SJC, see https://tinyurl.com/yagsxyyv.

tradition according to which Jews do not allow themselves to be cremated. We need to be buried in a simple wooden casket, in accord with Jewish tradition. The idea of not being buried as a Jew in the traditional way is one that I cannot live with. I needed to find a Jewish cemetery. So, I became active in co-chairing a committee to get a Jewish cemetery for Seaside Jewish Community. After much work and congregational politics, we established a cemetery for ourselves—a Jewish section—within the cemetery grounds of St. Peter's Episcopal Church in Lewes. The church was wonderful about it. They allotted us about sixty plots. It's been designated as the Cemetery of the Seaside Jewish Community. Many congregants of SJC have been buried there by now, and all of the plots are accounted for.

After much discussion and hunting, Connie and I have already installed our own headstone—a natural medium-sized stone from upstate New York—to which brass plaques will be attached at the appropriate times.

RA: This is fascinating. When you helped found the Seaside Jewish Community and then became a co-chair for the cemetery committee, you joined a community of interpreters. The community culture wasn't ready-made for you.

Michael: That's right.

RA: Yours is an altogether compelling narrative. Now, I'd like to probe you a little further.

Michael: Please do.

RA: From what you have said, what strikes me in your story is the conflict between the feeling of being welcome in the world—as the Swiss Romande orchestra celebrated your birth—and feeling displaced. At the same time, you are a true cosmopolitan. Your trips to India have been formative experiences for you, and you have worked closely with musicians in the United States and in Eastern Europe. So clearly you have lived and worked in different parts of the world and have felt at home.

Anywhere you go, you seem at home and familiar with people and places. This cosmopolitanism must have come, to some extent at least, from your family, perhaps especially from your father. I would like to know whether you have deliberately cultivated it, or whether you have been uncomfortable with it at times. You describe having grown up with a sense from a very early age that there was no place for you in this world, or for your family. I wonder how internalizing this may have influenced your work.

Michael: As for cosmopolitanism, I'm not sure that I have actually cultivated that. I guess though that for a long time, I have adopted the practice of imagining what it would be like to be in another person's situation, to be in another person's shoes.

RA: This is precisely what's so interesting about your style of philosophy, which comes through powerfully in your book, *Oneness and the Displacement of Self*. Your four fictional characters each represent a type; they're not necessarily actual individuals, but agents who interact with one another, without anybody feeling threatened by what others say. They pursue ideas. There's a certain intellectual openness that knows no limits.

I don't think it's simply an artifice that your invented character Nina does not get upset and leave the room when her view conflicts with the other characters—Barbara, Ronnie, or Adam. I think you really are committed to a distinction between the content of ideas and attitudes toward them. How have you managed to internalize that in your own conduct?

Michael: I'm not sure I have an adequate explanation. My father was keen on reminding me though, that when getting up in the morning, everyone has to put on their pants one foot at a time. In important ways, we're all the same in the end. And despite some of my disparaging remarks about Popper's behavior, he impressed upon me that however considerable we think our knowledge may be at a given stage, it is meager in relation to our infinite ignorance. It is an ignorance that remains forever infinite. So, it is best to be modest about what we think we know.

RA: I'm beginning to see a pattern here. You seem to invite a certain warmth and openness from various kinds of people you know—for example being under Gingold's violin, the Dalai Lama's forehead touching your forehead, and your warm greetings with an unknown rabbi in Bucharest. I don't know where it comes from, but all of this seems to suggest that you are a warm and empathic person as well.

Michael: Thank you for that kind thought. You know, I recognize my father in that description. That's the way he was—despite everything he endured.

RA: You are most welcome! Now, I'd like to discuss more fully your two books in dialogue form, *Oneness and the Displacement of Self*, which we've already begun to discuss, and *Dialogues on Relativism, Absolutism, and Beyond*, which came first. Both of them are written in the voices of the same four characters. Who are they really?

Michael: I chose the names of those fictional characters in accord with their respective views. I picked their names according to their first letters. Adam starts with A and stands for Absolutist; Ronnie starts with R and stands for Relativist. Barbara starts with B and stands for Both absolutist and relativist. And Nina starts with N and stands for Neither absolutist nor relativist. Those names were given to help the reader to keep track of who held what positions.

Adam, the absolutist, is a scientist in Washington at the National Bureau of Standards. He believes there are uninterpreted facts of the matter, which provides a kind of baseline that we need to keep in view for any admissible interpretation of whatever it is we're talking about. Ronnie, the relativist, is preoccupied with reference frames. It's appropriate for him to be an anthropologist. And why not give him his job at the school that he graduated from? And then there is Barbara, who, in *Relativism, Absolutism, and Beyond*, wants to make peace with the two protagonists, Adam and Ronnie. She wants to salvage what she can from both the absolutist and the relativist views. She offers two ways for doing this, neither of which turn out to be fully satisfactory. Nevertheless, she's inventive and conciliatory. So, as I gave her a therapeutic role, why not assign her the job of psychotherapist? And then there's Nina. She is an Advaitic meditator. She brings the message of the neither—neither relativism nor absolutism. Her view takes her beyond relativism and absolutism. Also, her underlying aim differs from the others.

RA: So you put a lot of thought into character development. I did notice, however, that you assigned the Advaitic vision to Nina instead of introducing her guru as a separate character, as a distinct interlocutor who might otherwise play an explicit role in the dialogue. Why is that?

Michael: Here's why. As I perceived the real-life Swamiji, he was often less concerned to propound a philosophical theory as he was concerned to facilitate the self-realization of his devotees, each coming to hear him with unique needs and concerns. What he said to one devotee might be different from what he said to another. And when he spoke to a group, each person in the group could hear his message differently. Sometimes, Swamiji would say one thing, which was appropriately taken to mean something quite different by another devotee. Thus, in my dialogue, instead of attempting to capture Swamiji's message, I presented what one unique fictionalized individual heard.

RA: I can see that it would be difficult to have a four-way discussion of philosophical positions if one of them were to have a different purpose from the other three about the purpose of the discussion itself.

Michael: That's a significant issue that has led me to speculate about elucidation in contrast with edification. That topic will come up again in our discussion of the aims of interpretation, I'm sure.

RA: So, in your thinking, who was behind the other fictionalized characters in *Dialogues on Relativism, Absolutism, and Beyond*? Were there real-life persons who inspired those characters?

Michael: The absolutist character, Adam, was inspired by Karl Popper and my friend Michael McKenna.[4] Relativist Ronnie was inspired by Nelson Goodman. The character Barbara was inspired by a particular devotee at the ashram, whose own mother—also a devotee—had shunned her for the simple reason that her daughter was a human being. Her mother had concluded from Swamiji's words that human beings do not exist. She had renounced human relationships. But her daughter insisted upon the reality and value of being human. Without much success, she would tell her mother, "Okay Mom, you know, a letter, an e-mail, a phone call from you once a month maybe would have been very much appreciated." Finally, the character Nina is inspired by another devotee, who has renounced human relationships. This devotee distanced herself from her own daughter, mother, father, and her friends for the sake of the pursuit of the meditative monkish life. She even refused to go to her dying brother when he asked for her. My thoughts about these women have helped me to discover that I am a kind of humanist.

RA: Your book, *Oneness and the Displacement of Self* starts by recounting the death of Norris, who is Nina's brother as well as Barbara's close friend.

Michael: Before his death, Barbara had a relationship with Nina's twin brother Norris. He is characterized as someone who's had an engaging life. He valued

---

4 See Michael McKenna, "A Metaphysics for Krausz," 129–146.

his relationships with all those around him. The opening scene of the book has Nina, Barbara, Adam, and Ronnie gathered at the New Delhi airport, waiting for their plane to take them to Philadelphia for Norris's memorial service. Much to Barbara's surprise, Nina is not mourning Norris's death. She feels no sorrow. Rather, she sees Norris—as she views everyone—as ultimately never having existed. Nina sees Norris as an embodiment of the One. For her, it's something like a category mistake to deny that the One was never born or will never die. Nina takes herself to have transcended the human realm, including human relationships and human love.

In the meantime, Barbara cannot understand Nina's lack of attachment to her brother Norris. For Nina, nothing exists except the One, of which individuals are non-existent embodiments. The One alone Is. So there is no question of human beings having been 'displaced' to begin with. In turn, Ronnie reasserts his existence and his human relationships. He rejects Nina's program of self-realization. Ronnie notes that Nina's program denies the existence of any human beings who would have sought solace in the first place. That is, if you deny the ultimate existence of individual human beings, then there would be no human beings to seek or receive solace.

RA: Thank you for that sketch of the characters. Now, can you say more about why you chose the dialogue form for these two books?

Michael: Yes. In a standard analytic treatment, for example, you would expect to see arguments in defense of a thesis. Generally, that kind of genre does not reveal the ambivalences of its author. It does not reveal the philosophical struggle that's part and parcel of philosophical life. But to *show* that struggle is revealing. The dialogue form is useful for me in that regard. I think there is lots to be said for each of their views. Even though I'm closest to Barbara for a number of reasons, I find that philosophical discourse is most fruitful when strengths and weaknesses of beliefs and arguments are identified and shown side-by-side. The dialogue form does that nicely.

RA: So I see that your choice of dialogue was deliberate, and you had philosophical reasons to choose these characters and to construct them as you did.

Michael: That's right. One of the charms about writings in dialogue form is that it allows me to linger more upon ambivalences about my present philosophical attitudes. I offer it as a present report, with no presumption of finality. I'm grateful to have had extraordinary opportunities to experience opposing cultural, philosophical, and religious settings—and the means to create bridges, at least for myself, between them. They have allowed me to locate and relocate myself.

RA: It sounds like an intellectual space similar to that which existed in the eighteenth-century salon or in Plato's *Republic*. It's that kind of space where you can pursue an idea of interest to its last consequence. More than just believing that such a space could exist, you have carefully crafted such a space. That in itself seems very optimistic.

Michael: Yes. I am optimistic about the power of dialogue.

RA: So, maybe it's time to consider an underlying issue for you concerning what philosophy itself is.

Michael: Yes. And I have operated between two conceptions of it.

RA: How so?

Michael: Amongst my various talks with Isaiah Berlin, I once asked him what he thought philosophy was. In reply, he asserted, "Philosophy is an activity in which one creates the conceptual space in which one can live." Notice, that it's an *activity*, in which one *creates* a kind of *space*. Most important is the space in which one might *live*. For me, the central point concerns life—human life. Berlin's definition has become important for me, for it emphasizes the praxial nature of philosophy.

RA: That's very interesting. How different is Berlin's definition of philosophy from other definitions?

Michael: Well, another useful definition of philosophy is one that Joe Margolis shared with me. It captures the way in which most analytic philosophy is conducted. He asserts that philosophy is a *second order inquiry into first order practices*. For example, philosophy of science is about scientific practice, including salient concepts. Joe's definition is good, too. It seeks to do something quite different from what Berlin's tries to do.

RA: Both of those definitions seem to capture different aspects of what you do. On the one hand, you have a passion for argumentative precision. On the other hand, you wrestle with concepts that seek to capture who you take yourself to be.

Michael: You're right. My training in analytic philosophy—to be as clear and precise as possible—has served me well. At the same time, I want my philosophy to be responsive to life experiences, to edify human beings.

RA: That sounds like a *Lebensphilosophie*, which prizes meaning, value, and purpose of life as the foremost focus of philosophy. Is that not a direction that differs from the usual trajectory of an analytical philosopher?

Michael: When I write about my personal program or about the mantras of Advaitists as speech acts, I am both pointing to human experience and engaging in second-order analytic philosophy.

RA: What's interesting to me is that in presenting various philosophical commitments such as relativism or absolutism, realism or constructivism, singularism or multiplism—even contemplating the combinations among them—you are not simply being agnostic to avoid getting caught in the mires of fairly complex arguments. Your ecumenism, for me, comes down to entertaining multiple possibilities at the same time in order to understand and honor each of them as much as possible. Ultimately, that's an enriching way of conducting a philosophical inquiry to my mind because you are making sure that you are giving each position its due.

Michael: Yes. That's what I try to do.

RA: You mentioned that many of your life choices had to do with 'whom you take yourself to be.' Can you say something about the idea of self-recognition?

Michael: Although Berlin didn't thematize it, it was in the context of his discussion of determinism and free will. He remarked that even if he were presented with conclusive arguments for a determinism that precludes free-will, for example, he could not embrace it.

RA: Why not?

Michael: Because if he did embrace it, he could no longer recognize himself to be the person he took himself to be.

RA: Is that not just a personal matter?

Michael: It is a personal matter, but not *just* a personal matter. Self-recognition prompts an attitude which has consequences in our relationships with others and our communities. It also enters into our philosophical strategies and the intensity with which we pursue them.

RA: So what is it that you recognize yourself to be?

Michael: First, I recognize myself to be a human person. That may sound obvious or trivial. But it is not. It turns out to be a contentious starting point. Notice that it is as a human being that I ask about purposes and interests. That's the perspective from which such questions arise in the first place. And it's a perspective that I take to be basic!

RA: It seems that, in following Berlin, you set self-recognition as a condition for embracing philosophical claims. For you, self-recognition functions as something of a fulcrum upon which the practice of philosophy turns. It means that argumentation and evidence—characteristically taken to be at the heart of rational discourse—is perhaps parasitic of something existentially deeper. Am I right?

Michael: Yes. So much of what we take ourselves to be is just that—what we *take* in one way or another. That is, there is an ineliminable constructivist element in taking ourselves to be one sort of being rather than another. And it is as a human being that I take myself to be a human being.

Now, if we agree that self-recognition functions in this way, then a fresh set of questions arises. For example, "What is involved in taking ourselves to be the kind of being we should strive to be?" As I take myself to be a human being, I take myself to be the sort of being who can deliberate upon and choose one or another personal program, or, one or another tradition.

Were I not able to do such things, I would not be able to recognize myself to be the Michael Krausz that I take myself to be. Of course, this does not preclude the possibility that as I age, for example, I may no longer be able to recognize myself to be the being I now take myself to be.

RA: So, who you take yourself to be is not cast in stone, so to say. That could change.

Michael: Yes. At every stage, who I take myself to be, would be basic. Yet what I take myself to be need not be permanent.

RA: Given what we've already discussed about your personal identity, I would imagine that you may appear to be different things—philosopher, artist, or musician, for example—depending upon who is viewing you.

Michael: Yes. From a philosopher's point of view, I am an artist or a musician; from an artist's point of view, I am a musician or philosopher; from a musician's point of view, I am an artist or philosopher. From an atheist viewpoint, I am a religionist; from a religionist point of view, I am an atheist. From a Jewish point of view, I am Hindu or Buddhist; from a Hindu point of view, I am Jewish or Buddhist; from a Buddhist point of view, I am Jewish or Hindu.

RA: Which is right?

Michael: They are all right.

RA: Have you ever felt the need to be discrete with members of some of those communities about your involvement with the other communities?

Michael: Yes. For awhile, I was uneasy about it being generally known that I was a member of three different communities—academic, artistic, and musical—partly because I expected that if any one community, particularly the academic community, knew that I was so involved in the others, my credibility in that community would be diminished. For a long time, I was somewhat defensive about that. As prudent as that might have been at the time, I don't do that anymore. Why waste that psychical energy?

RA: Perhaps, in sharing these reflections on the fabric of your life, you will realize how esteemed you are in each of those fields.

Michael: Thank you for that.

RA: Maybe it's time to turn to a more systematic discussion about your key philosophical preoccupations—relativism, interpretation, creativity, and self-realization.

Michael: Yes. Let's!

Else and Moritz Strauss

Francesca and Simon Krausz

Laszlo Krausz, mid-1970s

Susan Krausz, mid-1980s

Peter Krausz, early 1980s

Constance Costigan, 1996

Michael Krausz conducting The Great Hall Chamber Orchestra, 2013

PART 2

Philosophical Reflections

∴

CHAPTER 9

Relativisms

RA: Your name is closely associated with a key concept in philosophy, and that is the concept of relativism. In addition to several essays that you published earlier in your career, you have also edited an authoritative collection on the topic of relativism, that being *Relativism: A Contemporary Anthology*, which was published in 2010.

Michael: Yes, I think the question of relativism is pivotal in philosophy and so much more. So many other issues turn on it.

RA: So, where do you finally come out on that question?

Michael: As in so many things in philosophy, that depends on what you mean by the word 'relativism.' The term has been so loosely badgered around, and so many strong attitudes have been associated with it. If my work on relativism has been of help, it is primarily in getting clearer about what those terms and attitudes mean and what their implications are. My approach is to clarify what relativism claims and to contrast it with its opposite, namely absolutism.

RA: Okay. Then generally speaking, what do you take relativism to claim?

Michael: Of course, relativism is what Wittgenstein would call a 'cluster concept.' No one, fixed definition can be taken to fully capture its meaning. So, the best I can do is to offer what I take to be a characteristic definition, which I think captures its typical usages.[1]

RA: Okay, then. How do you define relativism?[2]

Michael: I take relativism to be the view that *such values as truth, goodness, or beauty are relative to a reference frame, and no absolute, overarching standards to adjudicate between competing reference frames exist.*[3]

---

1 See Ludwig Wittgenstein, *On Certainty*.
2 The following discussion of relativism is adapted from my paper, "Relativisms and Their Opposites."
3 Richard Bernstein provides another standard definition: "in its strongest form, relativism is the basic conviction that when we turn to the examination of those concepts that

RA: That seems fairly straightforward.

Michael: Actually, it's not all that straightforward, because the variables it mentions are themselves not all that straightforward. At the least, it embeds ideas of truth, goodness, beauty, reference frames, standards of adjudication, or varieties of absolutism that a relativist might oppose.

RA: Okay, I see what you mean.

Michael: So I'll need to say something about each of those. Notice that the definition provides for such values as 'truth,' 'goodness,' or 'beauty.' One reason for the 'or' rather than 'and' is that it allows for either *global* or *piecemeal* treatments of relativism. That is, one might affirm relativism with respect to all values or with respect to only one or some values. For example, one might affirm relativism with respect to any of the following combinations: truth, goodness, and beauty; with respect to goodness and beauty, but not truth; with respect to goodness, but not truth or beauty; with respect to beauty, but not truth or goodness; with respect to truth, but not goodness or beauty; or with respect to neither truth, goodness, nor beauty.

In fact, there may be other such multivalent values, such as 'indeterminacy,' 'reasonableness,' and the like. But we can stick with truth, goodness, or beauty for our present purposes.

RA: Do those values necessarily coincide with particular domains of inquiry?

Michael: Good question. While some such values are typically associated with particular domains of inquiry—for example, beauty, with respect to the aesthetic domain—such values may also apply to other domains. For example, some might consider a solution to a mathematical or scientific problem to be 'beautiful,' while moral or aesthetic claims may be taken to be 'true.' So, no necessary line-up between certain values and particular domains exists. Values and domains may overlap, but they need not be co-extensive.

---

philosophers have taken to be the most fundamental—whether it is the concept of rationality, truth, reality, right, the good, or norms—we are forced to recognize that in the final analysis all such concepts must be understood as relative to a specific conceptual scheme, theoretical framework, paradigm, form of life, society, or culture ... For the relativist, there is no substantive overarching framework or single meta-language by which we can rationally adjudicate or univocally evaluate competing claims of alternative paradigms"; see Bernstein's *Beyond Objectivism and Relativism*, 8.

RA: Okay. What about other variables in your definition? What about reference frames?

Michael: Reference frames come in many varieties. They may include paradigms, symbol systems, world-versions, systems of belief, languages, points of view, perspectives, standpoints, forms of life, or conceptual schemes. They may include cultures, tribes, communities, countries, civilizations, societies, historical periods, religions, races, or genders. This list of cognates is not exhaustive. Neither are they mutually exclusive. Some of these cognates of reference frames overlap; some do not. Some of their boundaries are easily delineable; others are not. Sometimes we can easily distinguish what is inside and what is outside a reference frame; sometimes we cannot. For example, the boundaries between Hindu and Buddhist traditions are vague, while those between Medieval, Renaissance, and Baroque periods are indeterminate. Boundaries between guilt and shame cultures are difficult to delineate.

RA: It seems that the relativist is saying that we can't appeal to facts of the matter independent of some reference frame. But couldn't absolutists press their case by observing that frames of reference are attached *onto* something, and that to which a frame attaches must be frame-independent?

Michael: Yes, but a relativist may counter by suggesting that frames may attach on to other frames. Accordingly, it would be a mistake to presume that there must be some frame-independent *thing* that reference frames are *of*. For example, there is no frame-independent fact of the matter whether the shortest distance between two points is a straight line, that is, independent of a given geometry. The shortest distance between two points *is* a straight line in Euclidean geometry, but it *isn't* so in a non-Euclidean geometry, say in a Riemannian geometry.

RA: But can't absolutists press their point still further by conceding that while we may understand the world via reference frames, such frames *distort* or to some measure *falsify* our knowledge of the world? And to say that much, mustn't we postulate a frame-independent world, without which we could not understand the very idea of distortion or falsification in the first place?

Michael: In reply to that question, the relativist may say that the idea of distortion or falsification doesn't require an absolutist construal of the world, because what we take to know is always already framed. That is, a relativist can agree that some statements are truer than others—truer, that is, in virtue of their fittingness with a constellation of other entrenched frame-dependent beliefs. Such an approach would disallow talk of 'getting at' or 'not getting at' frame-independent matters.

RA: But couldn't an absolutist still insist that behind all that we know is some kind of order, some kind of being that reference frames have to be about, an order that our frame-dependent efforts are still trying to 'get at' as you put it? Couldn't the absolutist affirm that such an underlying order provides absolutist standards to adjudicate between reference frames?

Michael: When you mention an underlying order, I presume you mean something like what Kant called the 'noumenon'—an indeterminate, frame-independent, undifferentiated realm, an 'I know not what' as he put it. Now that I think of it, in some respects, Kant's idea of the noumenon sounds a bit like the idea of the Atman.

But then, even if one were to embrace the idea of such a noumenal order, could it provide the grounds to adjudicate between reference frames? Could it have any methodological bite? Could it have the practical resources to adjudicate between reference frames?

RA: It's interesting that insofar as it's concerned with adjudication, your definition of relativism actually allows the possibility that one might embrace something like Kant's noumenon or the Hindu's Atman, as you say, just because they seem not to be the sorts of things that can adjudicate between reference frames.

Michael: Right. And there would be no contradiction in allowing that. Kant's idea of the noumenon, or the Hindu vision of Atman may look 'absolutist' in some sense of that term. But it is not the sense of absolutism that is invoked in our working definition of relativism. The sense of absolutism that our definition denies concerns *adjudication* between reference frames.

RA: Michael, can you say a bit more about the Advaitic idea of Atman or Oneness, as it relates to relativism and adjudication?

Michael: Sure. As I explained earlier, Advaitists embrace the notion that ultimate reality is the undifferentiated, non-countable, ineffable One. That Advaitic notion embraces non-dualism. It affirms that ultimate reality is the totality of existence, and not any or all countable objects. Therefore, appeals to that Advaitic notion would be ineffectual as regards adjudication between competing reference frames. Yet, insofar as the relativist is concerned with adjudication, a relativist could—without contradiction—embrace the Advaitic notion of Oneness.

RA: That's an interesting finding. We've been talking about adjudication. But now, by the relativists suggesting that no absolute standards exist to adjudicate between reference frames, I would think that they would need to be clear about what might be meant by 'absolutist.' What sense of absolutism do relativists characteristically oppose?

Michael: That's an important question, and a lot hangs on it. Absolutism might be variously understood as 'realism,' 'universalism,' or 'foundationalism.' Who knows? An absolutist might understand his absolutism in other terms, too. But for present purposes, let's consider these three: realism, universalism, or foundationalism. It is tempting to say that a strong absolutism affirms all three of these 'isms,' and a strong relativism opposes all three of them.

RA: So how do you understand those three isms?

Michael: By realism, I mean the view that frame-independent facts of the matter exist, that there is a way that things are that is logically independent of human representations, and that they are knowable.

RA: You mean that realists assert that there are facts.

Michael: Yes. But we need to be careful here about so-called facts. Realists assert that there are uninterpreted facts. Now, relativists might agree that there are facts, which, on the face of things, might sound as if they agree; but relativists hold that all facts are inevitably interpreted facts. Thus, when relativists speak of facts, they mean it in a sense different from the realist's sense. A relativist is free to say, for example, "It is a 'fact' that the shortest distance between two points is a straight line," understanding by that that such a claim is made within the reference frame of Euclidean geometry. So, we should not presume that any talk of 'facts' mandates a realist construal.

RA: Okay. Now, what about universalism? How do you understand that 'ism'?

Michael: Universalism asserts that designated characteristics apply to all peoples in all cultures. For example, universalists may hold that human rights exist for all peoples. Or, universalists may assert that peoples in all cultures can *know* whether all peoples share pertinent characteristics, for rationality itself is universally exemplified. In contrast, anti-universalists hold that some characteristics may apply only to some peoples in some cultures. They may claim that some human rights, for example, exist for some people and not for others. They may claim that rationality itself is not universally exemplified in all peoples or cultures. An anti-universalist could affirm that there are no universal grounds for deliberation shared by all peoples in all cultures.

RA: So, when a universalist claims that all peoples might share human rights or the ability to know that they might share human rights, such universalities could be a matter of contingency. It would just so happen that all peoples would share these features. Nothing would guaranty such universalities. Even if those universalities were exemplified, it could be otherwise. It could be different under different circumstances. So, if those universal conditions did exist, it would be something of a miracle that they would do so.

Michael: That's right. And that's why universalists are often driven to go beyond a claim of contingent universalism. They may be driven to embrace a foundationalism.

RA: So what is foundationalism?

Michael: A good way for me to introduce foundationalism is to make a distinction between two kinds of universalism—foundational and nonfoundational. 'Foundational' universalism holds that all peoples share some common characteristics by virtue of what—*inherently* or *intrinsically* or *essentially*—it is to be a human being. 'Nonfoundational' universalism holds that all peoples may share common characteristics without presuming that they do so by virtue of what, inherently or intrinsically or essentially, it is to be a human being. Foundational universalism is a claim of inherence or intrinsicality or essentiality. In contrast, nonfoundational universalism is a claim of historical or cultural or biological contingency. Put otherwise, foundationalism is the view that characteristics of pertinent subjects are what they are in virtue of their being inherent or intrinsic or essential to those subjects. In turn, at the epistemic level, knowledge can be acquired in virtue of foundational principles of rationality, such as the principle of non-contradiction. They are self-evident and not further reducible. They constitute the rock-bottom basis for rationality, argumentation, or justification.

RA: Can you give an example?

Michael: Here is a different example of foundational universalism. Consider the claim, "All persons have biological mothers." This example would amount to a foundational universalism if it were conjoined to the further claim that having a biological mother is an inherent or intrinsic feature of what it is to be a human being. In contrast, a nonfoundational universalist might urge that the fact that all persons have biological mothers is contingent and—considering possible developments in human cloning—it could be otherwise. This would leave open the possibility that one day, a being without a biological mother could be rightly considered to be a human being. So, contingently understood, universal commonality does not amount to a foundational universalism. Yet still, the foundationalist might reply that the universal instantiation of characteristics that all peoples share needs to be foundationally grounded in order to explain the otherwise miraculous fact of universality. That is, without foundational universalism, the commonality of shared characteristics seems miraculous.

RA: Okay. I think I have a pretty good idea of what you mean by realism, universalism, and foundationalism. Now what is the relation between them?

Michael: Realism, universalism, and foundationalism are logically distinct. While you could embrace all three of them without contradiction, realism entails neither universalism nor foundationalism; universalism entails neither realism nor foundationalism; and foundationalism entails neither realism nor universalism.

RA: Okay. So, how do these different ways of understanding absolutism relate to your claim that relativism need not be self-refuting?

Michael: Good. I'm glad you're bringing us back to that age-old classical argument against relativism. That argument holds that relativism is self-refuting.[4] If someone says, "Relativism is true," we might inquire in what sense of truth it is said that relativism is true. If our interlocutor says relativism is absolutely true, the claim that relativism is absolutely true is obviously self-contradictory. This charge of self-contradiction is often taken to be decisive. But this argument doesn't work.

---

4 See Myles F. Burnyeat, "Protagoras and Self-Refutation in Later Greek Philosophy."

RA: Why doesn't it work?

Michael: It doesn't work because it is insensitive to what 'absolutism' might mean. However, having untangled some possible meanings of absolutism—into realism, universalism, or foundationalism—we are now equipped to unseat the charge of contradiction.

RA: So how does that go?

Michael: Recall our initial definition of relativism. It is the claim that such values as truth, goodness, or beauty are relative to a reference frame, and no absolute, overarching standards to adjudicate between competing reference frames exist. Now, for the term 'absolute' in the latter part of this definition, substitute its unpacked meanings—'realist,' 'universalist,' or 'foundationalist.' Such a substitution yields the more refined formulation of relativism, namely, "Such values as truth, goodness, or beauty is relative to a reference frame, and no realist, universalist, or foundationalist overarching standards to adjudicate between competing reference frames exist."

Whatever misgivings you might have about varieties of realism, universalism, or foundationalism, no contradiction follows when the relativist negates any one or all of them. Neither the negation of realism, nor the negation of universalism, nor still the negation of foundationalism is self-contradictory. Put otherwise, if we conceive of relativism as a negation of one or more of the offered strands of absolutism, relativism is not self-refuting. In this way, the self-refuting argument against relativism dissolves.

RA: I follow that. It seems to me to be a significant insight.

Michael: Thank you. But let's be clear. This argument does not establish the rightness of relativism. It only shows the invalidity of the classical self-referential argument against relativism.

RA: Got it. As you say, all of this depends upon your initial definition of relativism.

Michael: Yes. As I said earlier, I think the definition I offered pretty well captures characteristic formulations. Of course, Joseph Margolis has offered an uncharacteristic definition that warrants its own treatment. His definition arises from a rich conception of interpretation and the metaphysics of culture. He characterizes what he calls 'robust relativism,' by citing, as he says:

two essential doctrines: (1) that, in formal terms, truth values logically weaker than bipolar value (true or false) may be admitted to govern otherwise coherent forms of inquiry and constative acts, and (2) that substantively, not merely for evidentiary or epistemic reasons, certain sectors of the real world open to constative inquiry may be shown to support only such weaker truth values. That is all.[5]

In other words, his so-called robust relativism urges that opposing judgments that would be contradictory on a bivalent logic would turn out not to be so on a multivalent logic. In this sense, opposing judgments based on a multivalent logic would be 'incongruent' rather than contradictory. Accordingly, two incongruent judgments may be reasonable, appropriate, or apt. Again, while I think his logic of multivalence is compelling, it deviates from what is characteristically understood to be the doctrine of relativism. Of course, Margolis might offer it as an account of what one should mean by relativism. But that's another matter.[6]

RA: Okay, then. Keeping in mind something like your definition of relativism, relativism often comes under attack from those who have serious moral concerns. They ask how one can be a relativist about evil—the Holocaust for example. Your own family had profoundly painful experiences as European Jews during WWII. Your family encountered evil.

Michael: Of course, I am concerned how relativists can deal with the fact of the Holocaust. The Nazi extermination of six million Jews, and so many other so-called undesirables as well is a fact.

RA: On the other hand, there are Holocaust deniers.

Michael: Yes, and they are wrong to deny that the Holocaust existed!

RA: How can a relativist say they are wrong?

Michael: The relativist can affirm that the Holocaust—as in all past events—is a post-dictive reconstruction based upon our present 'best evidence' that makes sense of our understanding of a series of instances of murder in the name of the Nazi ideology. The Holocaust remains one of the most morally

---

5 Joseph Margolis, "The Truth about Relativism."
6 I discuss this point more fully in my "Interpretation, Relativism, and Culture: Four Questions for Margolis."

heinous events in Western history. This is a fact—while still an interpreted fact. Being interpreted though does not entail the conclusion that it is not real. And it does not make the claim that it existed less true.

RA: How is that possible? Doesn't the 'fact' that it is an interpreted construction make it less real? Doesn't it make the assertion of its existence less true? Don't we have to be realists to insist upon the uninterpreted facts that ground all interpretations in order to preserve claims of reality and truth?

Michael: That's the linkage that realists often insist upon. But it's not necessary. And you know what? Not insisting upon a realist understanding of reality or truth robs us not one whit of asserting the moral outrage of the Holocaust. Put otherwise, we lose nothing by being non-realists about it.

RA: But how is that possible?

Michael: Okay. Take another example. Take the statement, "Peter Krausz existed and was born in Lausanne, Switzerland on August 18, 1938." That seems uncontroversial enough, wouldn't you say?

RA: Of course.

Michael: Do you take 'Peter Krausz' to be the name of a person, who was born to his mother, in the country of Switzerland, in a year designated as such-and-such, according to the Gregorian calendar?

RA: Yes.

Michael: So, notice that 'Peter Krausz' is a name given to a person by his parents, designating a person, born of a mother, in a city, and a country, on a particular date, as designated according to a particular calendar. All of these properties are interpreted. And yet we say that Peter Krausz was real and the statement that he was real is true, don't we?

RA: Yes.

Michael: And still, sometimes we believe things so strongly as to die for them—despite their being interpreted. Nevertheless, the world is not transparently given. We never see nor understand anything without an interpretive veil of some sort. What's more, even if there were a fact of the matter beyond interpretation, it would not be transparently available to human interpreters independent of interpretations.

RA: So what are we to say to the Holocaust denier?

Michael: The best solution to this conundrum was one suggested to me by Margolis. When a Holocaust denier rejects the assertion that the Holocaust existed on the grounds that it is 'merely' an interpretation, we may point out that what he, himself, has accepted as most basic is interpreted. For example, he accepts that he was born on such and such a date to such and such a mother, and so on. Such beliefs are interpreted. The fact that they are interpreted does not disqualify our holding that they are true!

RA: But sometimes, Holocaust deniers do not claim that the deaths never occurred. Instead, they interpret the deaths in ways other than the result of evil. They say that the deaths amounted to political maneuvers. Still other deniers argue over how many died and whether the term genocide is correctly used.[7]

Michael: Those sorts of deniers are debating between interpretations, and not interpretations in relation to interpretation-free, realist facts of the matter.

RA: Still, they hold that their interpretations are true.

Michael: Okay, but my point is that anti-realists can speak about facts and truth as well as realists can. They can argue about whether particular claims about numbers, for example, are admissible—all the while disagreeing about what each means by 'fact' or 'truth.' Anti-realist arguments about which historical events took place can be as powerful as realist ones. Their second-order disagreements about what they mean by 'real' or 'fact' are quite detachable from whether "The Holocaust happened" is admissible in a historical narrative. To agree that the Holocaust happened does not uniquely entail either realism or anti-realism.

RA: You have been talking about the strategic arguments open to realists, universalists, and foundationalists—all in answer to the question, "What is relativism?," or at least what you offer as the characteristic definition of relativism. Can we stand back now? I'm very interested to hear where you stand in regard to relativism. Can you give a summary of that?

---

7 See Imre Kertész, "Who Owns Auschwitz?," 267–272.

Michael: Sure. Assertions about what is and is not real cannot be based on some privileged access to the way the world is, independent of practice. There are no concepts that are applicable at all times and in all linguistic communities. Concepts are social products and are applicable insofar as thinkers of a common tradition find them useful. Human beings are never cognitively 'prior to' communities. Persons find themselves *in* communities in virtue of their development as appropriators of the common procedures of their culture. They do not start in the beginning. They start in the middle.[8]

RA: Thank you for that. With all of that said, can you place yourself in the conceptual landscape you've offered? For example, where do you stand with regard to foundationalism?

Michael: I embrace a version of nonfoundationalism, which I call 'polymorphism.' What polymorphism makes explicit in foundationalism is that there is no ultimate level of description. In other words, polymorphism affirms that no description can be taken to capture an inherent or ultimate constituent of reality. For example, if we describe water in a glass as thirst quenching, one might take that description as a truth about a frame-independent way of the world. Yet a polymorphist emphasizes that the water—understood as a middle-sized phenomenon—is thirst quenching. It affords satisfactions to middle-sized organisms such as human beings, dogs, and cats, for example. Yet, when we re-describe water in terms of electrons in empty space, the property of thirst-quenchingness does not apply. In this way, polymorphism holds that relevant properties must be understood elliptically, that is, within one reference frame or another. And no level of description captures an inherent or ultimate constituent of what there is.

Here is another example of how a polymorphist might handle things. In everyday contexts, one might say, "This is my hand." While a cell biologist might say that it is a collection of cells, a particle physicist might say that it is a collection of subatomic particles in empty space.

The polymorphist allows that subatomic particles are most basic in physics, and the polymorphist allows that cells are most basic in biology. But neither subatomic particles nor cells need be regarded as inherent constituents of reality irrespective of domains of inquiry. While such claims can be taken as most

---

8 For a fuller exposition, see Harré and Krausz, eds. Conclusion in *Varieties of Relativism*, 222–224.

basic within any given frame of reference, polymorphism refuses to make a claim about the inherent or ultimate nature of things. Further, what appears to be basic in an inquiry is basic only after a choice has been made about what reference frame one wishes to pursue in accord with one's purposes and interests.

When we talk about purposes and interests, it's natural to ask *whose* purposes and interests. In that sense, the postulation of 'human being' is privileged, in that we determine that it is human beings who do the choosing. But that privileged position—which I call the default position—need not be foundational. By the way, these ideas regarding human agency will be relevant again when we discuss self-realization and humanism.

RA: I look forward to that. But for now, you speak of the human being as the agent who chooses. But could that change?

Michael: The agent who chooses is revisable. Given evolutionary change, the agent of choice—with purposes and interests—might be a non-human, conscious, sentient being. In that sense, the default position of the human can be overridden. In other words, the assignment of priority to the 'human' is itself a human judgment, and that judgment need not be permanent. Conceivably, in the future, the assignment of purposes and interests may not be made by human beings. I leave that possibility open. However, at least to be choosers, they must be sentient conscious beings.

CHAPTER 10

Interpretation

RA: You have written a lot about the idea of interpretation, about its ideals and aim and about how we should understand objects of interpretation. I wonder if you might review some of your central claims.

Michael: By all means. Let's start by talking about two competing ideals of interpretation, namely, singularism, and multiplism.[1]

RA: OK. What is singularism?

Michael: Singularists hold that for *any* object of interpretation—say, a work of art, music, or literature—only one single admissible interpretation exists.

RA: And multiplism?

Michael: Multiplism is the view that holds that, for *some* objects of interpretation, more than one admissible interpretation exists.

RA: Can you give me an example how these ideals might apply?

Michael: Consider Vincent Van Gogh's painting, *The Potato Eaters*. It has been variously interpreted as answering to formalist, Marxist, Christian, feminist, or psychoanalytic treatments. Singularists think that, ideally, one and only one interpretation is admissible; so, we should seek the single right interpretation of the painting. In contrast, at least for this sort of case, multiplists will allow that more than one interpretation is ideally admissible.

RA: But if one said that, say, the Christian interpretation is true, wouldn't that mean that the others would be false?

Michael: That's just it. The multiplist allows that while there is some kind of logical tension or incongruence between those interpretations, they do not exclude one another.

---

[1] For a recent treatment, see Michael Krausz, "The Ideals and Aim of Interpretation." The present view is compatible with the thought that the concept of interpretation is essentially contested, in the sense developed by WB Gallie, "Essentially Contested Concepts."

While singularists think of opposition between contending interpretations in exclusive terms, multiplists holds that opposition between contending interpretations need not be understood in exclusive terms. A multiplist allows that there may be opposition between some contending interpretations, but that that would be an opposition without exclusivity. In other words, multiplists allow that incongruent interpretations may be jointly defended. That idea that opposing interpretations may under certain circumstances be jointly defended I owe to Joe Margolis in his idea of robust relativism. As he says, incongruent interpretations may appear to be contradictory according to a bivalent logic, but they are not contradictory according to a multivalent logic.[2]

RA: I don't get it. Wouldn't we say that one interpretation is true or false? And if we do, wouldn't we be endorsing the singularist idea that there is one truth?

Michael: That's just it. Particularly in cultural cases, we don't ordinarily talk about an interpretation being true in a bivalent way. We characteristically talk in terms of its reasonableness, or appropriateness, or aptness or the like. When we say one interpretation is reasonable that doesn't commit us to the idea that an opposing interpretation can't also be reasonable. That's what Margolis means when he says that, at least mostly in the cultural realm, evaluative concepts are multivalent.

RA: Wait a minute. Couldn't one say that such predicates like reasonableness, appropriateness, and aptness really reduce to bivalent concepts like truth or falsity? I mean, couldn't one hold that by saying that the psychoanalytic interpretation of Van Gogh's *The Potato Eaters* in reasonable, what one really means is that it is true?

Michael: That's what Monroe Beardsley argued in "The Authority of the Text."[3] He insisted that by reasonable or plausible we mean reasonable as to truth, or plausible as to truth, and so on. But underneath Margolis's treatment is the idea that the way we think about cultural phenomena is fundamentally different from the way we deal with natural phenomena. At least we can say this much. Margolis's approach—one with which I basically agree—affirms that such multivalent values like reasonableness are characteristically invoked when interpreting cultural phenomena, and those values are not reducible to bivalent values like true versus false.

---

2   Joseph Margolis, "Robust Relativism"; see also Joseph Margolis, *Interpretation Radical but Not Unruly*, IX.
3   Monroe Beardsley, "The Authority of the Text."

RA: OK. Now I see what you mean when you say that the difference between singularists and multiplists is reflected in their tolerances for opposed but not exclusive interpretations. Singularists think of opposition in bivalent terms, such that opposed interpretations contradict one another. In contrast, multiplists hold that opposition need not be understood in such bivalent terms. Opposed interpretations need not logically exclude one another.

Michael: Exactly so. Now here is another thing to notice about singularism and multiplism. As I define them, singularism and multiplism are asymmetrical in the sense that singularism mandates a single admissible interpretation for *all* objects of interpretation. In contrast, multiplism affirms that multiplist conditions may obtain in *some* but not *all* cases. Multiplism allows that some singularist conditions may obtain.

RA: I now see that your definition of multiplism allows that—while more than one interpretation may be admissible—still more are inadmissible.

Michael: That's right. The multiplist is just as concerned as the singularist is to jettison inadmissible interpretations.

RA: I've noticed that your definition of singularism speaks of the single right interpretation as *existing* and the definition of multiplism speaks of the multiply-admissible interpretations as *existing*. What do you have in mind when you say 'existing?'

Michael: I'm glad you mentioned that. It allows me to distinguish between singularism or multiplism in an *existential* sense from singularism or multiplism in a *regulative* sense.

The existential singularist or multiplist holds that for any object of interpretation, a single or multiple admissible interpretation actually exists. The regulative singularist or multiplist holds that for some objects of interpretation one should conduct one's inquiry *as if* those respective interpretations exist, without necessarily assuming one or more admissible interpretations actually exist.

RA: Why is that distinction important?

Michael: Well, consider this. Existential multiplists might find it useful to conduct their inquire as if only one interpretation exists, for it might motivate them to narrow the range of admissible interpretations, even if not to a limit of one interpretation. Put otherwise, trying for a 'singularly perfect' interpretation, for example, is not inconsistent with the belief that no such interpretation actually exists. Or, to consider another sort of case, reaching for a singularly perfect musical performance is not inconsistent with the belief that no such performance exists.

RA: OK. So here is a question about reasons: When multiplists argue with each other over competing interpretations, and they agree that their reasons are not offered in the name of settling upon the single right interpretation, how must they understand reasons? I mean, usually, when somebody offers a reason for an interpretation, it's offered in the name of settling upon the right—that is, the singularly right—interpretation. If that's not the aim of reasons for multiplists, how must they understand the reasons that they would offer?

Michael: In treating multiplist cases—where more than one interpretation is taken as admissible, one may still give reasons for one's preferences amongst admissible interpretations. In those cases, the aim is not singular truth but justified preferences. Look at it this way. Multiplism allows that admissible interpretations *may not be equally preferable*, yet good reasons may be offered for preferred interpretations.

RA: Perhaps an example would help.

Michael: Okay. Consider a musical case. Good reasons might be offered for *preferring* Arturo Toscanini's interpretation of Brahms's Symphony no. 4 over that of Wilhelm Furtwängler—or vice versa—without disallowing either interpretation as inadmissible. In such cases, good reasons for preferences need not be sufficiently strong to unseat alternative interpretations as inadmissible. Having good reasons for preferences does not mandate singularism.

RA: That's a useful example.

Michael: I can actually sharpen my point by invoking a distinction between *determinative* and *ampliative* reasons.

RA: What's that?

Michael: A *determinative* reason is one that is characteristically invoked to persuade an interlocutor of the admissibility of one interpretation over another. In contrast, an *ampliative* reason seeks to amplify upon, or to fill in, or to provide a rationale why one embraces the interpretation that one does. But it does not seek to bring an interlocutor over to her side. Rather, it provides an understanding as to why she embraces the view that she does.

RA: Can you put this point still otherwise?

Michael: Of course. Singularists characteristically think that if you have reasons for a preferred interpretation that means that you are necessarily arguing for the exclusive rightness of your interpretation. Accordingly, the aim of reasons would be taken to convince someone of the exclusive rightness of the interpretation in question. But, one may have reasons for one's preferences without aiming to convince someone of exclusive rightness.

RA: Can you give another example of how that might work?

Michael: Actually, the Indian philosopher, Vibha Chaturvedi, has provided a way to see that preferences with good reasons need not aim toward a singularist condition. Her example is that of a sacred text. Let me quote her:

> Can one say that there are good reasons for preferring one interpretation to others as implied by multiplism? Let me take the case of different interpretations of the same sacred text. You might say that if an interpretation can competently explain or account for the whole text or most of the text that interpretation is preferable to others that fail to do so. But to expect that the preferred interpretation must account for the essential or more significant parts of the text is reasonable, even if it fails to do so with respect to large sections of the not so essential parts. There can be difference of opinion about what constitutes essential or most crucial parts ... we can give reasons for favoring one over others. But these reasons in most cases may reflect the purpose or the preference of the person giving the reasons.[4]

As Chaturvedi says, an interpretation may be justified with good reasons to prefer one interpretation over another because it accounts for the essential or more significant parts of the text. Moreover, there may be a difference of opinion about what constitutes essential or most important parts. What is 'essential' or 'significant' is characteristically contestable. Different people with different purposes may identify different features as more or less salient or

---

4 Vibha Chaturvedi, "Reflections on the Interpretation of Religious Texts," 308–309.

significant—giving rise to different patterns of significance. Two interpreters may have good reasons for assigning salience in different ways.

RA: That helps. But there is one thing that puzzles me. It concerns the very idea of ideals of interpretation.

Michael: What's that?

RA: Well, it concerns a presupposition that both singularists and multiplists seem to make. They both assume something like an end of inquiry, where all relevant arguments and information are *in* and are available. Yet, one might object that inquiry has no end; no such thing as an end of inquiry exists. Consequently, the very idea of an *ideal* cannot apply; therefore, neither singularism nor multiplism can apply.

Michael: I take your point. Nonetheless, we might still deploy a serviceable notion of an ideal of interpretation if we understand it as depending upon an agreement by qualified practitioners that all pertinent information is effectively in, where they can reasonably judge whether all pertinent information is in. Here the notion of 'ideal' would be understood as a limiting concept. Pertinent ideals might best be understood within pragmatic, provisional, and unfolding interpretive conditions. Of course, there may be significant disagreement about what a *qualified* practitioner is, about what information is *pertinent*, and about what judgments are *reasonable*.

RA: Here is another worry I have. It concerns the countability of supposed objects of interpretation.

Michael: What do you have in mind?

RA: Well, it would seem that both singularists and multiplists would require that an object of interpretation must be *countable*. Without the numerical identity of the object of interpretation, neither singularism nor multiplism could apply. Competing interpretations must address the numerically identical object of interpretation. Numerical identity of an object of interpretation seems to be necessary before the possibility of *conflict* between contending interpretations can arise.

Michael: You're right about that. And there are interesting consequences if the numerical identity of the object of interpretation is not secured. Without that identity, neither singularism nor multiplism might apply. We might even go so far as to say that, without it, they are not interpretable.

RA: That would be a significant exception.

Michael: Indeed. For example, the Advaitic conception of the Divine as ineffable, unbounded, and indeterminate is not numerically identifiable or re-identifiable. That to which the Advaitic Hindu points as the Divine is purportedly the Atman, the One, the Supreme Self. But it is not re-identifiable. It is beyond numerality.

RA: How did you come upon the idea that an object of interpretation must be countable or re-identifiable for it to answer to either singularism or multiplism?

Michael: You'll recall that when I inquired of Swamiji whether—when inquiring about ultimate reality—he thought the Hindu and the Buddhist are talking about the same thing, his reply was quick and to the point: "Yes, the Hindu and the Buddhist are talking about the same thing. But the Buddhist is wrong." Whereas the Dalai Lama, answered the same question, unhesitatingly, by saying, "No. We are not talking about the same thing."

Of course, each of these thinkers might have construed my question in different ways to start with. Yet, those exchanges revealed to me that if two persons are not talking about the same re-identifiable thing, they would be talking past each other. In order to disagree, they must first be talking about the same thing. Indeed, here were two persons effectively disagreeing about whether they were disagreeing with each other.

Yet, here is yet another possibility. Perhaps both respondents were wrong. Perhaps they should have said that they *cannot say* whether they are talking about the same thing. So they should have said that they *cannot say* whether they are disagreeing. The lesson I learned was that if otherwise competing interpretations do not address a common numerically re-identifiable object of interpretation, they cannot be said yet to be in conflict with one another.

RA: Can you say how this would apply to the Advaitic vision of Oneness?

Michael: Yes. As I've previously explained, Advaitic Hindus affirm that one who seeks self-realization must transcend all subject-object dualities. As put by Swami Vivekananda,[5] "The ultimate aim of life is the realization of the *Brahman* where all consciousness of diversity and multiplism is negated." Vivekananda seeks to transcend all dualisms.[6] Where such realization obtains, there can be no distinction between one or another would-be object of interpretation.

RA: Now I see what you mean when you say that the Atman in not countable. It is not re-identifiable. It cannot answer either to singularism or multiplism. Maybe it's not interpretable at all.

Michael: It wouldn't be interpretable if singularist and multiplist cases exhaust the cases that would be interpretable. That's something I'm not sure about.

RA: When talking about interpretation, so far you have also been talking about objects of interpretation. So what are you building into that phrase? What is an object of interpretation?

Michael: Good question, and not so easy to answer. It's controversial. I've been using the phrase, 'object of interpretation' to mean an intentional object. By that I mean we should not take 'object' as signifying a reified entity, an *object as such*. Intentional objects are endowed with meaning or significance within a field of cultural codes, norms, or the like. They are objects upon which meaning has been conferred, presented as having the meaning they do. Intentional objects are nodes of culturally endowed complexes. I find Peter Lamarque to be helpful about this when he talks about the idea of a work. For him, *works* are intentional objects. He says that works:

> are human creations; they depend on human intentions and cultural conditions. They are intentional objects not only because they owe their origins to intentional acts but also because their identity conditions are partly determined by how they are *taken* or *thought to be* by relevant cultural communities ... They cease to exist when there is no longer the possibility of their eliciting the appropriate kind of responses (being identified, being understood, being appreciated, being valued) among suitably qualified respondent.[7]

---

5   Vivekananda, is the chief disciple of the Hindu mystic, Ramakrishna.
6   As quoted Vivekananda, ibid.; see also, Swami Vivekananda, *Vedanta Philosophy*.
7   Peter Lamarque, "Object, Work, and Interpretation," 5–6, emphasis added.

RA: I get that. So what is so controversial?

Michael: The story does not end there, because the natural question arises, "What is the relation between intentional objects to non-intentional objects?"—the sort of non-intentional objects you might find in nature. Going further, Lamarque asks:

> To accommodate non-intentional as well as intentional objects—rather than embrace a two-tiered structure between interpretation and object of interpretation—should we not embrace a three-tiered structure, one that includes interpretation, intentional objects and associated objects as such?

Lamarque formulates his tripartite framework this way. He says:

> My tripartite scheme, for artworks, is between object, work, and interpretation. Interpretations apply strictly to works, not to objects per se ... so I believe there could be multiple interpretations of *works*. But I don't think there are interpretations of *objects*, as such, except in a rather special sense ... Works are necessarily associated with some object or other ... but they are not identical with the objects that constitute them. The statue is not identical with the piece of marble, because they have different identity conditions.[8]

I agree with Lamarque's three-tiered account. It allows us to see that the question of numerical identity arises for intentional objects (or for works) and not for objects as such. Whether "The Potato Eaters," for example, is one or more works is, itself, a matter of interpretation.

RA: So, what would constrain the range of admissible interpretations? If we allow that the Marxist and psychoanalytic interpretations of Van Gogh's painting are admissible, what would disallow our admission of an astrological interpretation?

Michael: While that which is interpreted may be constituted within webs of interpretations rather than appeal to would-be objects *as such*, there are constraints on the range of admissible interpretations *at any particular historical moment*. And only a handful of interpretations would be available for serious consideration by qualified practitioners at a given historical moment. So, being

---

8 Ibid., 5.

a function of the consensual agreement of pertinent practitioners, the range of admissible interpretations would be socially determined. What makes an interpretation admissible at a given historical moment would depend upon the consensus of the pertinent community of researchers and not by appeal to an object as such—one which has not yet been numerically individuated.

RA: So where does the idea of an uninterpreted world fit in your account?

Michael: I agree with Bernard Harrison, who postulates a world without epistemic resources to adjudicate between contending interpretations.[9]

RA: I understand your account of singularism and multiplism as competing ideals of interpretation. Now, more generally, I'm wondering what you might say about the status of your account itself taken as an object of interpretation. That is, does your account itself answer to a singularist or multiplist condition? I mean, if it is admissible, is it singularly or multiply admissible?

Michael: Good question. Are you asking whether my account of ideals seeks to fulfill the singularist or multiplist ideal? Is that it?

RA: Precisely.

Michael: I take my account to be a reasonable one in much the way that a multiplist would treat other cultural phenomena. In turn, I do not offer my account as the single right interpretation of ideals of interpretation. Rather, I would say that my account of interpretation applies to itself. It is reasonable to the extent that it illuminates certain interpretive practices. I do not say that it is the only admissible interpretation of interpretive practice. But its reasonableness certainly does not depend upon its correspondence with an uninterpreted fact of the matter.

RA: As I recall, one of the central concerns in your theory of interpretation is what you have called the 'detachability thesis.' Could you explain what you mean by that term?

Michael: My detachability thesis is a central feature of my work on interpretation. It is straightforward, even self-evident. As I have said, the detachability thesis claims that neither singularism nor multiplism entails realism,

---

9   See Patricia Hanna and Bernard Harrison, *Word and World*; see also, Harrison, "Robust Multiplism, Or, New Bearings in the Theory of Interpretation," 55–66.

constructivism, or constructive realism. Conversely, neither realism, constructivism, nor constructive realism entails either singularism or multiplism. In short, neither of the ideals of interpretation entails any of the ontologies I mentioned—and vice versa. None of those ontologies entails either of the ideals in question.[10]

RA: Can you put that claim in another way?

Michael: Yes. From a strictly logical point of view of entailment, you can, without contradiction, mix and match each of these ontologies with either of the ideals of interpretation. The ideals of interpretation are logically detachable from the ontologies I mentioned. That's all.

At the same time, my detachability thesis does not urge one to desist from engaging in ontology, including discussions about whether realism or constructivism or constructive realism is right. My claim is a narrow, strictly logical one about entailment.

RA: So, if you don't excuse yourself from engaging in ontologizing, whose do you embrace?

Michael: I favor one worked out by Harrison and Hanna. They emphasize the praxial foundation of meaning, and argue that the creative inventions of language and culture are as real as any extra-linguistic reality.[11] While granting the existence of extra-human reality, however, they assert such reality is conceptually unorganized, but nevertheless, cognitively accessible by way of sense-perception and physical manipulation.

I might add that Harrison agrees with my detachability thesis. He agrees that ideals of interpretation do not entail the ontologies that I've inventoried, including his own 'relative realism,' which I have included under the umbrella category of 'constructive realism.'[12] And he most assuredly has pursued the project of ontology.[13]

---

10   Constructive realism, as I use the term, is a hybrid of constructivism and realism; see Chap. 4, "Realism and Constructivism," and Chap. 5, "Toward a Constructive Realism," in my *Limits of Rightness*.
11   See Hanna and Harrison, *Word and World*, 58–60.
12   See Harrison and Hanna, "Interpretation and Ontology," esp. 103–104.
13   Harrison, "Robust Multiplism."

For me, the world exists—even if it is not countable—and it incorporates human achievements. It is a world whose ways are multiple, while its boundary conditions are beyond human cognitive resources.

RA: OK. Let's move on from our discussion of ideals of interpretation to talk about the aim of interpretation. Singularism and multiplism seem to fall under the general aim of elucidation.

Michael: For all that we have said about singularism and multiplism, both fall under the larger heading of the *aim* of interpretation. That aim is to get at the meaning or meanings of objects of interpretation. That aim is elucidation, which means to explain, or to make intelligible.

RA: I hear you saying that elucidation is an aim of interpretation. Do I hear you saying that it's the only aim of interpretation?

Michael: OK. Before I answer whether it's the only aim, let's consider another possible candidate for an aim of interpretation.

RA: What could that be?

Michael: I have puzzled whether edification might also be an aim of interpretation.

RA: So what do you mean my edification?

Michael: Let me give different sorts of examples to elucidate the meaning of the concept. First consider what philosopher Arthur Danto has to say about 'high moments of artistic work.' He says:

> When artist and work are not separated by a gap of any sort, but fuse in such a way that the work seems to bring itself into existence. At such points—and any creative person lives for these— ... [materials] are ... agents of selflessness, which is the state at which ... so much of Oriental philosophy ... aims.[14]

Or consider composer Alexander Goehr's comments about special moments in his work:

---

14 Arthur Danto, *Mysticism and Morality*, 110–111, emphasis added.

the music writes itself ... There is no longer a composer who pushes the material about, but only its servant, carrying out what the notes themselves imply. This is the exact experience I seek and which justifies all else ... at this moment, I find myself overcome by an *oceanic sensation of oneness* with all around me.[15]

Or consider what artist Robert Henri says about an 'ontological experience' of Oneness behind every true work of art. He says:

The object, which is back of every true work of art, is the attainment of a state of being, a state of high functioning, a more than ordinary moment of existence ... its result is but a by-product of this state, a trace, the footprint of the state ... This state of spiritual exaltation is fundamental to creative activity, while skills and measurements are secondary. It is the manifestation of an ontological experience.[16]

In converging ways, these writers point to a kind of experience that motivates their work. These are special edificatory experiences of creators. At the same time, appreciative recipients of pertinent works may undergo corresponding edificatory experiences, as suggested by John Dewey, who speaks of this as *an* experience:

We have *an* experience ... when the material experienced runs its course to fulfillment. Then and only then is it integrated within and demarcated in the general stream of experience from other experiences ... [It] is so rounded out that its close is a consummation and not a cessation. Such an experience is ... *an* experience.[17]

When living *in* or *through* a work one may be moved, enriched, or enlivened. Sometimes such edificatory moments are understood to contribute to one's self-cultivation, one's self-fulfillment, or one's self-realization.

RA: These are useful examples to get at what you mean by edification. Given your understanding of it then, would you say that edification qualifies as an aim of interpretation?

---

15   Alexander Goehr, quoted in Anthony Storr, *Music and the Mind*, 97, emphasis added.
16   Robert Henri (1865–1929) quoted in Chang Chung-yuan, *Creativity and Taoism*, 203–204.
17   John Dewey, *Art as Experience*, LW: 42.

Michael: While, as a matter of lived experience, edification may occur at the same time as elucidation, it is *analytically distinct* from elucidation. This has led me to endorse Ken-ichi Sasaki's observation: "Interpretation has the unique aim of 'elucidation' ... To interpret a text or a phenomenon is not as such an act of 'edification.' Even if the edificatory concern may intervene, it can be as a *use* of the elucidatory result."[18]

Edification may arise from interpretive activity, but it is not constitutive of such activity. So, I conclude that edification is not an aim of interpretation.

---

18   Ken-Ichi Sasaki, "Limits of Interpretation."

CHAPTER 11

Creativity

RA: I understand that you came to formulate your theory of creativity in the course of articulating your personal program in art. Am I right?

Michael: Not quite. I'd been thinking about creativity in connection with the idea of a creative life, particularly when facing choices about whether to pursue the implications of life-altering experiences, starting around my late twenties. That preceded my art-making. Coincidentally, my meeting Larry Briskman occasioned serious philosophical reflection about the idea of creativity.

RA: Really? How did you meet Larry?

Michael: There's an interesting story there. Occasionally, uninvited people would show up in one of my classes. I was giving a senior seminar in the early 1970s—which included about eight or ten students—when Larry, whom I'd never met before, accompanied one of my students to class one day. At first, I paid no particular attention to him. By chance, during the class—I think it was when I was critiquing Popper's Three Worlds hypothesis—he shouted out, "You can't mean that!" He proceeded to set out his alternative view. I answered. He rebutted. I rebutted his rebuttal. We quickly both recognized each other as worthy opponents. By the end of the hour, we had had a feisty, engaging, enlivening, and memorable exchange—which we both obviously loved. It was only after that hour that my student introduced Larry to me. That was the start of a great friendship. At that time, Larry was a faculty member in the Philosophy Department at the University of Edinburgh, and he was a former student of Karl Popper's.[1]

What started as a disagreement turned into a series of discussions about creativity—both at Bryn Mawr and in Edinburgh, which eventually issued in fruitful published papers by each one of us separately.[2]

---

[1] Interestingly, Nick Sclufer was another one of those who showed up in my classes, this time in my Philosophy of Science Graduate Seminar.

[2] See Michael Krausz, "A Painter's View of Self-Development and Creativity." Also of interest is Briskman's unpublished, "Creativity and Self-Development: Comments on Michael Krausz's 'Creating and Becoming.'" An abridged version of this paper was presented at a symposium entitled, "Creating and Becoming," at the annual meeting of the Society for Philosophy of

RA: So, what was your point of disagreement with Briskman?

Michael: Well if, as Larry does, you distinguish between a creative person, a creative process, and a creative product, you might be tempted to emphasize one or another of those in your account of creativity. Larry emphasized the creative product as that which bears the philosophical weight of an adequate account of creativity. In so doing he followed Popper's idea that a work of music, for example, embodies objective contents of thought. It's what he called a third-world entity. That's part of his Three Worlds Hypothesis.[3]

In contrast, I emphasize the creative process over the creative product in order to accommodate the thought that it is a creative life that bears the conceptual weight. On my account, the creative product is a by-product, a consequence of, a creative life. I favor a program that values process over product, one that accommodates human experience in a significant way.

RA: Can you say more about your artwork in relation to your personal program?

Michael: Okay. I work with special handmade brushes. They are made of the hairs of deer, elk, and fox. They take on their own lives. After dipped in a solution—like India ink or dried pigment mixed in water—with a slight pressure on museum board, they make very fine, thin lines. With greater pressure a brush's bulbous base releases a swath of pigment on to the surface.

RA: Do you have a very precise idea of what you will paint before you start? That might be useful as an illustration of your program.

Michael: I usually have a general idea of what the painting will look like. But, as I say, the materials take on a life of their own. They suggest their own possibilities. The unintended spontaneous movements of my fingers and arms allow brush and pigment to respond as they may. Sometimes, the unintended emergent results are welcome, sometimes not. Sometimes, brush and pigment respond with extreme delicacy, variety, and wit. Other times they respond with ponderous contortions. Sometimes, the result is a scene that I could not have imagined. Sometimes, the scene provides a space that invites my entry.

Creativity, Eastern Division Meeting of the American Philosophical Association, Washington, DC, 28 December, 1978, and published as "Creating and Self-Development."

3   See Popper, *Objective Knowledge*; and "Three Worlds."

RA: When you make a piece, do you think of it as separate from others you've done?

Michael: As I work on a particular piece, I do so with the foreknowledge of its place in a series of works. Just as a single work may give rise to emergent features, so too, may a series of related works give rise to emergent features. These features may become apparent when I see the series as whole body of work, as in a solo exhibition. I think of the series as an on-going journey. Yes, it's composed of individual products—but the journey is the thing.

RA: Are there other factors that have encouraged your process-centered view of creativity?

Michael: I've already recounted the story of my epiphany—some people might call it an oceanic feeling[4]—which started me off on my spiritual journey. That was when I had that non-dualistic experience in my friend's art studio. Surrounded by her large abstract shaped canvases, I suddenly experienced myself *in* the space of the work instead of looking *at* it. I suddenly became much more highly visually sensitive—to spatial relations, to coloration and more.

RA: You just used an expression, 'non-dualistic experience.'

Michael: Yes. I suppose that kind of experience made me open to the sort of experiences that Eastern philosophers and artists describe when speaking about self-realization, particularly experiences of Oneness or emptiness. In any event, I think of my art-making as a process in which who I am enriched and transformed. You might say that my art production fosters my self-transformation, and my self-transformation fosters my art-production.

RA: I'm just wondering. Somebody might react to your program by observing that your epiphanic experience might have gone in different directions. I mean, you could have had a oneness experience and not decide to paint. Or, you could have decided to paint, yet not make self-transformation a central feature of your personal program.

Michael: Indeed. Someone else might have gone in those directions. They could have had similar experiences and not be compelled to make art at all. I

---

4   Wassily Kandinsky, *Concerning the Spiritual in Art and Painting in Particular*; see also Jussie A. Saarinen, "A Conceptual Analysis of the Oceanic Feeling."

do not say that my program is generalizable. Certainly, different people might choose different programs.

Others might not connect self-transformation with artistic production, or, artistic production with self-transformation. In any event, I suggest that there is no single right personal program, neither at one time nor at different times.

In my own case, my painting is integrally related to my self-transformation, and my self-transformation is integrally related to my painting. My artistic production motivates my self-transformation and my self-transformation motivates my artistic production. Such is my *personal program*.[5] My personal program values process over product. It seeks to foster self-transformation, and accommodates non-dualistic experiences. It recognizes non-dualistic experiences as benchmarks of my creative life's journey.

Personal programs reflect what David Novitz usefully calls a narrative identity. He says:

> The construction of narrative identities, like that of works of art, is often highly inventive. Both are usually constructed with immaculate care, often with insight and sensitivity, and in a way, moreover, which must alter and contribute to the sorts of people we are.[6]

He continues, "Our narrative identities are neither God-given nor innate, but are painstakingly acquired as we grow, develop, and interact with the people around us."[7]

In this way, who we are—our selves—transforms. Sometimes our self may exhibit incongruent characteristics. The need and extent of their 'resolution'— whether in the form of a single self with a single set of fully congruent characteristics or numerous incongruent ones—also depends upon the requirements of our personal program. Novitz says:

> Most of us have, at best, a fragmented and changing view of self. We see ourselves successively in different, sometimes incompatible, ways, and

---

5   See my "Creativity and Self-Transformation," 191–203.
6   David Novitz, "Art, Narrative, and Human Nature," 72.
7   Ibid., 65.

we do so, on my view, because we are inclined to tell more than one story about ourselves.[8]

RA: Clearly, you want to allow for non-dualistic episodes in your idea of a creative life. You want to allow for subjective experiences in your account of creativity. Clearly, that's just what Briskman wanted to deemphasize in his account of creativity. Am I right?

Michael: Just so. Larry assigns logical priority to products. He agrees that there might be some connection between creative activity and self-transformation. But he sees self-transformation as a mere by-product of creative production.

He even suggests that, if we give priority to products, we will be in a better position to benefit from the potential self-transformation that can follow in its wake. Accordingly, self-transformation should not be pursued as an aim as such. He argues that 'losing oneself' in one's work—whether of the more common variety or of a non-dualistic variety—depends upon focusing upon making the work and not upon the self.

RA: Maybe you two are not all that far apart, then. I mean, it's one thing to say that you value non-dualistic experience in an account of creativity. It's another thing to say that you should consciously aim for it all the time.

Michael: Good point. An individual might have a personal aim without making it a perpetual focus of attention. For example, I may aim to have a meaningful relationship or a rewarding career without continually focusing upon those aims at every waking moment. Still, I may periodically call upon an aim and choose among various personal or vocational possibilities in light of it. Having an aim does not require that it be the object of my continual focus. We can keep self-transformation as an aim, even if it is best only occasionally to call it to mind.

RA: How do critics enter into this discussion?

Michael: That's interesting. In our monthly critiques at the Artist Exchange of Delaware, for example, I can hardly remember anybody actually talking about non-dualistic experiences. It's all very dualistic. We talk mostly about materials and techniques, about form and color, about how to promote recognition and sales, and the like.

---

8 Ibid., 62.

RA: So how does Briskman advance his argument against your view of creativity?

Michael: As I've said, he draws sharp distinctions between creative persons, creative processes, and creative products. Then, he asserts logical priority to creative products.

RA: What does he mean by logical priority?

Michael: By logical priority he means that creative persons and creative processes can be identified only after creative products have been identified as such. Briskman says:

> Creative people and creative processes can only be identified *via* our prior identification of their ... products as themselves creative. That is, the person is a creative one and the process was a creative process only in the light of our prior evaluation of the product itself as a creative product. If this is correct, then it follows that a[n] artistic product is not creative because it was produced by a creative person or a creative process, but rather that both the psychological process involved, and the person involved, are deemed to be creative because they succeed in producing a product deemed to be creative. It is the creativity of the product which has, so to speak, logical priority.

Briskman summarizes his view:

> A creative ... artistic, product has, I suggest, the following characteristics. First, relative to the background of prior products, it is a *novel* product. Second, it puts this novelty to a desirable purpose by *solving a problem*, such problems being themselves relative to this background and emerging from it. Third, it does so in such a way as to actually *conflict* with parts of this background, to necessitate its partial modification, and to supplant and improve upon parts of it. Finally, this novel, conflicting problem-solution must be favorably evaluated; it must meet certain exacting standards which are themselves part of the background it partially supplants.[9]

---

9 Briskman, "Creative Product and Creative Process in Science and Art," 17–42.

RA: I'm trying to locate the source of your disagreement with Briskman. Where is it?

Michael: Here it is in a nutshell. While Larry might be right to emphasize that as a matter of *identifying* creative persons and creative processes, as a practical matter, we as evaluators must start with creative products. But that doesn't mean that in our account of creativity we should disvalue the experiences of the creative person and her processes. It all comes down to how we understand the idea of logical priority. If logical priority is only a matter of which question to consider first—*identifying* a creative product in order to then identify a creative person and a creative process—then I agree with him. But for me, logical priority concerns what primary value we place on each of those dimensions.

RA: So you agree with Larry that creative persons and creative processes can be identified only via a prior identification of products as themselves being creative.

Michael: Yes, but I qualify my agreement. Sometimes, even the distinctions between persons, processes, and products cannot be sharply sustained.

Even within the terms that Briskman embraces, the situation is more complicated. First, creators need not be individuals; they may be groups of individuals. They may even be holistic collectives like institutions. More generally, creators need not be persons. They may be other sorts of beings, like computers.[10]

RA: But surely your disagreement with Briskman arises for a deeper concern, does it not?

Michael: That's right. The issues surrounding self-transformation complicate Briskman's taxonomy of persons, processes, and products. For we may regard self-transformation per se as a creative product, thus undermining a general and sharp distinction between creative process and creative product.

Larry relegates self-transformation to subjective experience, or, as inhabitants of World 2. On his account, that means that self-transformation could not be regarded as a creative product, or, inhabiting World 3. As he concedes:

> If creativity were to be located as an event in World 3—if creativity was held to be, in a logical sense, *fundamentally independent* of events in

---

10   See Margaret Boden, "Creativity: How Does It Work?," 237–250.

World 2—then it would follow that living per se, and self-development per se [or self-transformation per se], could not be considered creative.[11]

So he generates a dilemma: either we must abandon his Popperian objectivist World 3 requirement for creativity. Or, we must somehow 'objectify' the subjective self-transformation.

But actually we must do both. We must reject Briskman's construal of subjective and objective states as 'fundamentally independent,' and we must allow that self-transformation may be taken up as a possibly creative activity. Put otherwise, we may take up our self-transformation as a valued priority.

RA: So does that mean that we should adjust Briskman's idea of a product?

Michael: Right. My underlying misgivings about Briskman's tripartite distinctions are captured by the thought that Larry's idea of a product is too restrictive. He thinks of it as one of Popper's third-world entities.

RA: How then should we think of products?

Michael: For 'product,' it would be better to substitute the idea of a 'work.' Works may be construed as both process and product. That substitution allows for bracketing a project such as self-transformation as one's work. It allows for a vocation as one's work; it allows for a personal relationship as one's work; it allows for one's life as one's work. No doubt, thingly products partly constitute one's life; they punctuate it; they serve as its signposts. But we need the more ample idea of a work or a 'life-work' to provide the normative context in virtue of which thingly products may have meaning and significance. It is in that larger notion of work that my personal program finds its place.

RA: I see. You want to allow that a life work can be creative.

Michael: Yes. Where is the distinction between process and product in Leonard Bernstein's performance of Beethoven's Symphony no. 9 in D minor to celebrate the fall of the Berlin Wall, in November 1989? Where is the distinction between process and product in Christo and Jean Claude's wrapping and

---

11 See Briskman, "Creativity and Self-Development," n2.

unwrapping of the Reichstag?[12] Such examples suggest that we cannot draw a general and sharp distinction between process and product.

Accordingly, I take the idea of work to incorporate processes and products. It is both a verb and a noun. A work is a doing as well as that which is done. Accordingly, I think we can take up the self and its life as a creative work. In fact, such a notion of work is commonplace in psychotherapy and soteriology. So understood, our work may include more than thingly products. It may include our self-transformation. And, in some personal programs, it may accommodate non-dualistic experiences amongst its ingredients. Yet conceding this much requires a taxonomy somewhat different from one that takes creative persons, creative processes, and creative products as fundamentally independent.

---

12   See Christo. *Christo & Jeanne-Claude: Verhüllter Reichstag, Berlin, 1971–1995*; see also Christo and Jeanne-Claude, Wrapped Reichstag, https://tinyurl.com/cqgtqan; and https://tinyurl.com/yau6qeej.

CHAPTER 12

Self-Realization

RA: It seems that the question of self-realization has occupied your attention, at least since you began your trips to India. Is that right?

Michael: That's fair to say. The question, "Who am I?" has captured my attention from my first encounters with Hindus and Buddhists.

RA: Can you start by explaining what you mean by self-realization?

Michael: It's difficult to give a definition of it in a neutral way, one that is not biased according to some philosophical or religious tradition such as Hinduism or Buddhism. But let me try to give a general definition.

Let's start with the word 'realization.' That word is ambiguous. One sense of that word means to become aware of, or, to comprehend something. I could say, for example, that I just realized that today is Sunday.

There's another meaning of realization, which has to do with achieving or accomplishing something. For example, one might say that by practicing a musical instrument, a young person is realizing one's potential. In this second case, we might say that someone is realizing one's self.

RA: How about the *self* that might be realized?

Michael: To start, you might say that a self is an agent that performs an action. But that doesn't get us very far. A number of questions arise there, also. Is the self an existing thing that embodies an essence? Or, is it no 'thing' at all? Is the self merely a grammatical subject? Clearly, we may find conflicting definitions that implicate opposing metaphysical accounts. Accordingly, one of the most revealing questions we might ask about self-realization is whether it involves addition or subtraction.

RA: What do you mean by addition or subtraction in this context?

Michael: An 'additive idea' of self-realization—in contrast to a 'subtractive idea'—involves specifying what it takes to become an educated, cultured person. That includes acquaintance with language, symbols systems, and other such skills. It includes an acquaintance with and acceptance of some values or other. These are things that, in growing up, one 'adds to' one's nature. For example, Bronwyn Davies and Rom Harré assert: "An individual emerges through the processes of social interaction, not as a relatively fixed end product but as one who is constituted and reconstituted through the various discursive practices in which they participate."[1] In contrast, a subtractive idea of self-realization involves erasing all of that, to arrive at an un-alloyed 'core' of the self—before enculturation. It involves unveiling the mantels of history and culture that occlude our experiences and awareness of who we essentially are. In any event, there seems to be a tension between these two ideas of realization. One concerns construction and the other concerns deconstruction, between affirmation and negation, between addition and subtraction.

RA: Say more about that.

Michael: You can take realization as a kind of building up—say, emotionally, or intellectually, or spiritually, wherein you're making more of yourself than when you started. Or, you can take self-realization as amounting to a kind of building down, or, deconstruction. Of course, these are stark oppositions.

RA: Given what you have said so far, I would think that you would categorize Advaitists as embracing a subtractive conception of self-realization. Am I right?

Michael: Yes. It would be subtractive insofar as it seeks deconstruction of the human self.

RA: But what guarantee is there that after such deconstruction, it is the Atman, the One—the unalloyed Source—that is revealed?

Michael: You have identified a question that has inhibited my embracing the orthodox Advaitic view, if I may call it that.

RA: I recall that in your book, *Limits of Rightness*, you talk about the constructed self. Presumably that means the constructed human self.

Michael: Yes. In that book I offered a constructivist notion of the human self.

---

1   Davies and Harré, "Positioning," 46.

RA: Can you summarize that constructivist notion?

Michael: Yes. I wanted to emphasize that when we tell the story about how we came to be the person we have become, we posit what might be called a 'narratized self.' That self, as the subject of the story, is a posit from the vantage point of the present speaker.

RA: So, the subject of the story is no inherent being but a construction of the presently told story. Is that right?

Michael: Yes. One postdictively postulates the self, the grammatical subject, which makes the narrative intelligible. The natures of selves are postdictive constructs of plausibly entertained present narratives.[2]

RA: So, how does your idea of the constructed self relate to the approaches taken by the Buddhist and the Advaitist?

Michael: For the Buddhist, 'self-realization' should not presuppose an inherently existing self. I agree with that. In turn, for the orthodox Advaitist, the individual self also does not exist *as such*. Yet it exists as an embodiment or manifestation of the 'Supreme Self.' And that Supreme Self, that One, exists inherently. Correspondingly, the Advaitist and Buddhist understand the idea of self-realization in different ways.

RA: Yet, insofar as the Advaitic Supreme Self is essentialist, I would think you would distance yourself from that view.

Michael: Not quite. As I've mentioned before, Advaitists might accept the description of the Atman, the Supreme Self, as inherently existing. Yet, they would add that it is beyond inherence or non-inherence, beyond essentialism or non-essentialism, beyond existence or non-existence, beyond all dualisms. So any initial rejection of the Supreme Self on the grounds that it is essentialist would no longer apply.

RA: That leads me to wonder about the idea of enlightenment. If you are so opposed to essentialism, what sense could you make of the idea of enlightenment? I don't see how one could embrace the idea of enlightenment without essentialism.

---

2 Krausz, *Limits of Rightness*, 144.

Michael: I allay that worry by introducing the idea of a regulative aim, where one might adopt an attitude of *as if* or *make believe*. Accordingly, one would assume the goal *as if* it were achievable and proceed in a pragmatic way, without assuming an essential or inherent Self.

RA: So, you are thoroughly anti-essentialist. At the same time, you do not foreclose something like the Advaitic Oneness–if, that is, you modify it in such a way as to render it not essentialist. You do that by casting it in a hypothetical mode. From a functional point of view that, at least to a degree, might alleviate the suffering and vicissitudes of human life. While valuing human being in a way that the orthodox Advaitist does not, the vision of Oneness, taken in a hypothetical way—an *as if* way—provides a measure of consolation for the human self. Is that a fair summary?

Michael: Yes. That's fair. And I came to that conclusion after witnessing what the more orthodox Advaitic understanding of Oneness actually did to one of Swamiji's devotees.

Andrea: So what did you see?

Michael: The devotee—whose name will remain anonymous—confided in me that she had achieved enlightenment. For her, that meant the dissolution of her human self. She also mentioned—rather ironically—that she had a *mixed reaction* to being without the burdens and challenges associated with being a human being.

RA: What was your reaction to that?

Michael: First, her remark, if true, would entail that for her, the 'I' that would have been liberated is no longer there. Now that would mean that liberation itself, as a human phenomenon, would no longer apply. Seen another way, the price of enlightenment is the loss of the human self. So the human self doesn't get enlightened. It is left behind. Of course, the orthodox Advaitist might respond that the human self never existed in the first place.

For me, her orthodox interpretation of "Thou art That," overshoots her aim. By that I mean that—should the process of realization succeed and displace the individual person to the Supreme Self in an effort to overcome human suffering—the very idea of liberation from such suffering would no longer apply. That is, the cost of such a liberation would be the dissolution of the human being altogether. One result of her supposed liberation involves the loss of her human self. And with that loss goes a renouncing of relationships with other human beings as well. In contrast, for me, liberation celebrates freedom *for* the human being, and not the dissolution *of* the human being. Her testimony confirmed my suspicion that a liberation *from* human being is not tantamount to liberation *for* human being.

Let me make my point in still another way. The promise for liberation of the human being prescribes the deconstruction of the human being. There would just be no human self there any more to receive the fulfillment of the initial promise. Finally, I am not surprised by the devotee's *mixed* reaction to her supposed liberation. For it signals that to some degree there is still a human being there. At least, that gives me hope for her.

RA: Could you say more about how the assertions and claims you encountered in Dharamsala and Kullu compare with your own philosophical views, especially your anti-essentialism and your humanism?

Michael: First, I need to make clear that my understanding of orthodox Advaita is filtered through my interactions at the ashram in Kullu. And my understanding of Buddhism is filtered through my conversations with Tibetan Buddhists, particularly with the Dalai Lama and Lobsang Gyatso in Dharamsala, and Geshe Ngawang Samten in Sarnath.[3]

RA: Still, I gather that your understanding must have been informed by your anti-essentialist orientation in your analytic philosophy.

Michael: Yes. In my analytic work, I embrace a thorough anti-essentialism. And you will see that that orientation is incongruent with the orthodox Advaitic view with regard to the Atman, the One. At the same time, the Atman is also said to be beyond characterization, beyond the sayable. That means that the Divine is thought to be beyond essentialism or non-essentialism.

RA: I'm puzzled. You are anti-essentialist all the way down. So, your personal affinity with the Advaitic view of the One seems odd in a way. It would seem that you would have to deny its status as 'essentialist.'

---

3   For further information, see Drakpa, *Ocean of Reasoning*; Srinivasa Rao, *Advaita*; and Ranganathananda, *Practical Vedanta and the Science of Values*.

Michael: You've put your finger on one of my philosophical challenges. Namely, how can I, an anti-essentialist, embrace something like the Divine if it is taken to be essentialist? The answer is, I cannot. So, either I disallow the Divine in my account, or, modify my understanding of it in such a way as to make it answerable to an anti-essentialist construal. Or, in turn, I might embrace the thought that, in this case, the essentialism versus non-essentialism issue is altogether misplaced, because it is a product of a vocabulary that is inappropriate when reflecting on the Divine.

RA: So, that leads me to wonder what attracted you to the Advaitic path.

Michael: For different reasons, I have found both the Dalai Lama and Swamiji to be compelling. Each, in his own distinctive way, exuded a spiritual energy and effulgence that I had never encountered before or since.

That's what brought me to Kullu and to Dharamsala. Upon reflection, it was both a matter of opportunity and the philosophical and spiritual challenge of it that led me to continue my inquiries into both Advaita and Tibetan Buddhism.

In regard to Buddhism, I found Lobsang Gyatso's tutorials intriguing and helpful as well. He was the founder of the Institute of Buddhist Dialectics in Dharamsala—very near to the Dalai Lama's residence—and a close associate of the Dalai Lama. He was a very clear scholar and a dear man.[4]

RA: You say 'was?'

Michael: Yes. In February of 1997, he was violently assassinated, along with two of his students.

RA: Who killed him? And why?

Michael: The initial suspicion was that it was done by the Chinese to send a message that the Dalai Lama, himself, was vulnerable. But that turned out not to be the case. The Indian police eventually determined that the murderers were connected with Dorje Shugden, a competing Buddhist faction.[5]

---

[4] For further reading on this subject, see Lobsang Gyatso, *The Four Noble Truths*; and *The Harmony of Emptiness and Dependent-Arising*.

[5] See Murder in a Monestary, by Newsweek Staff, *Newsweek*, 5/4/97; https://tinyurl.com/ybk9uutm.

RA: How did that affect you?

Michael: I have not returned to Dharamsala since Lobsang Gyatso was assassinated. But you are right to surmise that my philosophical affinities are more with the Buddhist, while my spiritual affinities are with a modified, non-orthodox Advaita.

RA: Did you have other close associations in the Tibetan Community?

Michael: The other close association in that regard was with Ven. Ngawang Samten, whom I already mentioned.

RA: So, how did all of this influence your trips to India?

Michael: I would continue my nearly annual trips to India, presenting papers at numerous universities, often managing to visit Swamiji as well. He would always receive me with extraordinary generosity of spirit, and would patiently respond to my questions and challenges.

As I've mentioned, I would try to modify his messages as they might apply to my own quest. In any event, since having met Swamiji in 1992, I had resonated with him, with a sense of self-recognition.

RA: Self-recognition?

Michael: Yes. Perhaps to a limited degree, Swamiji's vision of Oneness resonated with my own sense of Adoshem—a name for the Jewish God—notwithstanding my anti-essentialist biases.

RA: How does your understanding of Swamiji's version of Advaita Vedanta compare with your understanding Tibetan Buddhism?

Michael: As I understand them, Tibetan Buddhists embrace emptiness of inherent existence all the way down. All individuals are empty of inherent existence. No essentialist Atman appears in their ontology. As individuals we are not embodiments of a One that itself is un-characterizable. The Buddhist view is closer to my thoroughgoing non-essentialism.

RA: So how do you reconcile Tibetan Buddhism with Advaita Vedanta, at least as you understand them?

Michael: I am ambivalent. As I mentioned, I find Advaita to be more consoling, and I find Buddhism to be more philosophically perspicuous. Thus, philosophically, I'm more comfortable with the non-essentialism of the Buddhist principle of emptiness. On the other hand, while the Advaitic conception of Atman brings me a measure of solace, I have misgivings about that conception, at least as Swamiji sometimes presented it.

RA: Can you say more about your reservations about Swamiji's vision of Oneness—or at least what he has said about it? I guess I need to be careful here, because, as you have said before, what he said was geared to whom he was speaking and what he thought they needed to hear.

Michael: I'm glad that you ask with that proviso. My quandaries come down to understanding what the mantra, "Thou art That" really comes down to.

RA: What do you mean?

Michael: Consider the Advaitic mantra, "Thou art That," or its first person variant which Swamiji also featured: "I am I."

RA: Good. From a syntactic point of view, it seems like a curious utterance. What sense do you make of it?

Michael: You'll recall that I mentioned this puzzle when we first discussed my trips to India. The mantra is meant to invoke the ultimate truth that all individual persons are manifestations or embodiments of the Supreme Self, the One. Moreover, the One is both birthless and deathless. The One is 'pure, free, forever.' The grammatical strangeness of the utterance itself is meant to jog one into realizing that the individual person is an embodiment of something beyond itself that cannot be referred to directly. Thus, the utterance affirms the identity of the individual self with the Supreme Being.

RA: "The identity of the individual self with the Supreme Being?" Can you explain more about what that means?

Michael: In its strongest, or most orthodox version, it could mean that there are no individual selves, that only the One, the Supreme Being exists. In a softer version, it could mean individual selves are embodiments or manifestations of the Supreme Being. In both those cases, it can be taken as an assertion about the

SELF-REALIZATION

essential nature of the way things really are, including who we really and essentially are. Still taken as an assertion, that utterance looks like an essentialist claim.

In fact, at times, Swamiji categorically asserted, without reservation, that individuals—including persons—do not exist. When I first heard this, it seemed incredible, so completely counter intuitive. I asked Swamiji if individuals might at least *subsist*—in a way philosophically softer than existence. That is, I asked if there are degrees of existence. I wondered whether a distinction might be drawn between existence in a robust primary sense and subsistence in a secondary sense. That might allow us to concede at least a secondary place for humanity, in contrast to Swamiji's outright denial. That distinction might help accommodate the idea of embodiments of the One. As I saw it, embodiments would be afforded at least some existential standing.

RA: What did he say?

Michael: He flatly said, "No."

RA: Well, you must have given the idea more thought, yourself, didn't you? Is there any further benefit to your idea of subsistence?

Michael: Yes. While denial of full existence would foster a radical rejection of human beings, at least the allowance of subsistence would allow for the possibility of honoring human individuals to a degree.

RA: I'm struck by Swamiji's denial of human individuals. If no individuals exist, then persecution of individuals could not have occurred. What would he say about the Holocaust?

Michael: Actually, twice I asked him about that. The first time, he said that the Holocaust did not exist, because individual persons do not exist. The second time, he asked, "Who is asking?," which I took as a way to remind me that I am the One. That is all that would really matter.

By his redirecting my attention, the original question seemed to lose its urgency. Whether the Holocaust happened seemed to have no bearing on who I am. By recognizing who is asking, the question seemed to be short-circuited.

RA: How did you feel about that?

Michael: Curiously, his reply somewhat quieted my anger, my fear. Yet it did nothing to convince me that the Holocaust never happened.

RA: That sounds pretty extreme. Did you get the sense that he actually denied the existence of the Holocaust?

Michael: Again, I think that sometimes, he would say things for their effect on a devotee rather than to impart a belief that he literally believed to be true.

RA: It does seem that *you* want to assert the existence of the Holocaust, that human beings—including your grandparents—actually died in Auschwitz, and that that is a datum of your consciousness as a human being. Is that behind your thought?

Michael: Yes. That fact has been an enduring cloud in my life. Renouncing my grandparents' existence and cruel demise or renouncing my own humanness as a way to deal with that cloud is too much. Yet, that's not to say that I should not understand their existence as being empty of inherent existence.

RA: So, what do you think the Dalai Lama would say about that case?

Michael: I expect that the Dalai Lama would affirm that the Holocaust happened, and the Chinese suppression of Tibetans happened too, even while the perpetrators and victims need to be understood as non-inherent.

RA: I don't quite grasp the significance of that last qualifier. Can you say more about that?

Michael: Of course. As I've said, Buddhists embrace the thought that all that exists, is empty of inherent existence. That means it is empty of essences. For example, Lobsang Gyatso says that the fact that the thing that is before us now is a cup is not so because it embodies the form of cupness. Rather, it is a cup because we bring certain purposes and interests to it that makes it so. It allows us to drink water from it. In this way, it is endowed as a cup in virtue of its ability to satisfy certain purposes or interests. But there's nothing inherent that makes it a cup.

RA: Okay, I get that about the cup. What about the rest of what exists?

Michael: The Buddhist insight about the emptiness of inherent existence is generalized to everything that exists—including our individual selves. There is no such thing as an inherently existing self.

RA: So how does that differ from the Advaitic view?

Michael: Advaitists holds that our individual selves are embodiments of the inherently existing One. It is the Source and the basis of all that exists. So, in an ironic way, Advaitists could agree that individuals are empty of inherent existence, but they could do so because individuals do not exist. The only thing that exists—and exists inherently—is the One. Since Oneness *alone* exists—permanently and changelessly—personal identity does not exist.

RA: So what sense do you make of that?

Michael: For me, it's a question of embodiment. It is one thing to say that individuals are embodiments of the One. It is another thing to say that individuals do not exist at all. Sometimes, I heard Swamiji say that individuals do not exist. At other times, I heard him say that they are embodiments. The latter at least allows us to acknowledge that we do live in a causal world—which recognizes that we need to eat and sleep and protect our physical bodies.

RA: So, have you found any satisfactory way for you to modify the Advaitic view of Oneness in order to bring it into alignment with your non-essentialism?

Michael: Well, as I have indicated, Swamiji adds that the One is indescribable. That means that it is beyond any label, beyond either essentialism or non-essentialism. That's one way to avoid any difficulties about essentialism.

RA: Is there another way?

Michael: I think so. One could take the utterance "Thou art That," or "I am I" as no assertion at all, as neither true nor false.

RA: How might that work?

Michael: You could take it as a vehicle to displace one's preoccupations with one's human self—or, to at least to draw one's attention to a place beyond the human self. It could be taken as hortatory rather than descriptive.

RA: Is that how you see the mantra?

Michael: Yes. I have come to think that utterances like "Thou art That" or "I am I," could be taken not as assertions or descriptions of states of affairs, but rather as devices that put us in a non-ordinary state of no-thought, where there are no assertions or negations, no grammars or categories, no entanglements of the mind. Mantras may foster a meditative space.

RA: So, you see such utterances as transformative devices.

Michael: Yes. But to be effective, the mantric speech act[6]—at least to start with—might first depend upon tentatively accepting the supposition that an individual self does not exist.

RA: What then is the relationship between taking the speech act as a true assertion and taking it as a transformative vehicle? Can it be taken as both at the same time? Or, at different times?

Michael: We might need to take the speech act as expressing a provisional truth—as a hypothetical 'as if'—in order to take it as a transformative vehicle. Then, once taken as a transformative vehicle, the pertinence of its avowed truthfulness recedes. That isn't to say that one cannot revisit the question of its truth along the way.

RA: When we would do that, would we not be seeking consolations from the anxieties of the human condition?

Michael: That might be one way to do so. But in that regard, I am impressed by what philosopher Paul Thom has said about the relation of knowledge to consolation. He says:

> Consolation requires not knowledge but hope. A consoling message is not so much one that we know is true, as one that we hope will be fulfilled. We must believe fulfillment of the message to be possible. But belief in a possibility is a far cry from knowledge. The consolations offered by the great religions often concern matters about which no knowledge is possible, one way or the other. Precisely because we cannot know that their claims are false, we can cling to the hope that they may be realized ... You can try to make sense of death by telling a believable (but not knowable) story about its meaning, a story that gives us hope. Or, you can try to make sense of death by recounting all that is known about it, in a way that gives us understanding. But there need be no conflict between the two aims.

---

6   The theory of speech acts was first elucidated by John R. Searle; see his *Speech Acts*.

SELF-REALIZATION   213

> An attempt to provide consolation might come into conflict with an attempt to provide understanding, if for example it offered consolation on the basis of some proposition that can be known to be false. The consolation will be ineffective as soon as its recipient discovers that it is based on a falsehood. Such would-be consolers should ensure that they offer their wares only to the ignorant.
>
> But, so long as the recipient does not know that the basis of the consolation is false—even better, if that basis cannot be known to be false, because it is unfalsifiable—then no conflict occurs between consolation and understanding. I can know all to be known about death, and still take consolation from an interpretation that offers me hope, so long as that consolation is not based on falsifiable propositions. If knowledge offers me no hope, I derive hope from elsewhere.[7]

I agree with Thom. Clearly, speech acts have different aims in different contexts. Some speech acts may function in non-cognitive ways or in cognitive ways. Besides asserting, they may function in a metaphorical or mythical or hortatory way. So, the mantra, "Thou art That" or "I am I," may be either transformative or assertive. When taken transformatively, the mantra can be taken as an invitation, as in, "Be open to the mystery of the vastness," or, "Relax your preoccupations with human concerns," or "Be present for the One," or, "Do not dwell upon argumentation, justification or elucidation," or "Detach yourself from your ego concerns," or, "Seek the Divinity within you." These are invitations to adopt an attitude toward one's life experiences. These are performative utterances.[8] So understood such utterances invite an acceptance of an invitation of an attitude to a way of being. So understood, it is neither true nor false.

RA: Can you say more about the process of self-realization, especially about your view of human beings who would embark on the process of self-realization?

Michael: I do not regard human beings as non-existent or mundane. On the contrary, I regard human beings as fundamentally valuable. It is they who exercise choice. It is the human being who has purposes and interests. It is the human being who inquires. It is the human being who has doubts and questions. It is the human being who seeks solace. It is the human being who seeks realization. In this sense, it is the human being that holds the privileged, default position.

---

7   Paul Thom, "Constituents of Interpretation," 116.
8   On performative utterances, see Austin, *How to Do Things with Words*.

RA: Oh, I see. So, you oppose the view that consciousness itself might be taken to be the default, the place from which any account of realization should begin?

Michael: I leave that possibility open. Yet, I affirm the value of the individual human being as my default position, at least in matters of realization.[9] So, in such matters, the starting point is the individual human being who embarks on the process of self-realization.

RA: Okay, then. If—as a the orthodox Advaitist affirms—only the One exists and no individual human beings exist, it would follow that there would be no individual human beings to accept or reject the Advaitist view. Despite your affinity for Swamiji, your own philosophical inclinations sound different on doctrinal issues. Did you ever directly challenge his teachings?

Michael: On several occasions, I tried to ask what amounted to the questions you raise. But generally, he would not engage in speculations about the philosophy of language, for example. Theorizing about speech acts, for example, was not his concern. I took it that he meant primarily to displace our ordinary sense of our selves, to lead our attention to who 'we' essentially are—namely, that Being without ego, that egoless Self.

It was through a kind of iterative logic that he would replace the individual self with the Supreme Self as the default.

RA: You just used the phrase, 'iterative logic.' What is that?

Michael: Iterative logic is a kind of dialectical logic, which is displayed in uttering or chanting. As I say, it is deployed to alter—and presumably raise—the level of one's consciousness.

RA: How does that work?

Michael: Again, take the utterance, "I am I." As it stands, one might think that it is an uninteresting tautology, on a par with "A is A." But in this case something else is going on. Taken as a mantra, "I am I," amounts to "my individual human self is the Supreme Self." After one avowedly 'realizes' the truth that

---

9 See Samuel Scheffler, "Lecture 1: The Afterlife"; see also P.M.S. Hacker, "An Orrery of Intentionality" and "The Sad and Sorry History of Consciousness."

one's individual human self is the Supreme Self, the utterance turns out to be a report—an assertion—that one's individual self *is* the Supreme Self. In the first instance, the utterance is used to bring about a change in consciousness. And in the second instance, the utterance is deployed to report that such a transformation would have occurred.

RA: But what is going on when one realizes, as you say? I mean, how does saying so, or chanting so, make it so? How does the saying or chanting move one's consciousness so as to allow the realization that one's individual self is the Supreme Self?

Michael: It is a matter of recognition that—by removing the mantel of mental activity—we will recognize who we essentially are.

RA: But—and here is that old question—even if the chanting will bring us to another level of consciousness, how do we know that that new level of consciousness amounts to a recognition that we are the One, the Source, the Supreme Self? How do we know that involves a rise in consciousness?

Michael: You are right to raise that difficult question again. For now, all I mean to emphasize by invoking the phrase iterative logic, is the process in which by chanting a mantra such as "I am I," or, "I am That," and by focusing upon what is beyond ordinary mental human activities like believing, arguing, justifying and the like, we can place and find ourselves in a different level of consciousness. We might coax ourselves into a space that is free and unbounded.

Put another way, in the course of the speech act, "I am I," the referent of the 'I' will have shifted. Along with that shift goes a re-construal of who or what is speaking. In the process, human selves are being cajoled into shifting their self-awareness of who they really are.

RA: Suppose the repeated recitation, "I am I," would widen my 'field of vision' in that way. But that would not, in itself, get me to that innocent pure original place, would it? Might it not only get me to a more innocent frame or wider frame, but not to a perfect innocence or perfect field of vision?

Michael: But even if the result would never amount to a pure, original innocence, it remains that the retreat to relative innocence might help somewhat to relieve the burdens of ego domination. That would still be a lot.

RA: I understand that one aim of the iterative repetition of mantras is to alleviate or eliminate human suffering, especially the suffering associated with anxieties about old age, loneliness, and death. And I understand that realization of who I essentially am is meant to solve the problem of suffering. But isn't the question of who I essentially am different from the question of how to alleviate suffering? I mean, what if our suffering is alleviated by releasing ourselves from ego-domination? How would that tell me who I essentially am? How would it answer the question, "Who am I?." And, what if adopting that ontology is successful as a palliative, as reducing suffering? Is that a recommendation for the ontology as an ontology?

Michael: The Advaitist may well hold that engaging in ontology has no point unless it provides a means for reducing suffering. The Advaitist who discovers that embracing a given ontology is effective in alleviating suffering might hold that to be reason enough to embrace it.

Indeed, the Advaitist might go further by suggesting that, after a certain stage, even pursuing the question of ontological adequacy would occlude the effectiveness of its suffering-reducing power. The search for such truth might only deflect the effectiveness of the cure. Perhaps it would be best to accept Swamiji's advice: "Try it."

RA: Try it? What exactly would I be trying?

Michael: Of course, as an exercise of iterative logic, "I am I" may be taken as an utterance that is either true or false. That is, the mantra may be taken cognitively. Or, we may take it as neither true nor false, as non-cognitively. We can take it for its usefulness in shifting our attention from the human parade. It can be taken as an invocation, evocation, exhortation, a homiletic, or the like—such as, "see yourself as Divine!" In other words, they may be taken heuristically.

As I have surmised, Swamiji used language in unusual ways. Sometimes, he meant to use an utterance in a cognitive way when he affirms that individuals are embodiments of the One. On other occasions, he meant to conjure devotees to see themselves and experience themselves in different ways. He shifted between different aims when he spoke to different devotees or the same devotee on different occasions, depending upon what they need to hear.

Repetition of the mantras, "I am I," or "I am That," is meant to displace or replace the human speaker to the impersonal, cosmic, Supreme Self, the undifferentiated, Divine Being. In realizing one's true identity as the One, the speaker displaces its human individuality to 'realize' its true identity as the One. This iterative logic is meant to function as a vehicle toward enlightenment.

RA: After your interactions and studies in India, have you achieved some clarity about where you stand—if I may put it that way—about preserving the category of human being?

Michael: Yes, the orthodox Advaitic view holds that, what ultimately exists *is* the undifferentiated Being, the One. So, on that view, ultimately there can be no relations between individuals—human or otherwise—because there are no individuals between whom relations could occur.

I have become concerned with that view. I think the idea of Oneness needs to accommodate and honor—and not make mundane—the reality of human beings and their relations. Such relations are one of the blessings of life, my life, including my love for Connie.

RA: That's a significant accommodation, as you put it. So what is left of the Advaitic vision? I mean, once you allow that there may be non-mundane relations between human beings, what in Swamiji's vision do you honor?

Michael: While I privilege human being, I agree that we should not allow the parade of human affairs to overwhelm our consciousness.

RA: But wouldn't you agree that sometimes even attending to realization can be debilitating? Might it not lead your attention away from critical matters at the human level?

Michael: I agree. It depends upon circumstances. If you seek solace from death anxiety, attending to the vision of Oneness can be helpful. But if you are a surgeon, say, who must attend to careful diagnosis and precise incisions of a human body, then, concentration on the One might deflect practical attention from such critical activities. It depends upon your needs and your purposes. I leave open though whether one might function on dual tracks at the same time. After all, a musician may be mindful to play a particular note in tune while experiencing an at-one moment with his ensemble. Why not for the case of the surgeon?

RA: You suggested that Swamiji spoke of Oneness interchangeably with the Divine, the Pure, the Free, the Forever.

Michael: Yes. Swamiji also spoke of Oneness as Love. Of course, we often think of love as an emotion between human beings, or between a human being and pets or favored projects or the like. But that understanding of love does not accord with the idea of Oneness, because in Oneness there is no duality.

RA: I hear you saying that according to Swamiji, Divine Love is different from human love. Divine Love doesn't take any individuated object. It relates to no such object. So, what would Divine Love look like if one were to achieve it?

Michael: I am puzzled by the idea of Divine Love.

RA: At least might we think of Divine Love as achievable through a process of first embracing human love?

Michael: But the puzzle of Divine Love seems to me to arise from the more general view that if all that exists is the One, we could not speak of any relationship between the human and the Divine—for the very idea of a relationship is dualistic.

RA: I see. Without a differentiated intentional object—wouldn't undifferentiated Divine Love be no love at all?

Michael: Whatever it is, Divine Love is not what we have come to know by that word.

RA: Did you ask Swamiji about the more general question about the relation between the human and the Divine?

Michael: It was no surprise to me that when I asked about the relation between the human and the Divine—and I would ask that question numerous times in different ways—he would interrupt me. He would affirm that no relations exist, because only the One exists. When I would ask about love and the relations between lover and loved one, he would answer that only Love exists, that there is no relation between lover and loved one. He denied the realm of dualities.

RA: Perhaps he borrowed that word—love—the meaning of which is embedded in the human context, and recast it to serve as a bridge to consciousness of One.

Michael: Yes. That suggestion accords with what I have called his iterative logic.

RA: You've indicated that Swamiji said that the One you are is birthless and deathless. What thoughts do you have about death?

Michael: The best thing that I have heard about life after death was from a student of Collingwood, whose name was "Tom Brown" Stevens.[10] Many years ago, he reported to me that Collingwood had said, "if there is life after death, it must be so different from what we call 'life' that it is misleading to call it by that name."[11]

I have ruminated about Collingwood's remark for quite some time. Here is what I have come up with. First, Collingwood was not making a surface remark about the semantics of the word, 'death.' Rather, I imagine his having in mind a profound ontological point. Second, Collingwood leaves open the possibility that *something* might be going on after human death, and by implication, something before human birth. But as far as I know, he remained agnostic about what that might be. Since you asked, however, here are my own thoughts about death.

RA: Yes, I'd like to hear them.

Michael: Our anxiety about human death is connected with our anticipated loss of something, which is characteristically human, namely our sense of our individual self, our sense of what it is that makes us who we are, namely: our individuality. It is connected with what makes us the individual person we take ourselves to be.

Our anxiety is connected with our fear of loss of who or what we are, or what we take ourselves to be. In my case, that is the person that answers to the name Michael Krausz, or the philosopher, or the artist, or the musician, the teacher, the husband, the son, the brother—among a myriad of other roles. The list goes on for all of us human beings. If anything close to this thought is right, then there are significant consequences as to what might be appropriately said about the objects of our anxiety besides the concerns for our physical bodies

---

10   Personal communication, 1969. C.S. "Tom Brown" Stevens (1905–1976) was an Oxford historian, Fellow of Magdalen College, 1932–1972.
11   Collingwood might have thought something similar about Divine Love. If Divine Love is without duality, it must be so different from what we call human love, that it would be misleading to call it by that name.

as it inevitably deteriorates. I guess our anxiety about death concerns the deconstruction of our constructed self.

RA: But that, it seems, is what realization prescribes.

Michael: Perhaps, in an ironic way, in anticipation of one's human demise, one may wish to take some measure of control of that demise. Perhaps it is by rehearsing one's own death, by deconstructing one's individual 'I,' that one may affirm control of one's eventual death as one's body gives out. Perhaps that's what Swamiji meant when, on numerous occasions, he said, "I am already dead."

RA: That sounds consistent with the numerous occasions when he said that he is birthless and deathless.

Michael: The Advaitic assertion, "I am birthless and deathless" implies that who I ultimately and essentially am precedes bodily birth and continues after bodily death because ultimately only the One exists; human beings do not exist. Since human beings do not exist, the notions of 'birth' and 'death' do not apply. According to this vision, the recognition of who a human being essentially is involves not being a human being after all. It requires renouncing the category of human. In contrast, I suggest that inevitably, it is only as a human being that one can choose to pursue the path of realization.

RA: Among the things that have always attracted me to your philosophy are its sense of ecumenism and humanism.

Michael: Thank you. I welcome that term, humanism.

RA: OK. So how do you understand humanism? Can you explain what you take humanism to mean?

Michael: As I have indicated, my humanism arises from the thought that it is human beings who have purposes and interests. I have concluded that the conduct of inquiry—including inquiry as regards self-realization—inevitably depends upon the purposes and interests that human beings bring.

RA: Given your humanism, what, in the Advaitic tradition, as expressed in the mantra, "Thou art That," do you value?

Michael: I value the equanimity that it affords.

RA: How is that?

Michael: It's enough to simply suppose that "I am That" without believing it to be true. Just supposing it is enough to provide solace. There is no need to embrace the orthodox Advaitist's onto-theology as true to enter into the space of nonduality.

RA: I, too, gravitate more toward the attitude that encourages cultivation of the human being.

Michael: Indeed. How long can the denial of the human realm sustain itself while one is conscious of one's own bodily decline?

RA: And for someone who has renounced all relations, for someone who experiences no grief upon the death of a sibling, for someone who no longer has connections with friends and family, I would say such a person would have withdrawn from the realm of humanity.

Michael: Again, remember that the desire for solace from human suffering is a human interest to start with.

RA: So, your basic criticism of orthodox Advaita is that it rejects the human realm even though it is necessary for self-realization. Is that a fair summary of the difference between it and your humanism?

Michael: That's a provisional summary. But there is more.

RA: More? What do you have in mind?

Michael: Allow me to share a portion of a letter that I wrote to Swamiji on March 16, 2016, along with his reply. It is from the last letter I wrote to Swamiji before his death. At his suggestion, I had the opportunity to read it aloud to him at a *satsang*.

RA: Let's hear it.

Michael: Here it is:

Whomever it is that you are now addressing is moving between the individual Michael and the being who answers to the name Gyaan Swaroop. The first is involved with self-recognition. Yet, the achievement of that recognition at the same time displaces the very process of self-recognition, for recognition is a dualistic phenomenon which—if allowed to remain—inhibits the realization of the One. If I am on the right track, Michael recognizes that the realized Michael—the Gyaan Swaroop—is not in a position to recognize anything. Rather, in realization, there is a significant shift from a human individual to a transhuman Source, to which talk of self-recognition becomes inappropriate. I, Michael, am fully aware that the incommensurability between these voices—Michael and Gyaan Swaroop—lands me in a place of silence.

RA: What did he say when he heard this?

Michael: He said, "Your observation is correct."

Roots in the Air: A Postscript

My roots are like those of epiphytic plants. Rather than receiving their nourishment from a stationary ground, they are sustained by moisture and nutrients from the air. They have roots, but they are not grounded in a fixed place.

I take *roots in the air* as a metaphor—partial, of course—for several dimensions of my life. One dimension concerns my geographical displacements and locations—from Switzerland and America, to Canada, England and India, and many places in between.

Another dimension concerns my philosophical orientations with respect to culture and the human self. They include a kind of non-essentialism, a constructivism, a multiplism—all of which contribute to an attitude of impermanence or temporariness.

My non-essentialism permeates my treatments of interpretation and its ontologies. It runs through my treatments of creativity and self-realization. It runs through my attitudes about my Jewishness and my modified endorsements of Hinduism and Buddhism. My non-essentialism also runs through my modified humanism—one that invites a perpetual re-engagement and recommitment to the primacy of human being.

Yet certain incongruities remain. They concern an abiding recognition of a space of nonduality, one which affords consolation in regard to the vicissitudes of the human. In incalculable ways, my experiences of that space are reflected in the images in my art.

I look forward to furthering my investigations of these matters in the future. For now, I offer my story as an interim report. For I have come not to an end, but to a pause.

Michael Krausz

APPENDIX A

Chronology

1942

Born Geneva, Switzerland

1947

Emigrated to United States with parents, Laszlo and Susan, and brother Peter.

1960

Music: Organized and conducted the Youth Chamber Orchestra of Cleveland, first concert, Winter

1961–1962

Education: Entered Rutgers University, Philosophy Major

1963–1964

Education: General Courses student, London School of Economics and Political Science, J.O. Wisdom, Tutor; Instructors: Sir Karl Popper, Imre Lakatos, and Alan Musgrave

Music: Organized and conducted Ensemble Symphonique at Rutgers; strings with small choir; first concert in Kirkpatrick Chapel, May 9

1965

Education: BA, Philosophy, Rutgers University

1966

Education: MA, Philosophy, Indiana University, Thesis, "On Method in Metaphysics," Kenneth Schmitz, Supervisor

Appointment: Graduate Student Instructor in Philosophy, Glendon College, York University, Toronto

Article: "On Method in Metaphysics," *Rutgers Review*

1967

Appointment: Graduate Student Instructor in Philosophy, Glendon College, York University, Toronto

Appointment: Instructor, University of Toronto, Victoria College

1968
Education: Linacre College, Oxford, Patrick Gardiner, Tutor; Instructors: Isaiah Berlin, Rom Harré, Stephen Lukes, and Alan Montefiore
Article: "Popper and Wisdom on Method in Metaphysics," *Symposia*
Invited Lecture: Case Western Reserve University, Cleveland, OH

1969
Education: Linacre College, Oxford, Patrick Gardiner, Tutor; Instructors: Isaiah Berlin, Rom Harré, Stephen Lukes, and Alan Montefiore
Education: PhD, Philosophy, University of Toronto; Dissertation: "A Critique of R.G. Collingwood's Theory of Absolute Presuppositions," William H. Dray, Director
Appointment: Assistant Professor of Philosophy, Victoria College, University of Toronto
Appointment: Instructor, Trent University, Peterborough, Canada

1970
Appointment: Assistant Professor of Philosophy, Bryn Mawr College
Appointment: Instructor, Trent University, Peterborough, Canada
Invited Lecture: Swarthmore College, PA

1971
Appointment: Assistant Professor of Philosophy, Bryn Mawr College
Invited Lecture: University of Pennsylvania, Philadelphia
Epiphany: After which Krausz began to paint.[1]

1972
Appointment: Assistant Professor of Philosophy, Bryn Mawr College
Edited Volume: *Critical Essays on the Philosophy of R.G. Collingwood*
Chapter: "The Logic of Absolute Presuppositions," in *Critical Essays on...R.G. Collingwood.*
Art: Solo Exhibition, Provident National Bank, Bryn Mawr; Exhibition, Bryn Mawr College

1973
Appointment: Assistant Professor of Philosophy, Bryn Mawr College
Appointment: Visiting Assistant Professor of Philosophy, American University, Washington, DC
Article: "Relativism and Rationality," *American Philosophical Quarterly*

---

[1] See this volume, Chap. Five.

Art: Solo Exhibition, Bryn Mawr College; Solo Exhibition, Annenberg Center for Communication Arts and Sciences, University of Pennsylvania

1974

Appointment: Assistant Professor of Philosophy, Bryn Mawr College
Appointment: Visiting Assistant Professor of Philosophy, American University, Washington, DC
Article: "Popper's Objective Knowledge," *Dialogue*
Invited Lectures: American University, Washington, DC; Bryn Mawr Graduate School of Social Work and Social Research
Art: Solo Exhibition, Lawrence Gallery, Rosemont, PA; Solo Exhibition, Gulbenkian Gallery, Canterbury, England; Solo Exhibition, Jane Weiss Gallery, Cleveland, OH; Exhibition, Washington County Museum of Fine Arts, Hagerstown, MD

1975

Appointment: Assistant Professor of Philosophy, Bryn Mawr College
Invited Lectures: Hood College, Frederick, MD; Union College, Schenectady, NY
Art: Solo Exhibition, Tatem Arts Center, Frederick, MD; Solo Exhibition, Talbot Rice Arts Centre, Edinburgh, Scotland; Solo Exhibition, Dimock Gallery, Washington, DC

1976

Appointment: Associate Professor of Philosophy, Bryn Mawr College
Invited Lectures: Bryn Mawr College History of Art Colloquium; Conference on Value Theory, State University of New York at Geneseo; Fullerton Club at Bryn Mawr; Bryn Mawr College Seminar on the Limits of Growth; Villanova University, PA

1977

Appointment: Associate Professor of Philosophy, Bryn Mawr College
Appointment: Visiting Professorial Lecturer of Philosophy, Georgetown University, Washington, DC
Fellowship: Andrew W. Mellon Fellow, Aspen Institute for Humanistic Studies
Invited Lectures: Bryn Mawr College Graduate Philosophy Colloquium; Seven Sisters College Alumni Association; Aspen Institute for Humanistic Studies

1978

Appointment: Associate Professor of Philosophy, Bryn Mawr College
Appointments: Visiting Professor of Philosophy, Hebrew University of Jerusalem; Visiting Professorial Lecturer of Philosophy, Georgetown University

Fellowships: Resident Fellow, Ossabaw Foundation
Invited Lectures: Hollins College, Roanoke, VA; Van Leer Foundation, Hebrew University of Jerusalem; Tel Aviv University; Society for the Philosophy of Creativity, American Philosophical Association, Washington, DC
Art: Exhibition, Studio Gallery, Washington, DC

1979

Appointment: Associate Professor of Philosophy, Bryn Mawr College
Appointment: Visiting Professorial Lecturer of Philosophy, Georgetown University
Chapter: "Vision, Creation, and Object," in *Proceedings of the 10th Conference on Value Theory*
Invited Lecture: Bryn Mawr College Association of International Students
Art: Exhibition, Comfort Gallery, Haverford College

1980

Appointment: Associate Professor of Philosophy, Bryn Mawr College
Appointment: Distinguished Visiting Professor of Philosophy, American University in Cairo
Co-founder: Greater Philadelphia Philosophy Consortium (GPPC)
Fellowship: Resident Fellow, Ossabaw Foundation
Articles: "Historical Explanation, Re-enactment, and Practical Inference," *Metaphilosophy*; "A Painter's View of Self-Development and Creativity," *Leonardo*
Invited Lectures: Yale University; American University in Cairo; Cairo University
Art: Exhibition, Arlington Arts Center, Arlington, VA; Exhibition, Gross-McCleaf Gallery, Philadelphia

1981

Appointment: Associate Professor of Philosophy, Bryn Mawr College
Appointment: Haverford College (Faculty Exchange with Bryn Mawr College)
Edited Volume: *The Concept of Creativity in Science and Art*
Chapters: "Ferrater Mora's Continuum," in *Transparencies: Philosophical Essays in Honor of J. Ferrater Mora*; "Creating and Becoming," in *The Concept of Creativity in Science and Art*
Article: "On a Painter's View of Self-Development and Creativity" and Rejoinders to David Carrier, Larry Briskman, John Broyer, James Munz, and Joan Novosel-Beitel, *Leonardo*
Invited Lectures: Fourth International Conference on Culture and Communications, Temple University; Bryn Mawr College Symposium on the Philosophy of Jose Ferrater Mora
Art: Solo Exhibition, Barbara Fiedler Gallery, Washington, DC

1982
Appointment: Associate Professor of Philosophy, Bryn Mawr College
Appointment: Haverford College (Faculty Exchange with Bryn Mawr College)
Edited Volume: *Relativism: Cognitive and Moral*
Invited Lectures: Society for the Philosophy of Creativity, American Philosophical Association, Baltimore, MD; Bryn Mawr College
Music: Formed the Celebration Chamber Orchestra. Premier concert at Ethical Society Hall on Rittenhouse Square, Philadelphia, October 17

1983
Appointment: Acting Chair, Philosophy Department, Bryn Mawr College
Invited Lectures: Conferences on the Philosophy of the Human Studies, Villanova University; Haverford College; American Society for Aesthetics, Pacific Grove, CA; American Society for Aesthetics, Montreal
Music: Attended Murray Sidlin's conducting workshop at Aspen Music Festival

1984
Appointment: Professor of Philosophy, Bryn Mawr College
Articles: "Relativism and Foundationalism," *The Monist*; "The Tonal and the Foundational," *The Journal of Aesthetics and Art Criticism*; "Product and Progress in Artistic Creativity," *Kultura*
Invited Lecture: Greater Philadelphia Philosophy Consortium
Music: Co-founder, the Philadelphia Chamber Orchestra (PCO); President of the Board and Associate Artistic Director

1985
Appointment: Professor of Philosophy, Bryn Mawr College
Appointment: Visiting Professor of Philosophy, University of Nairobi
Invited Lectures: Kenyatta University College, Nairobi; Faculty Seminar on Interpretation, Bryn Mawr College; Williams College, Williamstown, MA
Music: Co-founder, the Philadelphia Chamber Orchestra (PCO); President of the Board and Associate Artistic Director

1986
Appointment: Professor of Philosophy, Bryn Mawr College
Appointment: Visiting Senior Member, Linacre College, Oxford
Edited Volume: *Rationality, Relativism, and the Human Sciences*
Chapter: "Art and Its Mythologies," in *Rationality, Relativism, and the Human Sciences*
Articles "Intentionality, Expressive Properties, and Popper's Placement of Music," *Internacional de Filosofia*;

Invited Lectures: Boston University; Greater Philadelphia Philosophy Consortium Workshop; University of Edinburgh; University of Helsinki; University of Essex, Colchester, England; University of Oxford; Villanova University

Music: Co-founder, the Philadelphia Chamber Orchestra (PCO); President of the Board and Associate Artistic Director; premier concert, April 27

Art: Exhibition, Delaware Center for Contemporary Arts, Wilmington; Exhibition, Dimock Gallery

1987

Appointment: Professor of Philosophy, Bryn Mawr College

Appointment: Visiting Senior Member, Linacre College, Oxford Invited Lectures: American Society for Aesthetics (Eastern Division), Rochester, NY; American University, Washington, DC; University of Oxford; University of Warwick, Coventry, England; University of Sussex, Brighton, England; Biotechnology Symposium, Bryn Mawr College

Music: Co-founder, the Philadelphia Chamber Orchestra (PCO); President of the Board and Associate Artistic Director; concert, October 25

1988

Appointment: Professor of Philosophy, Bryn Mawr College

Appointment: Visiting Senior Member, Linacre College, Oxford

Appointment: Research Associate, Linacre College, Oxford

Convener: Seminars on Philosophy of Music, University of Oxford

Participant: NEH Summer Institute: Interpretation in the Sciences and Humanities, University of California, Santa Cruz. Instructors: Stanly Cavell, Hubert Dreyfus, Clifford Geertz, David Hoy, Thomas Kuhn, Alexander Nehamas, Richard Rorty, Charles Taylor

Invited Lecture: Greater Philadelphia Philosophy Consortium, Workshop, Drexel University, Philadelphia

1989

Appointment: Professor of Philosophy, Bryn Mawr College

Appointment: Co-Instructor (with Bimal Matilal), All Souls College, Oxford University

Appointment: Visiting Senior Member, Linacre College, Oxford

Edited Volume: *Relativism: Interpretation, and Confrontation*

Chapters: "Mahler's Superstition," "Conducting Wagner," and "Beethoven's First Symphony," in *Puzzles about Art: An Aesthetics Casebook*; Introduction to *Relativism: Interpretation, and Confrontation*

Convener and Chair: Alumni NEH Institute on Interpretation, Philadelphia

Invited Lectures: University of Connecticut; Alumni NEH Institute on Interpretation, Philadelphia; American Society for Aesthetics, Eastern Division, The University of the Arts, Philadelphia; University of Oxford; University College, University of London; University of Lancaster, England; University of Bristol, England; Conference on the Philosophy of R.G. Collingwood, Trent University, Peterborough, Ontario, Canada; American Society for Aesthetics, New York City

1990

Appointment: Professor of Philosophy, Bryn Mawr College
Appointment: Visiting Senior Member, Linacre College, Oxford
Article: "Interpretation and Its Art Objects," *The Monist*
Invited Lectures: Institute of Pennsylvania Hospital, Philadelphia; State University of New York at Purchase; University of Cambridge, England

1991

Appointment: Milton C. Nahm Professor of Philosophy, Bryn Mawr College
Chapters: "Crossing Cultures," in *Cultural Relativism*; "Ideality and Ontology in the Practice of History," and Addendum, in *Objectivity, Method, and Point of View*
Articles: "History and Its Objects," *The Monist*
Invited Lectures: Swarthmore College, PA; American Society for Aesthetics, Eastern Division, Fredericksburg, VA; Conference on the Future of "Theory" in Social Theory, Temple University, Philadelphia; Bryn Mawr College; Greater Philadelphia Philosophy Consortium, Villanova University
Art: Solo Exhibition, Back Porch Cafe Gallery, Rehoboth, DE

1992

Appointment: Milton C. Nahm Professor of Philosophy, Bryn Mawr College
Appointment: Visiting Professor of Philosophy, Indian Institute of Advanced Study, Shimla, India
Chapter: "Intention and Interpretation: Hirsch and Margolis," in *Intention and Interpretation*
Invited Lectures: Hebrew University of Jerusalem; Tel Aviv University; Hong Kong University; Jadavpuhr University, Calcutta; Utkal University, Bhubaneshwar, India; University of Bombay; Humanities Institute, University of Michigan; Chaing Mai University, Thailand; Conference on Relativism and Interpretation, Temple University; Bryn Mawr College
Audiences: First audience with the Dalai Lama; First of numerous meetings with Swami Shyam Srivastava
Art: Solo Exhibition, Bryn Mawr College

1993

Appointment: Milton C. Nahm Professor of Philosophy, Bryn Mawr College
Appointment: Chair, Philosophy Department, Bryn Mawr College
Authored Volume: *Rightness and Reasons*
Edited Volumes: *The Interpretation of Music*; *Jewish Identity*
Chapters: Introduction, and "Rightness and Reasons in Musical Interpretation," in *The Interpretation of Music*; "On Being Jewish" and "The Culture of Identity," in *Jewish Identity*
Articles: "Culture and the 'Ontology' of Music," *Iyyun*;
Invited Lectures: University of South Florida, Tampa; American Society for Aesthetics, Eastern Division, Rhode Island School of Design, Providence; Rajasthan University, Jaipur, India; International Meditation Institute, Kullu, India; Tribhuvan University, Kathmandu, Nepal; American Society for Aesthetics, Santa Barbara, CA
Art: Solo Exhibition, Tatem Arts Center; Rehoboth Art League

1994

Appointment: Milton C. Nahm Professor of Philosophy, Bryn Mawr College
Invited Lectures: Greater Philadelphia Philosophy Consortium, Haverford College, PA; Curtis Institute of Music, Philadelphia; Interlocutors, University of Pennsylvania; Society for Philosophy in the Contemporary World, Estes Park, CO; American Society for Aesthetics, Charleston, SC; Penn State University, University Park
Art: Solo Exhibition, Rehoboth Art League; Exhibition, Carspecken-Scott Gallery, Wilmington, DE

1995

Appointment: Milton C. Nahm Professor of Philosophy, Bryn Mawr College
Article: "Three Meditations on Oneness." *Journal of the Indian Council of Philosophical Research*
Invited Lectures: University of Pennsylvania; Bryn Mawr College, Art History Department; Jefferson Medical College, Philadelphia; Society for Philosophy in the Contemporary World, Estes Park; St. Andrews School, Middletown, DE; Penn State University, Media; University of Ulm, Germany; University of Michigan; University of Pennsylvania
Audience: Second audience with the Dalai Lama
Art: Solo Exhibition, Penn State University, Media; Exhibition, Rehoboth Art League; Exhibition, Sussex County Arts Council, Lewes, DE

1996

Appointment: Milton C. Nahm Professor of Philosophy, Bryn Mawr College
Authored Volume: *Varieties of Relativism* (with Rom Harré)

Articles: "Interview with Ven. Lobsang Gyatso," and "On the Idea of the Single Right Interpretation in History." *Journal of Indian Philosophy and Religion*

Invited Lectures: Hampshire College, Amherst, MA; Conference on Population, Environment, and Development, Tata Energy and Resources Institute, Washington, DC; Institute of Buddhist Dialectics, Dharamsala, India; Saint Andrews School, Middletown; Beas Foundation Seminars on Philosophy and Development, University of Pennsylvania; Greater Philadelphia Philosophy Consortium; Art History Department, Bryn Mawr College; Beas Foundation Seminars on Philosophy and Development, Tata Energy Research Institute, New Delhi;

Art: Solo Exhibition, Gallery 10, Washington, DC; Solo Exhibition, Hampshire College, Amherst, MA; Solo Exhibition, Blue Moon Restaurant Gallery, Rehoboth; Rehoboth Art League; Exhibition, Sussex County Arts Council, Lewes

1997

Appointment: Milton C. Nahm Professor of Philosophy, Bryn Mawr College

Appointment: Visiting Senior Member, Linacre College, Oxford

Conference Director: Beas Foundation Seminars, "Human Rights, Asian Values and Civil Society," Bryn Mawr College and India International Centre (New Delhi)

Chapters: "Relativism and Beyond: In Tribute to Bimal Matilal," in *Relativism, Suffering, and Beyond*; "Choosing What One Is Cut Out To Be," in *Epistemology, Meaning, and Metaphysics after Matilal*; "Changing One's Mind, Changing One's Emotions," in *Philosophy from an Intercultural Perspective*

Articles: "The Interpretation of Art: Comments on Multiplism and Relativism," *JTLA*; "Interview with Ven. Lobsang Gyatso," *Journal of Indian Philosophy and Religion*; "Rightness and Reasons: A Reply to Stecker," *Journal of Aesthetics and Art Criticism*

Invited Lectures: The International Development Ethics Association, Madras, India; Society of Intercultural Philosophy, International Institute for Advanced Study, Kyoto; Philadelphia Psychoanalytic Society, Villanova University; University of Vienna; Collingwood Society, Oxford; Conference on Relativism, Society for Indian Philosophy and Religion, Calcutta; Society for Philosophy in the Contemporary World, Estes Park; University of Bremen, Germany; Queens University, Ontario, Canada; University of Toronto

Honors: The Hans Kupczyk Gastprofessur Lecture and Award, University of Ulm, Germany; The David Norton Memorial Lecture, University of Delaware

Art: Solo Exhibition, Blue Moon Restaurant Gallery; Exhibition, Nexus Gallery, Philadelphia; Exhibition, Rehoboth Art League

1998

Appointment: Milton C. Nahm Professor of Philosophy, Bryn Mawr College

Appointment: Visiting Senior Member, Linacre College, Oxford

Appointment: Visiting Fellow, University of Delhi, Centre for the Study of Developing Societies

Conference Director: Beas Foundation Seminars, "Human Rights, Asian Values and Civil Society," Bryn Mawr College and India International Centre (New Delhi)

Invited Lecture: The Elton Lecture at George Washington University, Washington, DC

Articles: "Two Aims of Cultural Interpretation: Explaining and Healing," *Studien zur interkulturellen Philosophie*; "Interpretation," *The Encyclopedia of Aesthetics*

Invited Lectures: Beas Foundation Seminar, India International Centre, New Delhi; Mohile Parikh Centre, Bombay; Ithaca College, Ithaca, NY; World Congress of Philosophy, Boston; Society for Philosophy in the Contemporary World, American Philosophical Association, Washington, DC

Art: Solo Exhibition, Yum Yum Restaurant Gallery, Rehoboth (2); Solo Exhibition, Peninsula Gallery, Lewes; Exhibition, Rehoboth Art League

1999

Appointment: Milton C. Nahm Professor of Philosophy, Bryn Mawr College

Edited Volume: *Interpretation, Relativism, and the Metaphysics of Culture: Themes in the Philosophy of Joseph Margolis*

Chapter: "Interpretation, Relativism, and Culture: Four Questions for Margolis," in *Interpretation, Relativism, and the Metaphysics of Culture*

Invited Lectures: Ninth Refresher Course in the Philosophy of Science, Jadavpuhr University, Calcutta; History of Art Colloquium, Bryn Mawr College; The Sudhakar Chattopadhyay Memorial Lecture, Visva-Bharati University, Shantiki Neketan, India; Jadavpuhr University, Calcutta; Central Institute for Advanced Buddhist Studies, Sarnath, India; University of Delhi; University of Pune, India; Society for Philosophy in the Contemporary World, Estes Park

Music: Conducted Pleven Symphony Orchestra, Bulgaria

Art: Exhibition, Rehoboth Art League; Exhibition, Touchstone Gallery, Washington, DC

2000

Appointment: Milton C. Nahm Professor of Philosophy, Bryn Mawr College

Authored Volume: *Limits of Rightness*

Article: "Interpretation and Its 'Metaphysical' Entanglements," *Metaphilosophy*

Invited Lectures: Curtis Institute of Music; University of Bucharest

Music: Conducted Pleven Symphony Orchestra, Bulgaria

Art: Solo Exhibition, Sugar and Spice, Lewes; Solo Exhibition, Edward Carter Gallery, Lewes; Rehoboth Art League; Exhibition, Canaday Gallery, Bryn Mawr College

CHRONOLOGY   235

2001

Appointment: Milton C. Nahm Professor of Philosophy, Bryn Mawr College
Invited Lectures: Society for Philosophy in the Contemporary World, Santa Fe, New Mexico; Smith College, Northampton, MA; Center for the Study of Visual Culture, Bryn Mawr College; Special Sessions on *Limits of Rightness*: International Development Ethics Association meeting held at the American Philosophical Association, Eastern Division, Atlanta, GA
Honor: Subject of Four-Day International Conference, University of Delhi
Music: Conducted Vratsa Philharmonic Orchestra, Bulgaria
Art: Solo Exhibition, Canaday Gallery, Bryn Mawr College
Art: Exhibition, Cloud Nine Restaurant, Rehoboth Beach; Exhibition, Nassau Valley Vineyards Gallery, Lewes

2002

Appointment: Milton C. Nahm Professor of Philosophy, Bryn Mawr College
Appointment: Instructor, Aesthetics, Curtis Institute of Music
Edited Volume: *Is There A Single Right Interpretation?*
Chapters: Introduction, and "Interpretation and Its Objects," in *Is There a Single Right Interpretation?*
Article: "Making Music: Beyond Intentions," *The Linacre Journal*
Invited Lectures: American Philosophical Association, Pacific Division, Seattle, WA (March); Greater Philadelphia Philosophy Consortium; Curtis Institute of Music; American Society for Aesthetics, Coral Gables, FL
Music: Conducted Plovdiv Philharmonic Orchestra, Bulgaria
Art: Solo Exhibition, Edward Carter Gallery, Lewes; Exhibition, Rehoboth Art League (2); Exhibition, The Artists' Museum, Washington, DC

2003

Appointment: Milton C. Nahm Professor of Philosophy, Bryn Mawr College
Review Panelist: Andrew W. Mellon Foundation, Emeritus Fellowship Program
Chapters: "Interpretation and Its Objects," and "Replies and Reflections," in *Interpretation and Its Objects*
Invited Lectures: University of Delhi; Conference on Philosophy, Interpretation, and Culture, SUNY Binghamton; Bryn Mawr College; McDaniel College, Westminster, MD; Jadavpuhr University, Calcutta; Hyderbad University, India; Delhi University; Indian Society for Art and Aesthetics, Delhi; Institute for Advance Buddhist Studies, Sarnath, India
Honors: Festschrift: *Interpretation and Its Objects: Studies in the Philosophy of Michael Krausz*, ed. Andreea Deciu Ritivoi; Annual Fellowship Lecture Tour, Indian Council of Philosophical Research

Music: Organized and conducted Conservatory Symphony Orchestra, Bryn Mawr College, February 18
Art: Solo Exhibition, Visual Arts Gallery; Solo Exhibition, Lavinia Street Gallery, Milton, DE; Zwaanendael Gallery, Lewes; Peninsula Gallery, Lewes

2004

Appointment: Milton C. Nahm Professor of Philosophy, Bryn Mawr College
Appointment: Instructor, Aesthetics, Curtis Institute of Music
Article: "Note on an Alleged Mistake in the Interpretation of Collingwood," *Collingwood and British Idealism Studies*
Review Panelist: Andrew W. Mellon Foundation, Emeritus Fellowship Program
Invited Lectures: Conference on the Philosophy of Donald Davidson and Chinese Philosophy, University of Beijing; Institute of Philosophy, The Chinese Academy of Social Sciences, Beijing
Music: Conducted Plovdiv Philharmonic Orchestra
Art: Exhibition, Rehoboth Art League; Exhibition, The Art League of Ocean City Center for the Arts, MD; Exhibition, Nassau Valley Vineyards Gallery, Lewes

2005

Appointment: Milton C. Nahm Professor of Philosophy, Bryn Mawr College
Review Panelist: Andrew W. Mellon Foundation, Emeritus Fellowship Program
Article: "Replies: Interpretation and Codes of Culture," *Philosophy in the Contemporary World*
Invited Lectures: Johns Hopkins University, Baltimore, MD; Society for Philosophy in the Contemporary World (Double Session), Western Carolina University, Cullowhee, NC; John Carroll University, University Heights, OH; Delhi University: St. Stephen's College, New Delhi
Honor: "Interpretation and Culture: Themes in the Philosophy of Michael Krausz." Special issue, *Philosophy in the Contemporary World*
Music: Artistic Director and Conductor, Great Hall Chamber Orchestra, Bryn Mawr
Art: Solo Exhibition, Tatem Arts Center

2006

Appointment: Milton C. Nahm Professor of Philosophy, Bryn Mawr College
Appointment: Instructor, Aesthetics, Curtis Institute of Music
Review Panelist: Andrew W. Mellon Foundation, Emeritus Fellowship Program
Chapter: "Relativism and Its Schemes," in *Philosophical Engagement*
Invited Lectures: American Philosophical Association, Pacific Division (Author Meets Critics), Portland, OR; Society for Philosophy in the Contemporary World
Music: Artistic Director and Conductor, Great Hall Chamber Orchestra, Bryn Mawr

Art: Exhibition, Rehoboth Art League; Exhibition, Academy Art Museum, Easton, MD; Exhibition, Delaware Center for Contemporary Art, Wilmington

2007

Appointment: Milton C. Nahm Professor of Philosophy, Bryn Mawr College
Review Panelist: Andrew W. Mellon Foundation, Emeritus Fellowship Program
Authored Volume: *Interpretation and Transformation*
Invited Lecture: J.P. College, Delhi University
Music: Artistic Director and Conductor, Great Hall Chamber Orchestra, Bryn Mawr
Art: Exhibition, Biggs Museum of American Art, Wilmington; Exhibition, Rehoboth Art League

2008

Appointment: Milton C. Nahm Professor of Philosophy, Bryn Mawr College
Appointment: Instructor, Aesthetics, Curtis Institute of Music
Review Panelist: Andrew W. Mellon Foundation, Emeritus Fellowship Program
Invited Lectures: American Philosophical Association, Pacific Division (Author Meets Critics), Pasadena, CA; Jawaharlal Nehru University, Delhi; Society for Philosophy in the Contemporary World, Eastern Division, American Philosophical Association; University of Ottawa, Canada; Carnegie-Mellon University, Pittsburgh
Music: Artistic Director and Conductor, Great Hall Chamber Orchestra, Bryn Mawr
Art: Solo Exhibition, Philip Morton Gallery, Rehoboth

2009

Appointment: Milton C. Nahm Professor of Philosophy, Bryn Mawr College
Review Panelist: Andrew W. Mellon Foundation, Emeritus Fellowship Program
Edited Volume: *The Idea of Creativity*
Chapters: Introduction, and "Creativity and Self-Transformation," in *The Idea of Creativity*
Invited Lecture: Jawaharlal Nehru University, Delhi
Music: Artistic Director and Conductor, Great Hall Chamber Orchestra, Bryn Mawr
Art: Awarded Master by Delaware by Hand; Solo Exhibition, Rehoboth Art League; Exhibition, Peninsula Gallery, Lewes

2010

Appointment: Milton C. Nahm Professor of Philosophy, Bryn Mawr College
Appointment: Instructor, Aesthetics, Curtis Institute of Music
Review Panelist: Andrew W. Mellon Foundation, Emeritus Fellowship Program
Edited Volume: *Relativism: A Contemporary Anthology*
Chapters: Introduction, and "Mapping Relativisms," in *Relativism*

Invited Lectures: Panjab University, Chandigarh, India; Greater Philadelphia Philosophy Consortium, College of New Jersey
Music: Artistic Director and Conductor, Great Hall Chamber Orchestra, Bryn Mawr
Art: Exhibition, "Delaware by Hand Masters," Peninsula Gallery, Lewes; Biennial Regional Show, Rehoboth Art League; Exhibition, Best of Beach Art Auction, Beebe Medical Center, Lewes

2011

Appointment: Milton C. Nahm Professor of Philosophy, Bryn Mawr College
Review Panelist: Andrew W. Mellon Foundation, Emeritus Fellowship Program
Authored Volume: *Dialogues on Relativism, Absolutism, and Beyond: Four Days in India*
Chapter: "Varieties of Relativism and the Reach of Reasons," in *A Companion to Relativism*
Invited Lecture: Panjab University
Music: Artistic Director and Conductor, Great Hall Chamber Orchestra, Bryn Mawr
Art: Best of Beach Art Auction, Beebe Medical Center, Lewes; Exhibition, Gallery 50, Rehoboth; Exhibition, Rehoboth Art League; Exhibition, Offices of Senator Chris Coon, Washington, DC

2012

Appointment: Milton C. Nahm Professor of Philosophy, Bryn Mawr College
Appointment: Instructor, Aesthetics, Curtis Institute of Music
Appointment: Co-Chair, Philosophy Department, Bryn Mawr College (Fall)
Review Panelist: Andrew W. Mellon Foundation, Emeritus Fellowship Program
Articles: "About My Art," *American Society for Aesthetics Newsletter*; "Relativisms and Their Ontologies," *Encyclopedia of Philosophy and the Social Sciences*
Invited Lecture: University of Utrecht, The Netherlands
Music: Artistic Director and Conductor, Great Hall Chamber Orchestra, Bryn Mawr
Art: Exhibition, Biennial Regional Show, Rehoboth Art League; Solo Exhibition, Gallery 50

2013

Appointment: Milton C. Nahm Professor of Philosophy, Bryn Mawr College
Review Panelist: Andrew W. Mellon Foundation, Emeritus Fellowship Program
Authored Volume: *Oneness and the Displacement of Self*
Invited Lecture: Central University of Tibetan Studies, Sarnath, India
Art: Solo Exhibition, Gallery 50; Solo Exhibition, Pairings Show, Rehoboth Art League; Exhibition, Biggs Museum of American Art

2014

Appointment: Milton C. Nahm Professor of Philosophy, Bryn Mawr College
Appointment: Instructor, Aesthetics, Curtis Institute of Music
Review Panelist: Andrew W. Mellon Foundation, Emeritus Fellowship Program
Chapter: "Bernard Harrison's 'World,'" In *Reality and Culture* Articles: "A Reply to Vaidya," *Comparative Philosophy*
Invited Lecture: "Relativism as Opposed to What?" Conference entitled *The Coherence of Relativism*, University of Bonn
Music: Artistic Director and Conductor, Great Hall Chamber Orchestra, Bryn Mawr
Art: Gallery 50

2015

Appointment: Milton C. Nahm Professor of Philosophy Emeritus, and Research Professor of Philosophy, Bryn Mawr College
Review Panelist: Andrew W. Mellon Foundation, Emeritus Fellowship Program
Invited Talk: Panjab University
Invited Lecture: 38th International Wittgenstein Symposium, Kirchberg, Austria
Honor: Awarded "Master," Delaware by Hand
Art: Exhibition, Rehoboth Art League Gala

2016

Appointment: Milton C. Nahm Professor of Philosophy Emeritus, and Research Professor of Philosophy, Bryn Mawr College
Review Panelist: Andrew W. Mellon Foundation, Emeritus Fellowship Program (2003–2016)
Art: Solo Exhibition, Gallery 50; Exhibition, Peninsula Gallery, Lewes; Exhibition, Rehoboth Art League

2017

Appointment: Milton C. Nahm Professor of Philosophy Emeritus, and Research Professor of Philosophy, Bryn Mawr College
Appointment: Adjunct Fellow, Linacre College, University of Oxford, UK
Appointment: Adjunct Member, Philosophy Department, Panjab University
Chapter: "Relativisms and Their Opposites," in *Realism—Relativism—Constructivism*

2018

Appointment: Milton C. Nahm Professor of Philosophy Emeritus, and Research Professor of Philosophy, Bryn Mawr College
Appointment: Adjunct Fellow, Linacre College, University of Oxford, UK
Honor: Festschrift: *Interpretation, Identity, and Relativism: Essays on the Philosophy of Michael Krausz*, edited by Chistine Koggel and Andreea Deciu Ritivoi

APPENDIX B

Select Bibliography of Michael Krausz

"On Method in Metaphysics." Rutgers Review (Winter 1966): 59–64.

"Popper and Wisdom on Method in Metaphysics." Symposia (1968).

"The Logic of Absolute Presuppositions." In *Critical Essays on the Philosophy of R. G. Collingwood*. Edited by Michael Krausz, 222–240. Oxford: Clarendon, 1972; reissued in Korean 2013.

"Relativism and Rationality." *American Philosophical Quarterly* 10, no. 4 (October 1973): 307–312.

"Popper's Objective Knowledge." *Dialogue* 13, no. 2 (June 1974): 347–351.

"Vision, Creation, and Object." In *Proceedings of the 10th Conference on Value Theory*. Edited by Ervin Laszlo and James B. Wilbur, 32–49. Geneseo, NY: State University College at Geneseo, 1979.

"Historical Explanation, Re-Enactment, and Practical Inference." *Metaphilosophy* 11, no. 2 (April 1980a): 143–154.

"A Painter's View of Self-Development and Creativity." *Leonardo* 13, no. 2 (Spring 1980b): 143–145.

The Concept of Creativity in Science and Art. Edited by Michael Krausz and Denis Dutton. The Hague: Martinus Nijhoff, 1981a; reissued in paperback, 1985.

"On a Painter's View of Self-Development and Creativity," *Leonardo* 14, no. 1 (Winter 1981b): 84–85.

Rejoinders to David Carrier, Larry Briskman, John Broyer, James Munz, and Joan Novosel-Beitel. *Leonardo* 14, no. 1 (1981c): 84–85; and no. 2 (1981): 173.

"Ferrater-Mora's Continuum." In Transparencies: Philosophical Essays in Honor of J. Ferrater-Mora. Edited by Priscilla Cohn, 91–95. New York: Humanities Press, 1981d.

"Creating and Becoming." In *The Concept of Creativity in Science and Art*. Edited by Denis Dutton and Michael Krausz, 187–200. The Hague: Martinus Nijhoff, 1981e.

Relativism: Cognitive and Moral. Edited by Michael Krausz and Jack W. Meiland. Notre Dame, IN: Notre Dame University Press, 1982; reissued in paperback, 1984; translated and reissued in Korean, 1990. In this volume, Krausz authored Introductions to the chapters: 1–9, 13–17, 30–33, 62–65, 81–83, 109–112, 149–151, 167–168, 186–188, 205–208; and 226–228.

"Relativism and Foundationalism: Some Distinctions and Strategies." The Monist 67, no. 3 (July 1984a): 395–404

"The Tonal and the Foundational: Ansermet on Stravinsky." *The Journal of Aesthetics and Art Criticism* 42, no. 4 (Summer 1984b): 383–386.

"Product and Progress in Artistic Creativity." Special Issue, Michael Mitias, ed. *Kultura* 64 (1984c): 64–70.

Rationality, Relativism, and the Human Sciences. Edited by Michael Krausz, Joseph Margolis, and Richard M. Burian. The Hague: Martinus Nijhoff, 1986a.

"Intentionality, Expressive Properties, and Popper's Placement of Music." Special issue dedicated to Popper. Edited by Marcelo Dascal. Manuscrito: Revista Internacional de Filosofia 9, no. 2 (October 1986b): 65–76.

"Art and Its Mythologies: A Relativist View." In *Rationality, Relativism, and the Human Sciences*. Edited by Joseph Margolis, Michael Krausz, and Richard M. Burian, 189–208. The Hague: Martinus Nijhoff, 1986c.

Relativism: Interpretation, and Confrontation. Edited and with an Introduction by Michael Krausz. Notre Dame, IN: Notre Dame University Press, 1989a; reissued in paperback, 1990.

"Mahler's Superstition; Conducting Wagner; and Beethoven's First Symphony." In *Puzzles about Art: An Aesthetics Casebook*. Edited by M.P. Battin, J. Fisher, R. Moore, and A. Silvers, 165, 172, and 142–143. New York: St. Martin's Press, 1989b.

"Interpretation and Its Art Objects: Two Views." *The Monist* 73, no. 2 (April 1990): 222–232.

"History and Its Objects." *The Monist* 74, no. 2 (April 1991a): 217–229.

"Crossing Cultures: Two Universalisms and Two Relativisms." In *Cultural Relativism*. Edited by Marcelo Dascal, 233–242. Leiden: Brill, and Mexico City: Fondo de Cultura Economica, 1991b; reprinted in Spanish as "Culturas encontradas: dos universalismos y dos relativismos." In *Relativismo Cultural y Filosofia: Perspectivas norteamericana y latinoamerica* [Cultural relativism and philosophy: Latin American and North American perspectives]. Edited by Marcelo Dascal, 315–327. Mexico: Universidad Nacional Autonoma De Mexico, 1991.

"Ideality and Ontology in the Practice of History." In *Objectivity, Method, and Point of View*. Edited by W.J. Van der Dussen and L. Rubinoff, 97–108. Leiden: Brill, 1991c.

Addendum to Objectivity, Method, and Point of View. Edited by W.J. Van der Dussen and L. Rubinoff, 108–111. Leiden: Brill, 1991d.

"Intention and Interpretation: Hirsch and Margolis." In Intention and Interpretation. Edited by Gary Iseminger, 152–166. Philadelphia: Temple University Press, 1992.

Rightness and Reasons: Interpretation in Cultural Practices. Ithaca, NY: Cornell University Press, 1993a.

"Rightness and Reasons in Musical Interpretation." In *The Interpretation of Music: Philosophical Essays*. Edited and with an Introduction by Michael Krausz, 75–87. Oxford: Clarendon, 1993b; reissued in paperback, 1996.

"The Culture of Identity, (with David Goldberg); and On Being Jewish." In Jewish Identity. Edited by David Theo Goldberg and Michael Krausz, 1–12; and 264–278. Philadelphia: Temple University Press, 1993c.

"Culture and the 'Ontology' of Music: Margolis' Anarchic Reconstruction." *Iyyun: The Jerusalem Philosophical Quarterly* 42 (January 1993d): 165–179.

"Three Meditations on Oneness." *Journal of the Indian Council of Philosophical Research* 12, no. 3 (May–August 1995a): 39–96.

"R. G. Collingwood's Aesthetics." In A Companion to Aesthetics: The Blackwell Companion to Philosophy. Edited by David E. Cooper and Robert Hopkins, 75–78. Oxford: Blackwell, 1995b.

Varieties of Relativism. (with Rom Harré). Oxford: Basil Blackwell, 1996a.

"Interview with Ven. Lobsang Gyatso." *Journal of Indian Philosophy and Religion* 1 (1996b): 104–134.

"On the Idea of the Single Right Interpretation in History." Special issue, *Journal of Indian Council of Philosophical Research* (July 1996c): 57–66.

"Relativism and Beyond: In Tribute to Bimal Matilal." In Relativism, Suffering, and Beyond: Essays in Memory of Bimal K. Matilal. Edited by P. Bilimoria and J.N. Mohanty, 93–104. Delhi: Oxford University Press, 1997a.

"Choosing What One Is Cut Out To Be." In *Epistemology, Meaning, and Metaphysics after Matilal,* special issue of *Studies in Humanities and Social Sciences*, edited by Arindam Chakrabarti 3, no. 2 (Winter 1996d): 185–199.

"Changing One's Mind, Changing One's Emotions: An Intercultural Perspective." In Philosophy from an Intercultural Perspective. Edited by Notker Schneider, Dieter Lohmar, Morteza Ghasepour, and Herman-Josef Scheidgen, 107–120. Amsterdam: Rodopi, 1997b.

"The Interpretation of Art: Comments on Multiplism and Relativism." *Journal of Technology, Learning, and Assessment* 22 (1997c): 33–42

"Interview with Ven. Lobsang Gyatso." *Journal of Indian Philosophy and Religion* 2 (October 1997d): 43–87.

"Rightness and Reasons: A Reply to Stecker." *Journal of Aesthetics and Art Criticism* 55, no. 4 (Fall 1997e): 415–418.

"Two Aims of Cultural Interpretation: Explaining and Healing." *Studien zur interkulturellen Philosophie* 9 (1998a): 133–144.

"Interpretation." In *The Encyclopedia of Aesthetics*, 2 vols. Edited by Michael Kelly, 2:520–523. New York: Oxford University Press, 1998b.

"Interpretation, Relativism, and Culture: Four Questions for Margolis." In *Interpretation, Relativism, and the Metaphysics of Culture: Themes in the Philosophy of Joseph Margolis*. Edited by Michael Krausz and Richard Shusterman, 105–124. Amherst, NY: Humanity Books, 1999.

Limits of Rightness. Lanham, MD: Rowman & Littlefield, 2000a.

"Interpretation and Its 'Metaphysical' Entanglements." *Metaphilosophy* 31, no.1/2 (January 2000b): 125–147; reprinted in *The Philosophy of Interpretation*. Edited by Joseph Margolis and Tom Rockmore, 125–147. Oxford: Blackwell, 1999b, 2000.

"Interpretation and Its Objects." In *Is There A Single Right Interpretation?*. Edited and with Introduction by Michael Krausz, 122–144. University Park: Penn State University Press, 2002a.

"Making Music: Beyond Intentions." *The Linacre Journal* (2002b): 17–27.

"Interpretation and Its Objects: A Synoptic View; and Replies and Reflections." In Interpretation and Its Objects: Studies in the Philosophy of Michael Krausz. Edited by Andreea Deciu Ritivoi, 11–22, 315–362. Amsterdam: Rodopi, 2003.

"Note on an Alleged Mistake in the Interpretation of Collingwood." *Collingwood and British Idealism Studies* 10 (2004): 98–102.

"Replies: Interpretation and Codes of Culture." In "Interpretation and Culture: Themes in the Philosophy of Michael Krausz." Edited by Michael McKenna, special issue, Philosophy in the Contemporary World 12, no. 1 (Spring-Summer 2005): 103–114.

"Relativism and Its Schemes." In Philosophical Engagement: Davidson's Philosophy and Chinese Philosophy. Edited by Bo Mou, 37–53. Leiden: Brill, 2006.

Interpretation and Transformation: Explorations in Art and the Self. Amsterdam: Rodopi, 2007.

The Idea of Creativity. Edited by Michael Krausz, Denis Dutton, and Karen Bardsley. Introduction and "Creativity and Self-Transformation" contributed by Michael Krausz, xvii–xxii; 191–203. Leiden: Brill, 2009a.

"Collingwood, R. G, " In *A Companion to Aesthetics*, 2nd ed. Edited by David Cooper, Stephen Davies, Kathleen Higgins, et al., 197–199. Malden, MA: Blackwell, 2009b.

"Mapping Relativisms." In *Relativism: A Contemporary Anthology*. Edited and with an Introduction by Michael Krausz, 13–30. New York: Columbia University Press, 2010.

Dialogues on Relativism, Absolutism, and Beyond: Four Days in India. Lanham, MD: Rowman and Littlefield, 2011a.

"Varieties of Relativism and the Reach of Reasons." In *A Companion to Relativism*. Edited by Steven Hale, 70–84. Malden, MA: Blackwell, 2011b.

"About My Art." *American Society for Aesthetics Newsletter* 32, no. 1 (Spring 2012a): 6–7.

"Relativisms and Their Ontologies, under Relativism." In *Encyclopedia of Philosophy and the Social Sciences*. Edited by Byron Kaldis, 810–815. Thousand Oaks, CA: Sage, 2012b.

Oneness and the Displacement of Self: Dialogues on Self-Realization. Amsterdam: Rodopi, 2013.

"A Reply to Vaidya." Comparative Philosophy 5, no. 1, article 5 (2014a) (Comments on Anand Vaidya's review of Michael Krausz, Dialogues on Relativism, Absolutism, and Beyond: Four Days in India).

"Bernard Harrison's 'World.'" In Reality and Culture: Essays on the Philosophy of Bernard Harrison. Edited by Patricia Hanna, 171–180. Amsterdam: Rodopi, 2014b.

"Interpretation in Art, under Interpretation." In *The Encyclopedia of Aesthetics*, 6 vols. Edited by Michael Kelley, 3:501–510. Oxford: Oxford University Press, 2014c.

"Relativisms and Their Opposites." In *Realism—Relativism—Constructivism*. Edited by Christian Kanzian, Josef Mitterer, Katharina Neges. Berlin: Walter de Gruyter, 2017.

APPENDIX C

For Further Reading

Appiah, Kwame Anthony. *As If: Idealization and Ideals*. Cambridge, MA: Harvard University Press, 2017. ISBN 9780674975002

Bo Mou. *Davidson's Philosophy and Chinese Philosophy: Constructive Engagement*. Boston: Brill, 2006. ISBN 9781435614895

Bstan-dzin-rgya-mtsho (Dalai Lama XIV). *Becoming Enlightened*. Translated by Gerard Manley Hopkins. London: Rider, 2010. ISBN 9781846041235

Bstan-dzin-rgya-mtsho (Dalai Lama XIV). *Beyond Religion: Ethics for a Whole World*. Boston: Houghton Mifflin, 2011. ISBN 9780547636351

Boghossian, Paul Artin. *Fear of Knowledge: Against Relativism and Constructivism*. New York: Oxford University Press, 2006. ISBN 9780199287185

Buber, Martin. *I and Thou*. New York: Charles Scribner's Sons, 1970. ISBN 9780684717258

Chomsky, Noam. *Syntactic Structures*. New York: Mouton de Gruyter, 1957/2002. ISBN 9783110172799

Cohen-Solal, Annie. *Mark Rothko: Toward the Light in the Chapel*. New Haven: Yale University Press, 2015. ISBN 9780300182040

DeLuca, David, ed. *Vivekananda, Lessons in Classical Yoga*. Anaheim, CA: Namaste Books, 2003. ISBN 9780972434874

Edmonds, David, and John Eidinow. *Wittgenstein's Poker: The Story of a Ten-Minute Argument between Two Great Philosophers*. New York: Ecco, 2001. ISBN 9780066212449

Findlay, J.N. "The Perspicuous and the Poignant." In *Aesthetics*. Edited by Harold Osborne. Oxford: Oxford University Press, 1972. ISBN 9780198750208

Gellner, Ernest. *Relativism and the Social Sciences*. New York: Cambridge University Press, 1985. ISBN 9780521265300

Gupta, Chhanda. *Realism versus Realism*. Lanham, MD: Rowman & Littlefield, 2002. ISBN 9780742513860

Harrison, Bernard. *What Is Fiction For?*: Literary Humanism Restored. Bloomington: Indiana University Press, 2015. ISBN 9780253014085

Hirsch, E.D. *The Aims of Interpretation*. Chicago: University of Chicago Press, 1976. ISBN 9780226342405

Israel Women for Ida Nudel. *Our Ida Nudel: Testimonies of Former Prisoners and Refuseniks*. Tel Aviv: Israel Women for Ida Nudel, 1980 OCLC: 8709541

Jakobson, Roman. "Closing Statement: Linguistics and Poetics (1960). In *Poetry in Theory: An Anthology 1900–2000*. Edited by Jon Cook, 350–358. Oxford: Blackwell, 2004. ISBN 9780631225539

Kandinsky, Wassily. *Concerning the Spiritual in Art, and Painting in Particular, 1912.* Translated by Michael Sadleir and Francis Golffing. New York: Wittenborn, 1963. OCLC: 4731758

Küper, Christoph. *Sprache und Metrum: Semiotik u. Linguistik d. Verses* [Language and Meter: Semiotics and Linguistics of Verses]. Tübingen: Niemeyer, 1988. ISBN 9783484105744

Lamarque, Peter. *Work and Object: Explorations in the Metaphysics of Art.* Oxford: Oxford University Press, 2012. ISBN 9780199655496

Larvor, Brendan. *Lakatos: An Introduction.* New York: Routledge, 1998. ISBN 9780415142755

Leddy, Thomas. "Creative Interpretation of Literary Texts." In *The Idea of Creativity.* Edited by Michael Krausz, Denis Dutton, and Karen Bardsley, 293–312. Leiden: Brill, 2009. ISBN 9789004174443

Lukes, Steven. *Moral Relativism.* New York: Picador, 2013. ISBN 9781429941822

Magee, Bryan. *Aspects of Wagner.* Oxford: Oxford University Press, 1988. ISBN 9780192177681

Margolis, Joseph. *Selves and Other Texts: The Case for Cultural Realism* University Park, PA: Pennsylvania State University Press, 2001. ISBN 9780271021508

Margolis, Joseph, and Jacques Catudal. *The Quarrel between Invariance and Flux.* University Park, PA: Pennsylvania State University Press, 2001. ISBN 9780271020648

Matilal, Bimal Krishna. *The Word and the World: India's Contribution to the Study of Language.* New York: Oxford University Press, 1990. ISBN 9780195655124

Matilal, Bimal Krishna. *Relativism, Suffering, and Beyond: Essays in Memory of Bimal K. Matilal.* Edited by Purusottama Bilimoria and J.N. Mohanty. New York: Oxford University Press, 2003. ISBN 9780195662078

McCormick, Peter. *Starmaking: Realism, Anti-Realism, and Irrealism.* Cambridge, MA: MIT Press, 1996. ISBN 9780585021201

Mohanty, J.N. *Classical Indian Philosophy.* Lanham, MD: Rowman & Littlefield, 2000. ISBN 9780847689323

Mohanty, J.N. "Levels of Understanding 'Intentionality.'" *The Monist* 69, no. 4 (Oct. 1986): 505–520. DOI: https://doi.org/10.5840/monist198669432

Norris, Christopher. *Against Relativism: Philosophy of Science, Deconstruction, and Critical Theory.* Malden, MA: Baldwin, 1997. ISBN 9780631198642

Novitz, David. "Against Critical Pluralism." In *Is There a Single Right Interpretation?.* Edited by Michael Krausz, 101–121. University Park, PA: Penn State University Press, 2002. ISBN 9780271021751

Popper, Karl R. *Popper Selections.* Edited by David Miller. Princeton, NJ: Princeton University Press: 1985. ISBN 9780691072876

Priest, Graham. *Beyond the Limits of Thought.* 2nd ed. Oxford: Clarendon Press, 2002. ISBN 9780199244218

Raphael, Frederic. *Anti-Semitism (Provocations)*. New York: Biteback, 2015. ISBN 9781849549622 (e-book)

Ritivoi, Andreea Deciu. *Yesterday's Self: Nostalgia and the Immigrant Identity*. Lanham, MD: Rowman & Littlefield, 2002. ISBN 9780742513600

Rothko, Mark, and Christopher Rothko. *The Artist's Reality: Philosophies of Art*. New Haven, CT: Yale University Press, 2004. ISBN 9780300102536

Rudolf, Max. *The Grammar of Conducting: A Practical Guide to Baton Technique and Orchestral Interpretation*. New York: Schirmer Books, 1980. ISBN 9780028722207.

Shyam, Swami. *Bhagavad Gita: The Most Precise and Comprehensive Rendering*. Montréal: International Meditation Institute, 1985. OCLC: 850933548

Shyam, Swami. *Shyam's Philosophy*. Edited by Nina Lehrman. Kullu: International Meditation Institute, 2003. ISBN 9788188352425

Steinhardt, Arnold. *Indivisible by Four: A String Quartet in Pursuit of Harmony*. New York: Farrar, Straus, Giroux, 1998. ISBN 9780374236700

Strasfogel, Ian. "Berenson's Life-Enhancing Art." Review of "The Passionate Sightseer" by Bernard Berenson. New York, The Harvard Crimson, September 30, 1960; available at http://www.thecrimson.com/article/1960/9/30/berensons-life-enhancing-art-pthis-is-bernard/.

Trungpa, Chogyam. *Cutting through Spiritual Materialism*. Berkeley: Shambala, 1973. ISBN 9780877730491

Tola, Fernando, and Dragonetti, Carmen. *Nagarjuna's Refutation of Logic* (Nyaya) : Edition of the Tibetan Text, English Translation and Commentary, with Introduction and Notes. Delhi: Motilal Banarasidass Publishers, 1995. ISBN 9788120809208.

Vivekānanda, Swami. *The Complete Works of Swami Vivekananda*. Calcutta: Advaita Ashrama, 1972–1978.

Vivekānanda, Swami. *Hinduism*. Vedana Pr., 1989. ISBN 9788171200016

Weiss, Paul. *Modes of Being*. Carbondale, Southern Illinois University Press, 1958/1968. OCLC: 225695

Bibliography

Adler, Mortimer Jerome, Clifton Fadiman, and Philip W. Goetz, eds. *Great Books of the Western World*, 61 vols., 2nd ed. Chicago: Encyclopedia Britannica, 1950/1990. ISBN 9780852295311.

Ansermet, Ernest. *Écrits sur la Musique* (Writings on Music). Neuchâtel: Éditions de la Baconnière, 1971. OCLC: 381351.

Austin, J.L. How to Do Things with Words, 2nd ed. The William James Lectures. Edited by J.O. Urmson and Marina Sbisà (Cambridge, MA: Harvard University Press, 1975. ISBN 9780674411524.

Ayer, A.J. Language, Truth, and Logic. New York: Dover, 1946/1952. ISBN 9780486200101.

Bandy, Alexander E. Chess and Chocolate: Unlocking Lakatos. Budapest: Akadémiai Kiadó, 2009. ISBN 9789630588195.

Beardsley, Monroe. "The Authority of the Text." In Intention and Interpretation, ed. Gary Iseminger, 24–40.

Bennett, Joan, and Lois Kibbee. *The Bennett Playbill: Five Generations of the Famous Theater Family*. New York: Holt, Rinehart, and Winston, 1970. ISBN 9780030818400.

Berlin, Isaiah. "Why Be Jewish?" In UJS Haggadah. Edited by Michael Marks and the Union of Jewish Studies. London: Free Press, 1996. ISBN: 9780952517016.

Bernstein, Richard. *Beyond Objectivism and Relativism: Science, Hermeneutics, and Praxis*. Oxford: Blackwell, 1983. ISBN: 9780812279061.

Boden, Margaret. "Creativity: How Does It Work?." In *The Idea of Creativity*, eds. Krausz, Dutton, and Bardsley, 237–50.

Briskman, Larry. "Creating and Self-Development: A Reply to Michael Krausz." *Leonardo* 13, no. 4 (Autumn, 1980): 323–25.

Briskman, Larry. "Creative Product and Creative Process in Science and Art." In *The Concept of Creativity in Science and Art*. Edited by Denis Dutton and Michael Krausz, 129–156. The Hague: Martinus Nijhoff Publishers, 1981. ISBN 9789400982307; reprinted in *The Idea of Creativity*, eds. Krausz, Dutton, and Bardsley, 17–42.

Burnyeat, Myles F. "Protagoras and Self-Refutation in Later Greek Philosophy." *The Philosophical Review* 85, no. 1 (Jan., 1976): 44–69. DOI: 10.2307/2184254.

Chang Chung-yuan. *Creativity and Taoism: A Study of Chinese Philosophy, Art, and Poetry*. New York: Harper Colophon, 1970. ISBN 9780061319686.

Chaturvedi, Vibha. "Reflections on the Interpretation of Religious Texts." In *Interpretation and Its Objects*, 303–311.

Christo, Wolfgang Volz. Christo & Jeanne-Claude: Verhüllter Reichstag, Berlin, 1971–1995 (Wrapped Reichstag, Berlin 1971–1995). Photographs by Wolfgang Volz. Köln: Benedikt Taschen; New York : Christo, 1995. isbn: 9783822886830.

Collingwood, R.G. *Speculum Mentis: Or the Map of Knowledge*. Oxford: Clarendon, 1924. oclc: 323012.

Collingwood, R.G. *An Essay on Metaphysics*. Oxford: Clarendon Press, 1940. OCLC: 368653.

Curtis, Michael. *The Great Political Theories: 1. From Plato and Aristotle to Locke and Montesquieu*. New York: Avon, 1961. OCCL: 760353.

Curtis, Michael.*The Great Political Theorie: 2. From Burke, Rousseau and Kant to Modern Times*. New York: Avon, 1962/1965. OCLC: 332057.

Danto, Arthur. *Mysticism and Morality: Oriental Thought and Moral Philosophy*. New York: Basic Books, 1972. OCLC: 548326.

Davies, Bronwyn, and Rom Harré. "Positioning: The Discursive Production of Selves." *Journal of Theory and Social Behaviour* 20, no. 1 (March 1990): 43–63. DOI:10.1111/j.1468-5914.1990.tb00174.x.

Dewey, John. *The Later Works 1925–1953*.Volume 10: 1934, *Art as Experience*. Edited by Jo Ann Boydston, with an introduction by Abraham Kaplan. Carbondale: Southern Illinois University Press, 2008. ISBN: 9780809312665.

Drakpa, Losang. *Ocean of Reasoning: A Great Commentary on Nagarjuna's Mulamadhyamakakarika*. Translated by Gesha Ngawang Samten and Jay L. Garfield. New York: Oxford University Press, 2006. ISBN: 9781429438414.

Dray, Wiliam H. *Laws and Explanation in History*. Westport, CT: Greenwood Press, 1957/1979. ISBN: 9780313207907.

Dray, Wiliam H. *On History and Philosophers of History*. Leiden: Brill, 1989. ISBN: 9789004090002.

Dray, Wiliam H. *History as Re-Enactment: R. G. Collingwood's Idea of History*. Oxford: Clarendon Press, 1995. ISBN: 9780198242932.

Dreyfus, Hubert L. *Being in the World: A Commentary on Heidegger's Being and Time*. Cambridge, MA: MIT Press, 1991. ISBN: 9780262041065.

Dworkin, Ronald. *Religion without God*. Cambridge, MA: Harvard University Press, 2013. ISBN: 9780674726826.

Ferrero, Shaul. "Switzerland and the Refugees Fleeing Nazism: Documents on the German Jews Turned Back at the Basel Border in 1938–1939. Shoah Resource Center, n.d. http://www.yadvashem.org/odot_pdf/Microsoft%20Word%20-%203212.pdf.

Forsén, Sture, Harry B. Gray, L.K. Olof Lindgren, and Shirley B. Gray. "Was Something Wrong with Beethoven's Metronome?" *Notices of the American Mathematical Society* 60, no. 9 (October 2013): 1146–1153, http://www.ams.org/notices/201309/rnoti-p1146.pdf.

Gablik, Suzi. *Progress in Art*. New York: Rizzoli, 1977. ISBN: 9780847800827.

Gallie, W.B. "Essentially Contested Concepts." *Proceedings of the Aristotelian Society*, n.s., 56 (1955–1956). DOI: http://dx.doi.org/10.1093/aristotelian/56.1.167.

Garelick, Herbert M. *The Anti-Christianity of Kierkegaard: A Study of Concluding Unscientific Postscript.* The Hague: M. Nijhoff, 1965. OCLC: 614888.

Geertz, Clifford. "Anti Anti-Relativism." *American Anthropologist*, n.s. 86, no. 2 (Jun., 1984): 263–278. DOI: http://www.jstor.org/stable/678960.

Gellner, Ernest. "Collingwood and the Failure of Realism. The Logic of Question and Answer" (review of Michael Krausz, ed., *Critical Essays on the Philosophy of R. G. Collingwood*). *The Times Literary Supplement* no. 3708 (March 30, 1973): 337–339.

Goodman, Nelson. *Ways of Worldmaking.* Indianapolis, IN: Hackett, 1978. ISBN: 9780915144525.

Griffin, James. *Wittgenstein's Logical Atomism.* Oxford: Clarendon, 1964. OCLC: 525515.

Grombich, E.H. *Art and Illusion: Study in the Psychology of Pictorial Representation.* 2nd ed. Princeton, NJ: Princeton University Press,1969. ISBN: 9780691017501.

Gyatso, Lobsang. *The Harmony of Emptiness and Dependent-Arising: A Commentary to Tsongkhapa's the Essence of Eloquent Speech Praise to the Buddha for Teaching Profound Dependent-Arising.* Dharamsala: Library of Tibetan Works and Archives, 1992. ISBN: 9788185102832.

Gyatso, Lobsang. *The Four Noble Truths.* Translated by Sherab Gyatso. Ithaca, NY: Snow Lion Publications, 1994. ISBN: 9781559390279.

Gyatso, Lobsang. *Memoirs of a Tibetan Lama.* Translated and edited by Gareth Sparham. Ithaca, NY: Snow Lion Publications, 1998. ISBN: 9781559390972.

Hacker, P.M.S. "An Orrery of Intentionality." *Language and Communication* 21, no. 2 (2001): 119–141, available at http://info.sjc.ox.ac.uk/scr/hacker/docs/Orrery%20of%20intentionality.pdf. DOI:10.1016/S0271-5309(00)00016-1.

Hacker, P.M.S. "The Sad and Sorry History of Consciousness: Being, among Other Things, a Challenge to the 'Consciousness-Studies Community.'" *Royal Institute of Philosophy Supplement* 70 (July 2012), available at http://info.sjc.ox.ac.uk/scr/hacker/docs/ConsciousnessAChallenge.pdf. DOI:10.1017/S1358246112000082.

Hanna, Patricia, and Bernard Harrison. *Word and World: Practices and the Foundation of Language.* Cambridge, UK: Cambridge University Press, 2004. ISBN 9781280457753.

Harré, Rom, and Michael Krausz, eds. *Varieties of Relativism.* Oxford: Blackwell, 1996. ISBN: 9780631184096.

Harrison, Bernard. *The Resurgence of Anti-Semitism: Jews, Israel, and Liberal Opinion.* Lanham, MD: Roman and Littlefield, 2006. ISBN: 9780742552265.

Harrison, Bernard. *Blaming the Jews: The Persistence of a Delusion.* Bloomington: Indiana University Press, forthcoming 2018.

Harrison, Bernard. "Robust Multiplism, Or, New Bearings in the Theory of Interpretation." In *Interpretation, Identity, and Relativism,* eds. Koggel and Ritivoi, 55–66.

Harrison, Bernard, and Patricia Hanna. "Interpretation and Ontology: Two Queries for Krausz." In *Interpretation, Identity, and Relativism,* ed. Ritivoi, 93–107.

Heidegger, Martin. "The Origin of the Work of Art" (*Der Ursprung des Kunstwerkes*). In *Poetry, Language, Thought*. Translated by Albert Hofstadter. New York: Perennial Library, 1971/1975. ISBN: 9780060904302.

Hesse, Herman. *The Journey to the East: A Novel*. Translated by Hilda Rosner. New York: Macmillan, 2003. ISBN: 9780312421687.

Horkheimer, Max, and Theodor W. Adorno. *Dialectic of Enlightenment: Philosophical Fragments*. New York: Herder and Herder, 1944/1974. ISBN: 9780804788090.

Hoy, David. "One What? Relativism and Poststructuralism." In *Relativism: A Contemporary Anthology*. Edited by Michael Krausz, 524–535. New York: Columbia University Press, 2010. ISBN: 9780231144100.

Iseminger, Gary, ed. *Intention and Interpretation*. Philadelphia: Temple University Press, 1992. ISBN: 9780877229711.

Kaprow, Allan. "The Legacy of Jackson Pollack" (1958). In *Essays on the Blurring of Art and Life*. Edited by Jeff Kelly, 1–9. Berkeley: University of California Press, 1993. Available at http://thenewschoolhistory.org/wp-content/uploads/2014/08/Kaprow-Legacy-of-Pollock_1958.pdf.

Kertész, Imre. "Who Owns Auschwitz?." Translated by John MacKay. Yale *Journal of Criticism* 14 (Spring 2001): 267–272. DOI:10.1353/yale.2001.0010.

Koggel, Christine, and Andreea Deciu Ritivoi, eds. *Interpretation, Identity, and Relativism: Essays on the Philosophy of Michael Krausz*. Lanham, MD: Lexington Books, 2018. ISBN: 9781498554749.

Krausz, Susan. *Piano Picture Book: Piano Solo*. New York: Edwin F. Kalmus, 1957; republication as *Krausz Picture Book*. Warner Bros Publications, 1957/1985/2000. Sheet music currently available: *Piano Picture Book*. OnlineSheetMusic.com, 2013. ASIN: B002GYI4TC.

Krausz, Michael. "A Critique of R.G. Collingwood's Theory of Absolute Presuppositions." PhD diss., University of Toronto (Canada), 1969. ProQuest NK06837.

Krausz, Michael, ed. *Critical Essays on the Philosophy of R.G. Collingwood*. Oxford: Clarendon, 1972. ISBN: 9780198243786.

Krausz, Michael. "A Painter's View of Self-Development and Creativity." *Leonardo* 13, no. 2 (Spring 1980): 143–145. DOI:10.2307/1577990.

Krausz, Michael. "On a Painter's View of Self-Development and Creativity." *Leonardo* 14, no. 1 (Winter 1981a): 84–85. DOI:10.2307/1574532.

Krausz, Michael. Rejoinders to David Carrier, Larry Briskman, John Broyer, James Munz, and Joan Novosel-Beitel. *Leonardo* 14, no. 1 (1981b): 84–85, and 14, no. 2 (1981): 173.

Krausz, Michael. "The Tonal and the Foundational: Ansermet on Stravinsky." *The Journal of Aesthetics and Art Criticism* 42, no. 4 (Summer 1984): 383–386.

Krausz, Michael, ed. *Relativism: Interpretation and Confrontation*. Notre Dame, IN: University of Notre Dame Press, 1989. ISBN: 9780268016364.

Krausz, Michael. "On Being Jewish." In *Jewish Identity*. Edited by David Theo Goldberg and Michael Krausz, 264–278. Philadelphia: Temple University Press, 1993a. ISBN: 9781566390392.

Krausz, Michael. Appendix, "From an Interview with a Luo Medicineman." In *Rightness and Reasons: Interpretation in Cultural Practices*. Ithaca, NY: Cornell University Press, 1993b), 167–169. ISBN: 9780801428463.

Krausz, Michael. *Rightness and Reasons: Interpretation in Cultural Practices*. Ithaca, NY: Cornell University Press, 1993c. ISBN: 9780801428463.

Krausz, Michael. "Rightness and Reasons in Musical Interpretation." In *The Interpretation of Music: Philosophical Essays*. Edited by Michael Krausz, 75–87. New York: Oxford University Press, 1993d. ISBN: 9780198239581.

Krausz, Michael. "Creativity and Self-Transformation." In *The Idea of Creativity*, eds. Krausz, Dutton, and Bardsley, 191–203.

Krausz, Michael. "Interpretation, Relativism, and Culture: Four Questions for Margolis." In *Interpretation, Relativism, and the Metaphysics of Culture: Themes in the Philosophy of Joseph Margolis*. Edited by Richard Shusterman and Michael Krausz, 105–124. Amherst, NY: Humanity Press, 1999. ISBN: 9781573926560.

Krausz, Michael. *Limits of Rightness*. Lanham, MD: Rowman & Littlefield, 2000. ISBN: 9780742511682.

Krausz, Michael. "Making Music: Beyond Intentions." Edited by Rom Harré. *The Linacre Journal: A Review of Research in the Humanities* no. 5 (2002a): 17–27. ISSN 2368–7263

Krausz, Michael, ed. *Is There a Single Right Interpretation?*. University Park: Penn State University Press, 2002b. ISBN: 9780271021751.

Krausz, Michael. *Interpretation and Transformation: Explorations in Art and the Self*. Amsterdam: Rodopi, 2007. ISBN: 9781429481267.

Krausz, Michael, Denis Dutton, and Karen Bardsley, eds. *The Idea of Creativity*. Bardsley. Leiden: Brill, 2009. ISBN: 9789047427902.

Krausz, Michael, ed. *Relativism: A Contemporary Anthology*. New York: Columbia University Press, 2010. ISBN: 9780231144100.

Krausz, Michael. *Dialogues on Relativism, Absolutism, and Beyond: Four Days in India*. New York: Rowman & Littlefield, 2011. ISBN: 9780742560321.

Krausz, Michael. *Oneness and the Displacement of Self: Dialogues on Self-Realization*. Leiden: Brill, 2013. ISBN: 941199416.

Krausz, Michael. "The Ideals and Aim of Interpretation." In *Interpretation and Meaning in Philosophy and Religion*. Edited by Dirk-Martin Grube. Leiden: Brill, 2016. ISBN: 9789004254992.

Krausz, Michael. "Interpretation and Its Objects." In *Is There a Single Right Interpretation?*, 122–144.

Krausz, Michael. "Relativisms and Their Opposites." In *Realism—Relativism—Constructivism*. Edited by Christian Kanzian, Josef Mitterer, and Katharina Neges, 187–202. Berlin: Walter de Gruyter, 2017. ISBN: 9783110467734.

Kuhn, Thomas S. *The Structure of Scientific Revolutions*. Chicago: University of Chicago Press, 1970. ISBN: 9780226458038.

Lakatos, Imre, and Alan Musgrave, eds., *Proceedings of the International Colloquium in the Philosophy of Science, 1965, London: 4: Criticism and the Growth of Knowledge*. Amsterdam: North-Holland, 1968–1972. OCLC: 525806.

Lakatos, Imre. *Proofs and Refutations: The Logic of Mathematical Discovery*. Cambridge: Cambridge University Press, 1976. ISBN: 9780521210782.

Lakatos, Imre. *The Methodology of Scientific Programmes: Philosophical Papers, Volume 1*. Cambridge: Cambridge University Press, 1978. ISBN: 9780521216449.

Lamarque, Peter. "Object, Work, and Interpretation." In *Interpretation and Culture: Themes in the Philosophy of Michael Krausz*. Edited by Michael McKenna. Special edition of *Philosophy in the Contemporary World* 12, no. 1 (Spring–Summer 2005): 1–7. DOI:10.5840/pcw200512110.

Magee, Bryan. "Jews—Not Least in Music." In *Aspects of Wagner*. Oxford: Oxford University Press, 1988. ISBN: 9780192840127.

Marcuse, Herbert. *One Dimensional Man: Studies in the Ideology of Advanced Industrial Society*. Boston: Beacon Press, 1964. ISBN: 9780807015759.

Margolis, Joseph. "Robust Relativism." *The Journal of Aesthetics and Art Criticism* 35 (1976): 37–46. DOI:10.2307/430843. Reprinted in *Philosophy Looks at the Arts*. Edited by Joseph Margolis. Philadelphia: Temple University Press, 1978. OCLC: 376557.

Margolis, Joseph. *Interpretation Radical but Not Unruly, The New Puzzle of the Arts and History*. Berkeley: University of California Press, 1995. ISBN: 9780520915145.

Margolis, Joseph. "The Truth about Relativism." In *Relativism: A Contemporary Anthology*. Edited by Michael Krausz, 100–123. New York: Columbia University Press, 2010. ISBN: 9780231144100.

Margolis, Joseph, Michael Krausz, and Richard Burian, eds. *Rationality, Relativism, and the Human Sciences*. The Hague: Martinus Nijhoff, 1986. ISBN: 9789024732715.

McKenna, Michael. "A Metaphysics for Krausz." In *Interpretation and Its Objects*, 129–146.

Medsger, Betty. *The Burglary: The Discovery of J. Edgar Hoover's Secret FBI*. New York: Alfred A. Knopf, 2014. ISBN: 9780307962959.

Meiland, Jack W., and Michael Krausz, eds. *Relativism: Cognitive and Moral*. Notre Dame, IN: University of Notre Dame Press, 1982. ISBN: 9780268016111.

Nehamas, Alexander. "The Postulated Author: Critical Monism as a Regulative Ideal." *Critical Inquiry* 8 (Autumn, 1981): 133–149. DOI:10.1086/448144.

Nehamas, Alexander. *Nietzsche, Life as Literature*. Cambridge, MA: Harvard University Press, 1985. ISBN: 9780674624351.

Nehamas, Alexander. "Art, Narrative, and Human Nature," *Philosophy and Literature* 13, no. 1 (April, 1989): 57–74. DOI:10.1353/phl.1989.0056.

Norton, David L. *Imagination, Understanding, and the Virtue of Liberality*. Lanham, MD: Rowman & Littlefield, 1996. ISBN: 9780847681273.

Nudel, Ida. *A Hand in the Darkness: The Autobiography of a Refusenik*. New York: Warner, 1990. ISBN: 9780446514453.

Nussbaum, Martha C., and Amartya Sen. "Indian Rationalist Traditions." In *Relativism: Interpretation, and Confrontation*. Edited by Michael Krausz. Notre Dame, IN: University of Notre Dame Press, 1989. ISBN: 9780268016364.

Nussbaum, Martha C., and Amartya Sen. "Internal Criticism and Indian Rationalist Traditions." In *Relativism: A Contemporary Anthology*. Edited by Michael Krausz. New York: Columbia University Press, 2010. ISBN: 9780231144100.

Oruka, Henry Odera. *Practical Philosophy: In Search of an Ethical Minimum*. Nairobi: East African Educational, 1997. ISBN: 9789966467041.

Popper, K.R. "The Nature of Philosophical Problems and Their Roots in Science." *The British Journal for the Philosophy of Science* 3, no. 10 (Aug. 1952): 124–156.

Popper, Karl R. "Three Views of Human Knowledge." In *Conjectures and Refutations: The Growth of Scientific Knowledge*, 2nd ed. London: Routledge, 1965, 97–119. OCLC: 2003787.

Popper, K.R. *The Open Society and Its Enemies*, 2 vols. Princeton, NJ: Princeton University Press, 1966. OCLC: 177688.

Popper, K.R. *Objective Knowledge: An Evolutionary Approach*. Oxford: Clarendon Press, 1972. ISBN: 9780198243700.

Popper, Karl R. "Three Worlds." In *The Tanner Lectures on Human Values. 1*. Edited by Eric Ashby and Sterling M. McMurrin, 141–167. Salt Lake City: University of Utah Press; Cambridge: Cambridge University Press, 1980. OCLC: 22262113.

Popper, Karl R. *Unended Quest: An Intellectual Autobiography*. London: Routledge, 1992. ISBN: 9780415086936.

Prausnitz, Frederick. *Score and Podium*. New York: Norton, 1983. ISBN: 9780393951547.

Prausnitz, Frederick. *Sessions : How a 'Difficult' Composer Got that Way*. Oxford; New York: Oxford University Press, 2002. ISBN: 9780195355208.

Putnam, Hilary. *Jewish Philosophy as a Guide to Life: Rosenzweig, Buber, Lévinas, Wittgenstein*. Bloomington: Indiana University Press, 2008. ISBN: 9780253351333.

Rao, Srinivasa. *Advaita, A Critical Investigation*. Bangalore: The Indian Philosophy Foundation, 1985. OCLC: 12978537.

Richards, Mary Caroline. *Centering in Pottery, Poetry, and the Person*. Middletown, CT: Wesleyan University Press, 1964a. OCLC: 1118782.

Ritivoi, Andreea Deciu, ed. *Interpretation and Its Objects: Studies in the Philosophy of Michael Krausz*. Amsterdam: Rodopi, 2003. ISBN: 9789042011670.

Ritivoi, Andreea Deciu, ed. *Intimate Strangers: Arendt, Marcuse, Solzhenitsyn, and Said in American Political Discourse*. New York: Columbia University Press, 2014. ISBN: 9780231168687.

Rorty, Richard. *Philosophy and the Mirror of Nature*. Princeton, NJ: Princeton University Press, 1979. OCLC: 5886457.

Rorty, Richard. "Solidarity or Objectivity?." In *Relativism: Interpretation and Confrontation*. Edited by Michael Krausz, 167–183. Notre Dame, IN: University of Notre Dame Press, 1989. ISBN: 9780268016364.

Rotenstreich, Nathan. "Metaphysics and Historicism." In *Critical Essays on the Philosophy of R.G. Collingwood*. Edited by Michael Krausz, 179–200. Oxford: Clarendon Press, 1972. ISBN: 9780198243786.

Roy, Krishna. *Hermeneutics: East and West*. Calcutta: Allied Publishers in collaboration with Jadavpur University, 1993. ISBN: 9788170232438.

Russell, Bertrand. *Why I Am Not a Christian*. New York: Simon and Schuster, 1957. ISBN: 9780671203238.

Saarinen, Jussie A. "A Conceptual Analysis of the Oceanic Feeling: With a Special Note on Painterly Aesthetics." Jyväskylä Studies in Education, Psychology, and Social Research (University of Jyväskylä, 2015. https://tinyurl.com/q29ljz2.

Salmon, Wesley C. *Causality and Explanation*. New York and Oxford: Oxford University Press, 1998. ISBN: 9780195108637.

Samuel Scheffler. Lecture 1: "The Afterlife (Part I)." *Death and the Afterlife*. Edited by Samuel Scheffler and Niko Kolodny, 15–49. New York: Oxford University Press, 2016. ISBN: 9780199982509.

Sasaki, Ken-Ichi. "Limits of Interpretation." In *Interpretation and Its Objects*, 69–78.

Schuller, Gunther. *The Compleat Conductor*. New York: Oxford University Press, 1998. ISBN: 9780195063776.

Searle, John R. *Speech Acts: An Essay in the Philosophy of Language*. London: Cambridge University Press, 1969. ISBN: 9780521071840.

Sen, Amartya, and Martha C. Nussbaum. "Internal Criticism and Indian Rationalist Traditions." In *Relativism: Interpretation and Confrontation*. Edited by Michael Krausz, 299–325. Notre Dame, IN: University of Notre Dame Press, 1989. ISBN: 9780268016364.

Sparkes, A.W., ed. *Talking Philosophy: A Wordbook*. New York: Routledge, 1991. ISBN: 9780415042222.

Storr, Anthony. *Music and the Mind*. New York: Free Press, 1992. ISBN: 9780029316214.

Tarkski, Alfred. "The Semantic Conception of Truth." In *Semantics and the Philosophy of Language*. Edited by Leonard Linsky. Urbana: University of Illinois Press, 1952. ISBN: 9780252000935.

Thom, Paul. "Constituents of Interpretation." In *Interpretation and Its Objects*, ed. Ritivoi, 109–118.

Vivekananda, Swami. *Practical Vedanta*. Calcutta: Advaita Ashrama, 1991/1995 9788175050877.

Vivekananda, Swami. *Vedanta Philosophy*. Calcutta: Swami Mumukshananda, July 1997 ISBN 9788175050372.

Waskow, Arthur Ocean. *Godwrestling—Round 2: Ancient Wisdom, Future Paths*. Woodstock, VT: Jewish Lights, 1996. ISBN: 9781879045453.

Waskow, Arthur Ocean. *Godwrestling*. New York: Schocken Books, 1978. ISBN: 9780805236910.

Whorf, Benjamin Lee. *Language, Thought, and Reality: Selected Writings*. Edited by John B. Carroll. Cambridge: Technology Press of Massachusetts, 1956. OCLC: 306502

Wittgenstein, Ludwig. *On Certainty*. Edited by G.E.M. Anscombe and G.H. von Wright. New York: Harper & Row, 1972. ISBN: 9780061316869.

Wong, David B. "Pluralism and Ambivalence." In *Natural Moralities: A Defense of Pluralist Relativism*. Oxford University Press, 2006, 5–28. ISBN: 9780199724840.

Wright, Georg Henrik von. *The Tree of Knowledge and Other Essays*. Leiden: Brill, 1993. ISBN: 9789004097643.

Name Index

Abramovic, Charles   120
Adams, Mark   81
Adorno, Theodor W.   24
Agassi, Joseph   56, 58
Ansermet, Ernest   9, 18, 19, 26, 38, 59
Arben, David   37, 111–113, 121
Athieno, Tago   93
"The Authority of the Text" (Beardsley)   179
Ayer, A.J.   52, 79

Bach, Johann Sebastian:
    Double Violin Concerto   14
    Mass in B minor   133
    Piano Concerto in D minor   13
    Suite no. 2 in B minor   112
    Violin Concerto in E major   112
Baltacigil, Efe   123
Bamborough, John   74
Bartley, William Warren   56
Beethoven, Ludwig van   116, 126
    Concerto in C major ("Triple Concerto")   123
    Coriolan Overture   117, 118, 120
    Marcia Funebre: Adagio Assai   126
    Piano Concerto no. 4 in G major   117, 118, 124
    Spring Sonata   66
    Symphony no. 1 in C major   39, 41
    Symphony no. 3 in E♭ major ("Eroica")   33, 118, 121, 124, 128
    Symphony no. 5 in C minor   122
    Symphony no. 6 in F major ("Pastoral")   134
    Symphony no. 7 in A major   120, 123
    Symphony no. 8 in F major   118, 121
    Symphony no. 9 in D minor   199
    Violin Concerto in D major   118, 122, 123
Begin, Menachem   85
Bell, Joshua   34
Bennett, Joan   11
Bent, Margaret   100
Berenson, Francis   100
Berlin, Irving   73
Berlin, Sir Isaiah   70–74, 77, 156–158
Bermanis, Cantor Simon   41
Bernstein, Carol L.   81
Bernstein, Leonard   133
Bernstein, Richard   79, 81
Biava, Luis   111, 119, 120, 131, 133
Bloch, Ernest:
    Baal Shem Suite (Vidui)   33
Bloom, Julius   113
Blumenschein, José   122, 123
Bober, Phillis   81, 88
Brahms, Johannes   18, 55, 116, 129
    Double Concerto in A minor   122
    Symphony no. 4 in E minor   115, 118, 119, 124, 130, 181
Braithwaite, R.B.   54, 63
Bretter, Zoltàn   21, 22
Briskman, Larry   107, 192, 193, 196–198
Brodsky, Joseph   78
Brom, Greta   15
Bruch, Max:
    Violin Concerto no. 1 in G minor   121, 122
Bruckner, Anton   55
Brusilow, Anshel   36, 37, 114, 121
Buber, Martin   61
Bujic, Bojan   99
Burian, Linda   112
Burian, Richard   82, 111
Busch, Fritz   18

Cage, John   107
Cambon, Glauco   67
Canellakis, Nicholas   122
Canfield, John   75
Carnap, Rudolf   62, 63, 65
Carroll, Gretchen   85, 88
Casals, Pablo   18, 19
Cassirer, Ernst   89
Cast, David   81, 82
Castaneda, Carlos   103, 108
Catudal, Jacques   82
Cavell, Stanley   98
Centering in Pottery, Poetry, and the Person (Richards)   107
Chakrabarti, Arindam   63
Chalifoux, Alice   36
Chattopadhyaya, D.P.   135

Chaturvedi, Vibha 182
Chausson, Ernest 34
Cherubini, Luigi 122
Christo 199, 200
Churchill, Winston 73
Cohen, Rabbi Armond 41
Cohen, Gerald Alan 'Jerry' 99
Collingwood, R.G. 64, 65, 68–72, 76, 84, 85, 97, 99, 108, 219
    Speculum Mentis 48
Costigan, Constance (Connie) 23, 29, 60, 81, 84, 88, 104, 106, 107–111, 121, 142, 144–146, 149, 151, 161, 217
Curtis, Michael 47
    The Great Political Theories 49

Dalai Lama (Tenzin Gyatso) 21, 100, 136, 139–146, 152, 184, 205, 206, 210
Danto, Arthur 189
Davenny, Ward 38
Davenny-Wyner, Susan 38
Davin, Daniel Marcus 'Dan' 71
Debussy, Claude 34
Denker, David 46
Desjardins, Paul 81
DeSousa, Ronald 68
Dewey, John 132, 133, 190
Diamond, David 113
Dick, Marcel 14, 19, 79
Dickson, Jennifer 106
Dimitrov, Micho 118
Dimov, Dimo 119
Donagan, Alan 65
Dorje, Shugden 206
Dray, William "Bill" 68, 69, 75
Dreyfus, Hubert "Bert" 64
    Being-in-the-World 98
Drinkel, Janet 33
Dudden, Adrienne 81
Dudden, Arthur Power 81
Duff, Cloyd 37
Dunn, Mary Maples 81
Durfee, Harold 84
Dvořák, Antonín 115
Dworkin, Ronald 43, 99
    Religion without God 44

Elwell, Herbert 14
Erb, Donald 14

Farinacci, John 35, 36
Fauré, Gabriel 123
Ferrater Mora, José 78, 79
Feuer, Lewis Samuel 68, 75
Fischer, Edwin 10
Francescatti, Zino 37
Franck, Cesar 34
Frank, Josef 67
Fuchs, Harry 36
Furtwängler, Wilhelm 18, 25, 126, 127, 181

Gablik, Suzi 97
    Progress in Art 103
Gardiner, Patrick 69–71
Garelick, Herbert 48
Garelik, Herbert 50
Gates, H. I. and Elaine 108
Geertz, Clifford 64
    "Anti Anti-Relativism" 96
Gellner, Ernest 71, 108
Geminiani, Francesco:
    Concerto Grosso in C minor 39
    Concerto Grosso in E minor 112
Gettier, Edmund 68
Gingold, Josef 14, 33, 34, 36, 37, 40, 45, 65, 66, 112, 114, 152
Gluck, Christoph Willibald:
    Iphigénia in Aulis 123
Goehr, Alexander 189
Goldstein, Raquel Krausz 28
Gombrich, Ernst 55
Goodman, Nelson 154
Gottlieb, Adolph 104
Greenberg, Michael 61
Grobstein, Paul 82
Grubart, Judy 27
Guarneri, Quartet 113
Gupta, Chhanda 135
Gyatso, Lobsang 143, 146, 205–207, 210

Habermas, Jürgen 91
Hacker, Peter 71, 99
Handel, George Frideric:
    Messiah 35, 38, 112
Hanna, Patricia 71, 187, 188
Harman, Abraham 86–88
Harré, Rom 70, 202
    Varieties of Relativism (with M. Krausz) 72

NAME INDEX

Harrison, Bernard   71, 187, 188
Haydn, Joseph:
   Cello Concerto no. 1 in C major   123
   Symphony no. 68 in B♭major   113
Haydn, Mary-Jean   120
Hebert, William   36
Hegel, G.W.F.   65, 97
Heidegger, Martin   65, 98
   "The Origin of the Work of Art"   53
Heifetz, Jascha   37
Hempel, Carl   62
Henri, Robert   190
Herzl, Theodore   73
Higgins, David   47
Hindemith, Paul   113
Hitler, Adolf   10, 18, 53, 95
Hochman, Benjamin   123, 124
Hood, Colleen   120
Hooper, Mark   117
Hoy, David   64
   "One What?"   98
Huberman, Bronislaw   22
Hume, David   54
Husserl, Edmund   59

Jacobi, Peter and Ritzi   108
Jakobson, Roman   89, 90, 106
Janschka, Fritz   102
Jarvie, Ian   56
Jean-Claude   199, 200
Jeffrey, Richard   62
Jewish Identity (Goldberg and M. Krausz)   149
Johns, Michael   119, 120

Kalmus, Edwin   13
Kant, Immanuel   49, 78, 168
Kavafian, Ida   122
Kelly, Ellsworth   101, 103
Kenny, Anthony   91
Kilbride, Philip   82, 92
Killmeyer, Peggy   35, 38
Kleiber, Otto   18
Kletzki, Paul   18, 20
Kline, Franz   104
Kline, George   78
Koggel, Christine   82
Krausz, Ezra Simon   28
Krausz, Franceska Spuller   20, 21

Krausz, Laszlo   11, 17, 21, 23, 46, 160
Krausz, Michael:
   "A Critique of R.G. Collingwood's Theory of Absolute Presuppositions"   68
   Between Lines, Beyond Words   104
   Beyond Between   104
   Critical Essays on the Philosophy of R.G. Collingwood   71
   Dialogues on Relativism, Absolutism, and Beyond   153, 154
   End of Texts   104
   Jewish Identity (with David Goldberg)   149
   Limits of Rightness   202
   Oneness and the Displacement of Self   152
   Opposition   102, 103
   Relativism: A Contemporary Anthology   98, 165
   Relativism: Interpretation and Confrontation   96
   The Interpretation of Music   66, 100
   Varieties of Relativism (with Harré)   72
Krausz, Peter   10, 11, 23, 24, 26–29, 32, 59, 61, 109, 161
Krausz, Ezra Simon   28
Krausz, Simon   20, 21
Krausz, Susan (Suzi) Strauss   9–17, 19, 20, 22, 23, 32, 33, 35, 42, 86, 110, 112, 130, 145, 149
   Piano Picture Book   13
Krausz-Bouille, Tami   28
Krausz-Nevo, Gilah   28
Krogh, Peter   84, 85
Kuhn, Thomas   62, 64, 66, 96, 103
   The Structure of Scientific Revolutions   63, 97

Lakatos, Imre   50, 52–54, 62, 63, 81, 98
   Criticism and the Growth of Knowledge (with Musgrave)   64
Lamarque, Peter   185, 186
Lane, Barbara and Jonathan   81
Lane, Luis   37
Langan, Thomas   65
Language, Thought, and Reality (Whorf and Carroll)   48
Lansbury, John and Coral   81
Laredo, Jaime   34, 112, 113
LeBlanc, Hughes   79

Lee, Robert 81
Leighton, Lawrence 112
Levine, Steven 81
Lichtenberg, Philip 81
Lieber, Gene 61
Lipatti, Dinu 10
Litwinko, Tony 81
Lopatnikoff, Nikolai 14
Lubar, Walter 106
Lukes, Stephen 70, 99

MacPherson, Mary Patterson "Pat" 79
Magee, Bryan 100, 129
Mahfouz, Afaf 88
Mahler, Gustav 55
   Symphony no. 9 in D major 133
Marchand, Jacques 47, 61
Margolis, Joseph 43, 82, 90, 156, 172, 173, 175, 179
Markevitch, Igor 15, 35, 38
Martin, Agnes 104
Martin, Frank 20
Mascagni, Pietro 18
Matilal, Bimal Krishna 71, 72, 100, 135
McCormack, Elizabeth F. "Liz" 82
McCormack, John 67
McKenna, Michael 82, 154
McLuhan, Marshall 68
McRay, Robert 67
Mendelsohn, Felix 117
Menuhin, Yehudi 20, 74
Miller, Gary (Guarav) 136
Mitropoulos, Dmitri 19
Mohanty, Jitendra (Jiten) 71, 82, 90, 100, 135
Montefiore, Alan 70, 99
Morini, Erica 37
Moskof, Martin "Marty" 115, 136
Motherwell, Robert 104
Mozart, Wolfgang Amadeus 116
   La Clemenza di Tito 122
   Idomeneo 124
   Overture to *The Marriage of Figaro* 117, 121, 124
   Piano Concerto no. 24 in C minor 119
   Sinfonia Concertante in E♭ major 113
   Symphony no. 29 in A major 114
   Symphony no. 35 in D major ("Haffner") 121
   Symphony no. 38 in D major ("Prague Symphony") 121
   Symphony no. 41 in C major ("Jupiter") 114
Munch, Charles 18, 19
Musgrave, Alan 50, 54
   Criticism and the Growth of Knowledge (with Lakatos) 64
Muti, Riccardo 113, 126, 133

Nagel, Thomas 95
Nahm, Milton Charles 78–81
Nehamas, Alexander 64
   "The Postulated Author" 98
Newton-Smith, William "Bill" 70
Neyer, Joseph 49
Nicholson, Ben 103
Nietzsche, Friedrich 98
Novitz, David 71, 195
Nudel, Ida 27–29
Nussbaum, Martha 99

Oberdiek, Hans 82
Oistakh, David 36
One Dimensional Man (Marcuse) 62
Ormandy, Eugene 19, 37, 114, 133
Oruka, Henry Odera 92
Otto, Rudolf 44

Paray, Paul 18, 20
Party, Lionel 118, 121
Pears, David 70
Pederson, Richard and Nelda 87, 88
Peirce, Charles Sanders 67, 78
Perr, Herbert 106
Pollock, Jackson 104
Popper, Karl Raimond 43, 50, 52, 56, 58, 63–65, 68, 70, 81, 97, 107, 152, 154, 192, 193, 199
   The Open Society and Its Enemies 53, 62
   "Three Views of Human Knowledge" 51
   Unended Quest 54, 55
The Potato Eaters (Van Gogh) 179, 186
Potter, Jean 78
Prager, Eddie 61
Prausnitz, Margaret 116
Putnam, Hilary 135

NAME INDEX

Rattle, Simon   123, 130
Raugh, Robert   49
Ravel, Maurice   18
Raz, Joseph   70, 99
Rehberg, Walter   10, 11
Reinhardt, Adolph Frederick "Ad"   104
Rhodes, Leah   101
Rockman, Arnold   68
Rilke, Rainer Maria   13
Rimsky-Korsakov, Nikolai:
   Scheherazade   34
Rorty, Amélie   62
Rorty, Richard   62, 64, 91
   Philosophy and the Mirror of Nature   96
Rosen, Charles   100
Rossini, Gioachino   119
Rotenstreich, Nathan   84, 85, 87
Rothko, Mark   103
Roy, Klaus   14
Rozsa, Miklos   11
Russell, Bertrand   42, 70
Ryan, Alan   74
Ryle, Gilbert   69, 70

Sadat, Anwar   84
Sai*nt-Saëns, Cam*ille   34
   Cello Concerto no. 1 in A minor   121
Salmon, John   81
Salmon, Wesley   65
Samten, Geshe Ngawang   143, 146, 205, 207
Sargent, Malcolm   18
Sasaki, Ken-ichi   191
Savan, David   67
Schachter-Shalomi, Rabbi Zalman   149
Schick, Fred   62
Schmitz, Kenneth   62
Schnabel, Artur   10, 12
Schönberg, Arnold   55
Schubert, Franz   116
   Symphony no. 9 in C major ("Great")   123, 131
Schuller, Gunther   20, 124
Schumann, Robert   123
Schuricht, Carl   18, 38
Schwarzkopf, Elisabeth   25
Sclufer, Anne   120
Score and Podium (Prausnitz)   116
Scott, Yumi   111

Scriven, Michael   65
Sen, Amartya   99
Serkin, Rudolf   37, 55
Sessions, Roger   116
Sharpe, Maurice   36
Shaw, Robert   20, 38
Shieren, Carl   88
Shteir, Ann Baron 'Rusty'   67
Shure, Leonard   12, 13, 20, 130
Sindell, Carol   40
Sindell, Steven   35, 38
Snowdon, Paul   70
Solti, Sir Georg   22, 23
Spaeth, Ned   109
Sparshott, Francis   75, 76
Stearns, Isabelle   78
Stern, Isaac   37, 74
Stevens, Courtenay Edward "Tom Brown"   219
Stevenson, J.T.   68
Stokking, Nancy Leichner   121
Stokking, William   37, 121
Stokowski, Leopold   19, 38
Storr, Anthony   132
Strauss, Else   11, 160
Strauss, Moritz   16, 160
Strauss, Richard   18
Stravinsky, Igor   18, 20, 59
Strong, George Templeton:
   "Choral sur un thème de Léo Hassler"   38
Swamiji (Shyamacharan Srivastava)   137–141, 143–146, 153, 184, 204, 206–209, 211, 214, 216–221
Szell, George   12, 19, 20, 35–37, 39, 114, 133
Szigeti, Joseph   19, 20

Taft, Tracy   82
Taylor, Charles   64, 97
Thom, Paul   212, 213
Tobey, Mark   103
Toscanini, Arturo   34, 129, 181
Toulmin, Stephen   34, 129, 181
Tree, Michael   34, 112, 113

Vallabha, Bharath   82
Van Beinum, Eduard   18

Van Sice, Robert   119
Verdi, Giuseppe:
    Requiem   133
Vivaldi, Antonio:
    Concerto Grosso in A minor   39
    Concerto Grosso in B minor   76
Von Karajan, Herbert   25
Von Magnus, Eric   38
Von Wright, Georg Henrik   95
    *The Tree of Knowledge and Other
        Essays*   96

Wagner, Richard   16, 55, 100
Walter, Bruno   124, 129, 131
Wanger, Walter   11
Waskow, Rabbi Arthur   149
Watkins, John   50
Watzek, Wilhelm   18
Weaver, George   79, 81

Weber, Carl Maria von   123
Weingartner, Felix   18
Weiss, Paul   79
Whorf, Benjamin Lee   48, 50
Winn, James   112
Wisdom, J.O.   50, 54, 63
Wise, John and Harriet   108
Wittgenstein, Ludwig   31, 57, 62, 72, 95, 165
Wittgenstein's Logical Atomism (Griffin)   54
Wofford, Harris   79, 80
Wolfe, Marvin   61
Wolf-Ferrari, Ermanno   61

Yang, Amy J.   124
Young, Judea   27
Ysaÿe, Eugène   34

Zádor, Eugen   11
Zimmerman, Robert   62

Subject Index

Abrahamic traditions   42
absolutism   96, 153, 157, 169, 171–173
   compared with relativism   165
   invoked in definition of relativism   168
   varieties of   166
adjudication   166, 168, 169
admissibility   181
Advaita Vedanta   43n9, 207
aesthetics   75, 118, 166
   a. experience   48, 60, 103
Akron Symphony Orchestra   19, 33–35, 38, 40, 112, 121
American University, Washington, DC   84
American University in Cairo   85, 87
anti-intellectualism   24
anti-Semitism   44, 72, 73, 100
anti-universalist view   170
art(ists)(works):
   a. products   107, 194, 196; *see also* c. products *under* creativity
   Costigan's   104
   as 'an' experience (Dewey)   132, 133
   high moments of artistic work (Danto)   189
   history of   55, 72, 97
   Krausz's   49, 77, 89, 92, 98, 101–106, 131
   minimalist a.   101, 103
   personal programs in   89, 103, 106, 107, 192, 193, 195; *see also* personal programs
   Popper's anti-expressionist attitude toward   55
   relationship between a., religion, and science (Collingwood)   48
   Tibetan children's a. exhibition   144
   tripartite scheme for artworks (Popper)   186
Artists Exchange of Delaware   105
ashram at Kullu   137, 146, 154, 205
Aspen Institute   84, 112
asymmetry thesis (Popper)   51
Atman   143, 168, 184, 185, 202, 203, 205, 207, 208. *See also* One(ness)
Auschwitz   20, 22, 210. *See also* Holocaust

beauty:
   in Dworkin's discussion of numinous experiences   44
   in Krausz's definition of relativism   165, 166, 172
belief(s)   45, 68, 83, 135, 155, 167, 210, 212
   frame-dependent   168
   interpreted   175
   religious   57
betweens and beyonds   147
beyonds   148
Black Mountain College   107
Boyer Conservatory   120
Brahman   185
Bryn Mawr College   90, 109, 111
Buddhism   140, 143, 144, 147, 201, 205–208, 223
Bulgaria   116–120, 130

Camp David Accords   84, 85
Canada   67, 148, 223
Case Institute Chamber Orchestra   39
causes and conditions   142
Celebration Chamber Orchestra   37, 111
Chiang Mai University, Thailand   135
Christendom   73
ciphers   103, 104, 131
Cleveland:
   Chamber Orchestra   19
   Composer's Guild   14
   Heights High School   27, 35, 38
   Institute of Art   19
   Krausz family in   12, 13, 18–20, 25, 31, 36
   Music School Settlement   12, 19, 33
   Orchestra   12, 16, 19, 20, 34, 36–38, 40, 46
   Basel Switzerland visit   133
   Seder in Moscow   85, 86
   Philharmonic Orchestra   36, 39, 40
   Youth Chamber Orchestra of Cleveland   38, 39
cluster concept (Wittgenstein)   165
commodity fetishism, Marx's critique of   24
communities   157, 158, 167
   barriers to communication among   97

cultural 185
  Krausz's various 148–150, 159
  linguistic 176
  philosophy of indigenous 92
compassion 57, 95, 141, 144
composer's intentions 131
concepts 156, 176
  bivalent/multivalent 179
Concerto Soloists 114
conclusiveness vs. decisiveness 131
conduct(ing)(or) 124, 127, 133
  conductor's intentions 125
  Krausz's 35, 40, 41, 77, 111, 115–118, 120, 127, 128, 161
confirming instances 51
consciousness 214, 215, 217
  dualistic 133
Conservatory Symphony Orchestra 119, 120
consolation 204, 212, 223
constructivism 157, 188, 223
consummatory experience (Dewey) 101n1
cosmopolitanism 151, 152
creativ(e)(ity) 198
  c. activity 190, 196, 199
  c. persons/processes/product distinction(Briskman) 197, 198, 200
  Jewish (Magee) 100
  Krausz's work on 89, 102, 103, 106, 192–194, 196–198, 223
  life as a creative work 200
  subjective experience and 196, 198
creator god 42, 43, 147
cultures 167, 169, 170
Curtis Institute of Music 55, 66, 111, 118, 121, 125

dead baby in the Ganges in Benares 83
death 212, 213
  d. anxiety 139, 145, 216, 217, 220, 221
  life after 219
  One is deathless 139, 208
decisiveness. See conclusiveness vs. decisiveness
Delhi University conference on Krausz's work 100

detachability thesis (Krausz) 187, 188. See also ontology
detachment 146
determinism 157
Dharamsala 136, 139, 140, 143, 144, 146, 205–207
dialogue:
  cultural 92
  inner d. (inner speech) 89
  between Israelis and Palestinians 88
  Krausz books written in d. form 153–156
  between reference frames 97
disagreement 141, 175
displacement:
  of individual self to essential Self 204, 211, 214, 216, 217, 222
  Krausz's geographical 151, 155, 223
the Divine 184, 205, 206, 216–219

East-West Concert 119, 120
edification 96, 154, 189–191
Egypt 85, 87, 148
Eldoret 92
elucidation 154, 189, 191, 213
embodiment:
  of the Buddha 142
  of an essence 42
  of the One 155, 203, 207–209, 211, 216
empirical verification 51, 64
emptiness of inherent existence 43, 140, 141, 144, 146, 194, 207, 208, 210
enlightenment 203, 204, 217
Ensemble Symphonique 113
Ensemble Symphonique de Genève 18
epiphanic experiences 133, 134, 194
epiphany, Krausz's art 101, 102, 147, 194
essence(s) 42, 51, 52, 201, 210
essentialism 42, 51, 59, 211
  anti-e. 42, 43, 51, 52, 141, 205
  beyond e. or non-e. 203
  e. vs. non-e. issue 206
  non-e. 43, 205, 207, 208, 211, 223
existence:
  Advaitic view 168
  Buddhist and Hindu view 142, 143
  degrees of 209
  inherent 43, 142–144, 207, 210, 211

SUBJECT INDEX 265

experience(s)   48, 57, 157, 192, 193, 202, 205, 223
    aesthetic   60, 103
    consumatory/epiphanic/at-one   101, 101n1, 102, 133, 134, 194
    edificatory (Dewey)   190
    lived   191
    numinous   43, 44
    oceanic   132
    ontological   190
    subjective   196, 198

fabric of inner life   57
facts   71
    anti-realist view   175
    facts of the matter   167, 174, 187
    realist and relativist view   169
    uninterpreted   153, 169
FBI office breakin at Media PA   80
5th element   132
Ford Foundation   91
Foreign Service School, Georgetown   84
forms of life   167
foundationalism   169–172, 176
    nonfoundationalism   176; see also polymorphism
frame-independent world   167
free-will   157

gebildet (cultured)   24, 25
goodness in Krausz's definition of relativism   165, 166, 172
Great Hall Chamber Orchestra   37, 92, 119, 120, 161
Greater Philadelphia Philosophy Consortium (GPPC)   90–92, 112, 144

Haverford College   79, 92
Haystack Mountain School of Crafts   84, 106
Hebrew University   61, 84–86, 88
Hinduism   143, 144, 147, 201, 223
history of science, sociological vs. permanentist approach   63
holism vs. individualism   62
Holocaust   20, 26, 44, 65, 94, 95, 142
    Dalai Lama's view of   210
    H. deniers   173–175
    Swamiji's view of   209, 210

hope   212, 213
human beings:
    communities and   176
    edification of   157
    embodiments of the One   155
    existence/reality of   154, 217
    priority of   177, 213, 220
    relationships with other   205, 209
humanism, Krausz's   177, 205, 220, 221, 223

identity   208
    i. conditions   185, 186
    Jewish   27, 149
    Krausz's   148, 149
    narrative   195
    numerical   183, 184, 186
    personal   70, 159, 211
India, Krausz's experiences in   44, 72, 83, 100, 102, 135, 140, 143, 146, 151, 201, 207, 208, 217, 223
    Christians in   147
Indian Council of Philosophical Research   100
Indian Institute of Advanced Study   100, 135
Indiana University   34, 65
individuality   217, 219
inductive logic   65
inquiry, end of   183
inscapes (Costigan)   104
intentionality   66
intentions   185
    assimilating the i. of another (Walter)   124
    composer's/conductor's   125, 126, 131
International Colloquium in the Philosophy of Science   63
interpretation(s)   82, 96, 159, 172, 213
    admissible   13, 130, 153, 178, 180, 181, 185–187
    aim of   189–191
    in art   103
    contending   179–182, 184
    ideals of   183, 187–189
    multiple interpretability   186
    in music   13, 66, 100, 127–129, 131
    objects of   178, 185
    theory of   71, 90, 91, 98, 141, 179, 187, 223
    uninterpreted facts that ground   174, 175

Israel   22, 27, 73, 109
　　Krausz's travels to   60, 61, 88, 94, 148, 150
　　peace treaty with Egypt   85
　　Zionism and   28, 29, 72

Jadavpur University   135
Jewishness   27, 44, 45, 73, 94, 147, 149, 223
　　J. Diaspora   136
judgment   177
　　dualistic   134
　　incongruent vs. contradictory   173
　　reasonable   183

Kenya   92–95, 147, 148
Kikuyu communities   92, 94
Kira (moral sins)   93
knowledge   170
　　consolation and (Thom)   212
　　hope and   213
　　justified-true-belief account of (Gettier)   68
　　meager in relation to infinite ignorance   152
　　non-foundationalist view of   43
　　objective   55
　　reference frames distort   167
　　scientific   63
　　subjectivist approaches to   56
Kullu   136, 137, 140, 143, 146, 205, 206

Lebensphilosophie   157
liberation (*moksa*)   204, 205
Linacre Philosophy Seminars   100
logic:
　　bivalent vs. multivalent   173, 179
　　dialectical   214
　　inductive   65
　　iterative   214–218
logical positivism (Ayer)   52
London School of Economics (LSE)   47, 49, 50, 52, 54–57, 59–61, 62, 97
love:
　　Divine vs. human   155, 218, 219
　　Oneness as   218

mantras   139, 208, 211, 213–216, 220
meditation   137
Mellon Foundation   84

metaphysics of interpretation   98, 172
Middle East exchange program   86
multiplism   98, 129, 130, 137, 178, 180–185, 187–189, 223. *See also* singularism
music:
　　balance, coordination, dynamics, tempo   126
　　epiphanic experiences in   133
　　m. interpretation   13, 66, 100, 127–129, 131
　　Popper anti-expressionist toward   55
　　silence in   131, 132
mysticism   72

NBC Symphony Orchestra   34
NEH Summer Institute at the University of California   64
New Jewish Agenda   149
New York College of Music   11, 12
numinous experiences   43, 44

objectivism (Popper)   55n14, 64
objects:
　　of anxiety   219
　　countable   168
　　intentional   185, 186
　　of interpretation   71, 98, 178, 180, 183, 185, 189
oneness, oceanic sensation of   190
One(ness), Advaitic   138, 139, 143, 145, 146, 168, 169, 184, 190, 194, 202, 204, 207, 208, 211, 212, 205, 207–209, 211, 213–220, 222. *See also* Atman; emptiness
ontology:
　　absolutist/objectivist   63
　　Advaitist   216
　　Buddhist   207
　　detachability thesis and   188
　　no-ontology o.   71
Orchestre de la Suisse Romande   9, 18
ornamentation, musical   129
Ossabaw Island Foundation   88
other, the   129, 150
　　feeling of Krausz as   94
Oxford community orchestra   111

paradigms (Kuhn)   64, 97, 167
Park Synagogue   26, 41
peace treaty between Egypt and Israel   85
Pécs, Hungary   21

SUBJECT INDEX

M. Krausz visit   22
Municipal Music School   17
personal programs   89, 103, 106, 107, 157, 158, 192–195, 199, 200
perspectives   167
perspicuous contrast, language of (Taylor)   97, 98
Pew Charitable Trust   91
Philadelphia:
    Chamber Symphony   114
    College of Art   106
philosophy *passim*
    definitions   156
    Indian   71, 72, 83
    Krausz's introduction to   47, 48
    sage (sagacious) philosophy   92
Pleven Symphony Orchestra   117, 128
Plovdiv Philharmonic Orchestra   117
polymorphism   176, 177
Popper-Kuhn debate   63
post-dictive constructs   173, 203
potential, personal   201
pragmatist vs. relativist view (Rorty)   96
presuppositions:
    absolute (Collingwood)/relative   64, 68, 76
    cultural   94
preunderstanding   150
Prisoners of Zion (refuseniks)   27
process:
    process-centered program   107, 194
    product-process distinctions (Briskman)   193, 197, 198, 200

quantum mechanics, multiple interpretability of   82
questions and answers, Collingwood's philosophy of   76

rationality   170
    irrationality   97
realism   157, 169, 171, 172
    anti-r.   175
    constructive   188
    Popper's   51
    relative   188
    singularism, multiplism, and   187, 188
reality   132, 174, 176, 217
    extra-human/linguistic   188

realist understanding of   174
    ultimate   168, 184
reasonableness   166, 179, 187
reasons, ampliative vs. determinative   181
reference frames   97, 98, 153, 177
    adjudication between   168, 169
    frame-independent things   167
    in relativism definition   165, 166, 172
relativism   95, 96, 157
    begins with diversity   135, 136
    definition   165, 166
    global vs. piecemeal treatments of   166
    Krausz's work on   165–177
    Kuhn's   97
    moral   82
    objectivism vs.   64
    perspicuous contrast consistent with   98
    robust (Margolis)   91, 172, 173, 179
    self-refuting argument   171, 172
religious:
    r. attitude   44
    r. beliefs   57
    as mode of experience   48, 132, 134
    opposing r. settings   155, 156
    r. space   150
    r. traditions   141
refutability in science   54
research programmes (Lakatos)   53
Roerich Hall Estate   137, 138
Roosevelt Junior High School   34
roots in the air (metaphor)   223
Royal Conservatory of Music, Toronto   77
Rutgers University   28, 46, 47, 49, 54, 61, 62, 67, 68, 74, 111, 113

science   48
    history and philosophy of   52, 63, 103, 156
    Krausz's interest in philosophy of   65, 66, 70, 82
    Kuhn's vs. Popper's views   64
    vs. non-s.   51
scores, music   40, 124, 125, 128, 129, 131, 132
    multiple interpretability of   130
Seaside Jewish Community (SJC)   148, 150, 151

self:
  egoless   214
  Supreme   139, 184, 203, 204, 214, 215, 216
self-:
  cultivation/fulfillment   190
  realization   60, 137, 139, 145, 147, 153, 190, 194, 201–203, 213, 214, 220, 221, 223
  recognition   72, 157, 158, 159, 207, 222
  transformation   89, 194–196, 198–200
Severance Hall   38
significance   183, 185, 199
silence in music   131, 132
singularism   13, 98, 130, 157, 178, 180, 181, 183–185, 187–189. *See also* multiplism
  singularist ≠ bully   129
situatedness (Heidegger)   53
soloists Krausz conducted   117, 118, 120–125
space   44. *See also* silence
  conceptual space in which one can live   156
  empty space   176
  free, unbounded   215
  intellectual   89, 156
  meditative   104, 212
  of nonduality   221, 223
  of painting   101, 193, 194
  between positive and negative   132
  religious   150
spirituality   72, 73, 150
subjectivism   54, 55
suffering   139, 204, 216, 221
suppositions   57. *See also* presuppositions
Supreme Being   208. *See also* One(ness)
Swiss Romande Orchestra   26, 151
symbol systems   43, 167

Temple University   82, 90, 91, 111, 120
tempo   126–128
Thou art That/ I am I   117, 139, 204, 208, 211, 213–216, 220. *See also* mantras
Three Worlds Hypothesis (Popper)   54, 63, 192, 193
Tibetan Diaspora   136
Toronto   67–69, 71, 75, 76, 78, 82, 102, 149

tribes   167
truth   176, 179, 181, 216
  ant-realist view   175
  provisional   212
  realist understanding of   174
  in relativism definition   165, 166, 171, 172
  semantic theory of (Tarski)   55n14
  ultimate   208
  t. values   173

universal hypothesis   51
universalism   169, 171, 172. *See also* foundationalism
foundational   170, 171
University of Helsinki   95
University of Oxford   29, 47, 52, 75, 76, 78, 86, 97, 99, 100, 111, 117
  All Souls College, Oxford   71, 72, 99, 100
  Balliol College   69
  Linacre College   69, 70, 74, 99, 100
  Magdalen College   69
University of Pennsylvania   81, 90–92
University of Toronto   67–69, 75, 82
urgency   60, 61, 209

Victoria College, University of Toronto   75, 76, 78, 82, 103
Vienna Circle   62
Vietnam War   61, 67
Villanova University   91
Vratsa Philharmonic Orchestra   117, 118

Western Reserve University   12, 13, 19
what is? questions   51, 52, 68, 80
witch doctor   93
Who am I? question   201, 216
works   185, 186. *See also* intentional objects
world-versions   167

York University   56, 67, 75, 102

Zionism   26–29, 72

Printed in the United States
By Bookmasters